IF THESE STONES COULD TALK

IF THESE STONES
COULD TALK

*The History of Christianity in
Britain and Ireland through
Twenty Buildings*

Peter Stanford

With illustrations by Stephen Tsang

HODDER &
STOUGHTON

First published in Great Britain in 2021 by Hodder & Stoughton
An Hachette UK company

2

Copyright © Peter Stanford, 2021
Illustrations by Stephen Tsang

Biblical references are taken from *The New Jerusalem Bible*
published and copyright © 1974 by Darton, Longman and Todd Ltd
and Doubleday, a division of Random House Inc.

A CIP catalogue record for this title is available from the British Library

Hardback ISBN 978 1 529 39642 3
eBook ISBN 978 1 529 39644 7

Typeset in Sabon MT by Hewer Text UK Ltd, Edinburgh
Printed and bound in Great Britain by Clays Ltd, Elcograf S.p.A.

Hodder & Stoughton policy is to use papers that are natural, renewable
and recyclable products and made from wood grown in sustainable
forests. The logging and manufacturing processes are expected to
conform to the environmental regulations of the country of origin.

Hodder & Stoughton Ltd
Carmelite House
50 Victoria Embankment
London EC4Y 0DZ

www.hodderfaith.com

To my parents-in-law, Lena and Jim Cross, with whom I have enjoyed wandering round many an old country church in Britain and in Lena's native Ireland. Though they are sadly no longer around to do it, their love, constancy, care and laughter continue to sustain us.

Contents

Timeline

Timeline

1170	Martyrdom of Thomas Becket in Canterbury Cathedral
1171	Henry II leads a force into Ireland and meets bishops at Cashel
1192	Pope removes Scottish bishops from English control
1208	Pope Innocent III places England under interdict
1209	Pope excommunicates King John
1215	Magna Carta signed
1215	Fourth Lateran Council meets
1221	Dominicans establish first house in England at Oxford
1285	Edward I celebrates victory over Welsh
1290	Jews expelled from England
1297	Irish Parliament established
1309–77	Avignon papacy
1337–1453	Hundred Years' War between England and France
1381	Peasants' Revolt
1384	Wycliffe dies working on English Bible
1395	Lollards present Twelve Conclusions to Parliament
1414	Council of Constance excommunicates Wycliffe
1415	English victory at Agincourt over French
1517	Martin Luther's Ninety-five Theses
1521	Henry VIII attacks Luther and named Defender of the Faith by Pope
1533	Henry divorces his first wife and marries Anne Boleyn
1534	Act of Supremacy
1536	Dissolution of Monasteries begins
1537	Irish Parliament endorses King as Head of Church
1540	Execution of Thomas Cromwell
1547	Occupation of St Andrews by Scottish Presbyterian reformers ended by French fleet
1549	First English Prayer Book

1549	Mary Queen of Scots betrothed to Dauphin of France
1552	Second English Prayer Book
1553	Death of Edward VI and accession of Mary
1556	Thomas Cranmer burnt at the stake
1557	Scottish Lords of Congregation demand church reform
1558	Death of Mary I, accession of Elizabeth
1559	Elizabethan Settlement
1560	Scottish Parliament votes in Scots Confession and establishes Presbyterianism as national Church as widowed Mary, Queen of Scots returns from France
1567	Mary, Queen of Scots goes into exile in England, leaving behind infant son, crowned James VI of Scotland
1570	Pope excommunicates Elizabeth
1587	Mary, Queen of Scots executed
1588	Spanish Armada defeated
1603	James VI of Scotland becomes James I of England
1605	Gunpowder Plot
1611	King James Bible published
1620	*Mayflower* sails for America with Puritans on board
1625	Charles I succeeds his father
1629	Charles I dissolves Parliament
1639–40	Scottish Bishops' wars
1640	Short then Long Parliament summoned by King
1641–52	Irish Confederate Wars
1642	English Civil War begins
1649	Execution of Charles I and declaration of Commonwealth
1653	Cromwell named Lord Protector
1656	Jews allowed to return to England

Timeline

1658	Death of Cromwell paves way for restoration of monarchy
1660	Charles II returns
1662	Revised Prayer Book and new Act of Uniformity
1685	Accession of Catholic James II
1688	'Glorious Revolution' restores Protestant monarchy with William and Mary
1689	James II defeated at Battle of Boyne
1701	Act of Settlement provides for continuing Protestant monarchy
1707	Acts of Union between England and Scotland
1714	Death of Queen Anne and start of Hanoverian monarchs
1738	Conversion of John Wesley and 'birth' of Methodism
1778	First Catholic Relief Acts followed by Gordon Riots
1800	Act of Union between England and Ireland
1818	Establishment of Church Building Society
1828	Repeal of Test and Corporation Acts
1829	Catholic Emancipation Act
1832	Great Reform Act
1845	Newman abandons Oxford Movement and becomes a Catholic
1850	Restoration of Catholic hierarchy in England and Wales
1869	Disestablishment of the Church in Ireland
1920	Disestablishment of the Church in Wales
1970	Church of England General Synod established
1972	Failure of Anglican–Methodist merger
1982	Papal visit to Britain
1985	Robert Runcie's *Faith in the City* report
1992	General Synod votes in favour of women priests

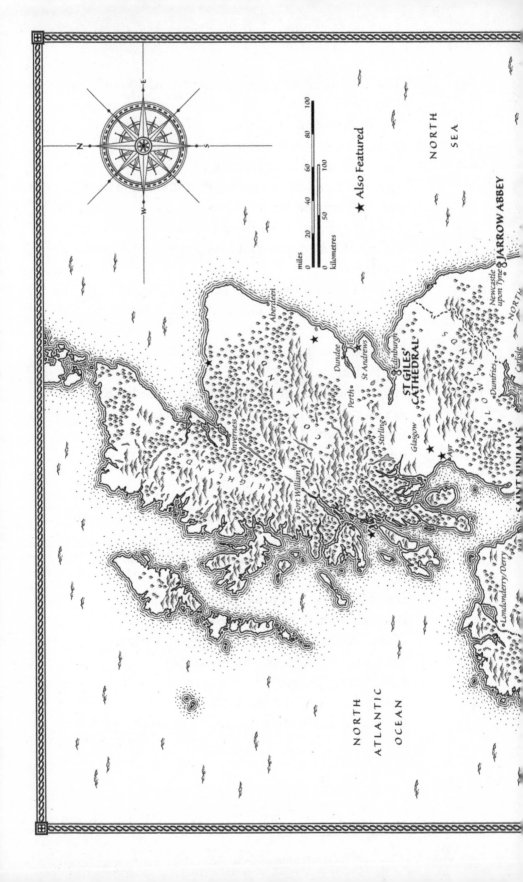

Prologue

I tried to add up everything that was in England. I began with
churches. Then the stones that the churches were built from.
Rose Tremain: Sacred Country (1992)[1]

THE ORIGINS OF Christianity in Britain and Ireland are impossible to establish. They lie somewhere in the second half of the first century, but exactly where and when is buried in a tangle of legend, folklore and the occasional tree. What I can be clearer about, however, is when my own habit began of searching out answers to this and other questions about the Christian history of these islands. It was the summer of 2006, and the method I stumbled upon was by wandering into whatever churches happened to be at hand.

That was the first school holiday our family had spent in north Norfolk. My wife had grown up there, so for her it was the return of the native. What had been edited out of her memories of big sandy beaches and even bigger blue skies, though, were the occasions, mercifully rare, when the blue was replaced by black clouds and the walk back over marshes in driving rain felt penitential. On one such drizzly, downcast day, knowing that I just had to get the children, nine and six at the time, out of a house that was too small to contain them any longer, I stumbled upon the idea of visiting a local medieval church. Such jaunts had played no part in my own childhood, but I had read somewhere that St Mary's had a roof decorated with angels. That promise seemed sufficient to stifle the protests of our offspring. We packed coloured pencils, notebooks and snacks and set off. And so began our 'church crawls'.

The choice of destination that day proved inspired – large, dry, empty of other people, but stuffed with fascinating things. Like the angels peering down benignly from the ceiling. There was even an ancient, wheeled device with angled mirrors on top of it so you could get a better look at the cherubim up in the rafters. Each was holding a different object. Drawing them and trying to work out what they were for, provided an activity that was a good deal cheaper than anything else on offer locally to make the rainy days wash by. Thereafter the combination of strange, colourful objects, layer after layer of stories, and access to what felt like secret places, though they stood in plain sight, turned such outings into regular stand-bys, our very own variation of the *Horrible Histories* books they were reading at the time. Only not horrible – or not very often. One statue in an isolated church depicting Saint Sebastian being shot through with arrows was graphic enough to be slightly disturbing, even for me.

When my church-crawling companions reached teenagerdom and moved on to other pursuits, I continued the habit. I always try, usually briefly and falteringly, to find one feature of whichever church I hit upon that illuminates something not just about its own past but also about the shape Christianity has taken down the centuries, and how that shape has shaped these countries too. Like the box pews, shut off from the hoi polloi by doors, usually found at the front of churches but sometimes at the back, and raised up, which were the product of a class system that dominated local churches as it did the world outside them, until the seismic changes of industrialisation began to sweep all such earthbound hierarchies away. Or the curious pagan nature symbols found in more ancient churches, lurking in the margins of elaborate carvings, especially on great stone crosses, cheek by jowl with details taken from the Gospel narratives, which reveal how an older set of beliefs co-existed with Christianity long after they were officially declared dead. Or even the inscriptions on tombs that line the aisles, suggesting that the orthodoxy of the history taught in our classrooms might not always be the whole story. In a remote Herefordshire church, a memorial to Elizabeth I's longest-standing lady of the bedchamber describes her mistress as truly the Virgin Queen.

There is no shortage in rural Norfolk of huge, grand, lavishly decorated churches in tiny villages, a legacy of the county's medieval prosperity and the anxiety of every wealthy family back then to establish their social status and endow a church in order to ease their ascent into heaven. My crawls, though, in search of history on the hoof, have over the years spread far and wide, though I am a novice compared with Britain's reigning church-crawling champion, Oxford historian, writer and broadcaster Diarmaid MacCulloch, who started young (his dad was a vicar, which may or may not have helped) and has clocked up by his own account an estimated six or seven thousand visits.[2]

Nevertheless, I, and many others I have bumped into during my own expeditions, share his enthusiasm for a pastime that, in an unpressured, entertaining and health-enhancing way (if you combine it with a hike), pieces together the history of what remains the dominant faith in our country. Yes, it requires going into a church, and we are not a particularly churchy nation any more; so much so that people often feel unsettled by not knowing the right words to use of the various areas – nave, chancel, apse, ambulatory and so on. And, unlike museums, there are often inadequate labels, or none at all, to explain the source, story and point of the objects to be found there. Yet most of the time you can have these buildings to yourself to work it out and give your imagination free rein. What they offer is more than a tale of popes and bishops, dogma and ritual. Collectively and individually they tell a human story about the how and the where and the why of the faith of the people who have used these buildings, and the ways in which that was reflected in the societies to be found beyond their walls. Being places that have always opened their doors to (almost) everyone, they have a rare power to connect us in a tangible way, even in our secular and sceptical times, to the everyday flow of history. When we stand before fittings and furnishings that have been there for a thousand years, or touch walls that have been witnessing events for even longer, there is an invitation to join the long chain that links us to those who were once in exactly the same spot. This is where we come from.

What follows is an ordering and assembling of Christian history as told by a selection of 'crawled' churches – and what surrounds them – so as to recount the story of faith over two millennia in England, Scotland, Wales and Ireland. Each nation, of course, has its own distinctive narrative, and these are reflected too, but what connects them in the Christian history of these islands goes a long way to explaining why we have ended up where we are now. To explore the fullness of the tale I have reached into every corner of the land with a building in each chapter heading that follows the pattern of the centuries, plus an additional small number of locations appended because they also illuminate that century in a remarkable and complementary way.

Some readers will disagree with my choices, but with thousands to pick from, that is part and parcel of the compulsion of church crawling. Everyone has their favourites because each one you go into is different, in big ways as well as small. Some can only be accessed on foot. Some require perseverance, following long, narrow lanes deep into countryside that give every appearance of being bound to lead to a dead end. Many are tiny and can be enjoyed in silence and solitude, though there are some bigger beasts in there too, well-known names that mean you have to learn to share if you are to get the best out of them.

Some family friends, on being told of those summer excursions of long ago, would tease me that it was all a cover for trying to indoctrinate my young children. If that had been my intention, it has certainly backfired now they are in their twenties and have made up their own minds; but it really wasn't. The point of church crawling is not an evangelical drive to repopulate churches or to revive institutional faith. It is much more modest and inclusive: to benefit from these free-to-access resources in our midst that are centuries old, historic and usually beautiful, and which have something about them that makes them stand apart from the rush of modern life and our own fleeting obsessions. They may once have been built 'to the glory of God', but their continuing meaning is subtler. They are close to the heartbeat of human history, giving expression to our longings and helping us to remember who we are.

CHAPTER I

The First Century

Glastonbury Abbey: And Did Those Feet in Ancient Times?

The rapidity with which the faith spread through the Roman Empire astounded the Christians themselves.

Professor Henry Chadwick[1]

THERE WERE ALMOST certainly Christians in the British Isles in the first century. The Church established by the followers of Jesus of Nazareth in the middle decades of the century, following his death and based on the conviction that he had risen from his tomb, expanded rapidly out of Palestine. It spread around the Middle East, into the imperial capital of Rome, and then onwards to all points of the far-flung Roman Empire, which, from AD 43, included the conquered province of Britannia. Yet, while it is possible to identify how the new religion would have reached these islands, exactly when it did and who embraced it still remain just out of reach, and therefore largely the stuff of legend.

One location in particular – Glastonbury in Somerset – boasts of being 'the cradle of Christianity in England'. The description appears on the information boards that greet today's visitors to its ruined Abbey, a much later creation, once one of the grandest and richest in the country but destroyed in 1539 as part of the Dissolution of the Monasteries during the English Reformation. Such an eye-catching assertion, however, rests precariously on medieval claims widely dismissed by scholars that Joseph of Arimathea, the disciple who, according to the Gospels, provided a tomb where Jesus' corpse could be laid after his crucifixion,[2] came to Glastonbury as part of the first-century missionary push. He is said to have established there, on the site subsequently occupied from the early 700s by the first of three abbey buildings, a simple Christian church that was the first of its kind in the land.

The strongest evidence to back up this story comes from 1130, when William of Malmesbury, sometimes referred to as second only to the Venerable Bede as a reliable source on early Christianity in Britain, wrote in his description of Glastonbury that it contained an 'ancient' church that was 'the oldest of all those that I know of in England'.[3] He makes no reference to Joseph of Arimathea. That only came as an addition to his writings, inserted by others in later editions that appeared after his death.

William's picture of this church, though, is a beguiling one for those searching for evidence of early Christianity in the British Isles:

> In it are preserved the bodily remains of many saints, and there is no part of the church that is without the ashes of the blessed. The stone-paved floor, the sides of the altar, the very altar itself, above and within, are filled with relics close-packed. Deservedly indeed is the repository of so many saints said to be a heavenly shrine on earth.[4]

This earliest of Christian churches, made, William suggested, of 'brushwood', was destroyed in 1184, when fire consumed the whole abbey complex. In the rebuilding that followed, it was reborn, at the request of the monastic authorities, as a chapel dedicated to the Virgin Mary, whose cult grew popular in medieval Christianity (compared to in its early centuries). Money was required to fund the construction, and it seems likely that the wily monks took liberties with a hazy Joseph of Arimathea legend that had become attached to the 'ancient' chapel. They rightly saw its potency in attracting pilgrims who would be inspired to dig ever deeper into their 'scrips', or wallets, by the suggestion that they were standing on the very spot where someone who knew Jesus had once walked.[5]

They were being misled. A 2018 archaeological study by academics from Reading University concluded that, while there were traces of a fifth-century structure buried underneath and around what are now the ruins of the twelfth-century Lady Chapel, there was no evidence of anything dating back to the first century.[6]

Christianity's arrival on British shores has, then, left no structure that, however distantly and indirectly, connects visitors with those early decades. It is a conclusion that fits with what we know of the circumstances of first-century Britannia. The new Jesus sect had been spreading rapidly. The Welsh monk and chronicler, Gildas, writing in the 540s in *De Excidio et Conquestu Britanniae* (*On the Ruin and Conquest of Britain*), claimed that Christianity had been established in the British Isles before the death of Emperor Tiberius in 37,[7] but most discount any suggestion that it predated the Roman conquest in 43. It is unlikely, though, to have been imported by the elite of colonial administrators, military and civil, who arrived after that date. They were the people who would have had to approve, or at least turn a blind eye to, the building of any Christian church, and the Roman Empire, while generally tolerant of local religious sects and cults within its borders, also insisted on formal adherence by all to its state pantheon of gods – Jupiter, Juno, Minerva, Mars and others – to whom was ascribed imperial success and prosperity. This top-down demand that all go through the motions as regards the official religion weighed most heavily on senior officials and their families. They were expected to set an example, leaving them little room to indulge their own private religious convictions.

For those lower down in the colonial ranks, including in the entourage of these high-ranking figures, there may have been a little more freedom to reject the official polytheism of the Roman state – but only as long as they, too, were seen in public to offer symbolic sacrifice, when required, to the gods. Such acts were akin to an oath of allegiance to the Empire.

However, before embarking for this Roman outpost, some among their number may have had some contact or connection with what we know from Saint Paul's letters was a growing, if still small, community of Christians in the imperial capital in the first century. In his epistle to the Romans, dating from the mid 50s, he greets Prisca and Aquila as 'fellow workers' and refers to 'the church at their house'.[8] In such settings, the talk was not of the vast official pantheon of gods, but of the one God who sent his Son, Jesus, to preach a radical, bottom-up message of reform to the world.

There may even have been some who were touched by the fledgling Christian communities that were springing up elsewhere in the Empire among the legions of soldiers who played their part in bringing and keeping most of Britannia under the rule of Emperor Claudius (41–54) (though Scotland remained free, and parts of the north and Wales were just too far from the centre of Roman power in southern England to see for many years any sustained efforts at effective imperial control). Many of those who made up the occupying force under Aulus Plautius had come from Roman-controlled Gaul (France), where Christianity is said to have spread especially quickly up from the Mediterranean coast and into the Rhône valley, making Avignon, Lyon and Marseille significant centres of Christianity in these early centuries. It grew so rapidly in numbers that its followers faced a major persecution by the authorities in Lyon by 177.

To mark the addition of Britannia to his empire, Claudius – nephew of and successor to the infamously louche Caligula (37–41) – paid a sixteen-day celebratory visit. He was accompanied, according to reports, by elephants when he arrived in triumph in the newly established Roman capital at Camulodunum (Colchester). In his retinue, as well as the generals and administrators (and those who answered to them) required to keep down the unruly locals in the patchwork of kingdoms and tribes now under his authority, was the first influx of traders. The Empire was not just about territorial power but also about economics, and Britannia's mineral reserves in particular had made it very attractive to the Romans. There were profits to be made, and so in the string of fortified towns, linked by the well-made, straight roads that are Rome's lasting mark on the countryside, merchants and dealers would gather. Again, among the less-regimented ranks of this commercial fraternity there may well have been some who had already encountered and carried with them the Christian faith.

A lot is written of the Roman persecution of Christians. Generations of schoolchildren have grown up on tales of those who refused to deny Jesus Christ being thrown to the lions in vast Roman arenas in front of baying crowds. Much of that brutal oppression came later, growing over the centuries as numbers of Christians and their network of churches and bishops expanded, causing official alarm that this new sect of believers posed an existential threat to the cohesion of the Empire itself. By contrast, in the first century only two flashpoints of anti-Christian violence stand out. Emperor Nero (54–68) blamed and punished Christians for the Great Fire of Rome in 64, during which, legend has it, he did nothing but play his fiddle as the flames took hold. The ensuing persecution may even have claimed the lives of both Saint Paul, the missionary par excellence who, more than any other figure, defined the Christian canon, and of Saint Peter, Jesus' chosen leader for his new Church.[9] Subsequent Christian accounts of their deaths in Rome sometime between 64 and 67 have, though, been widely challenged. Peter may never have been to the imperial capital at all. And the whole story of Nero's targeting of Christians rests on a single contemporary reference by the Roman historian Tacitus who, in his *Annals*, writes of the emperor inflicting 'the most exquisite torture' on adherents of a 'most mischievous superstition' called 'Chrestian'.[10]

The second outbreak of violence in the first century came with the persecution of Christians at the end of Domitian's reign (89–96). It provided the backdrop and inspiration for the apocalyptic scenes that dominate Revelation, the final book of the Bible, written at this time. Yet such purges were often confined to specific places and regions. While Domitian's imperial decrees and edicts would have applied equally to Britannia, prosecution relating to them was much less fierce in this new colony than elsewhere.

This may have been because there were just too few Christians around to pose a real threat, especially when compared to the much more pressing uprising against Roman rule in Britannia led by Boudica, queen of the Celtic Iceni tribe. Her forces destroyed Camulodunum, Londinium (London) and Verulamium (St Albans), leaving an estimated 60,000 dead, before being defeated in 60 or 61. Next to this, the private activities of a scattering of first-century Christians would scarcely have set alarm bells ringing, especially if they kept their beliefs to themselves and others of like mind, while all the time paying lip service to the official gods.

Christianity is, of course, an evangelistic faith, with Jesus urging his followers to go out and spread his message.[11] For those first British Christians, what might have proved just as inhibiting as fear of persecution may well have been the (baseless) reputation this new sect enjoyed in Roman society. 'Popular fear of this strange new group,' writes American historian Paula Fredriksen, 'fed also on rumour, which attributed terrible anti-social crimes to Christians – infanticide, cannibalism, incest.'[12]

As a consequence, the earliest manifestations of Christianity in Britannia would have been in the privacy of a family's home, and later other believers would be invited into what became a house church. These were not, then, the brushwood, rock, wooden, stone and bricks-and-mortar structures that tell so much of the subsequent story of Christianity in Britain and Ireland. 'Church' for these early Christians – taking their cue from the Greek noun ἐκκλησία (*ekklesía*), meaning assembly or congregation – was about people, whether it be an assembly of one or a gathering of several in a private home. And so signs of it are hard to detect twenty centuries on.

Later chroniclers of the rise of Christianity, nevertheless, fleshed out accounts of the faith in the British Isles in the first century by putting names and faces to that first generation, on the basis of little or no reliable evidence. Most prominent among these characters is Aristobulus of Britannia, referred to in *On The Seventy Apostles of Christ*. This is a second- or third-century text attributed to the theologian Hippolytus (170–235), who played a leading part in the early doctrinal disputes of the Church, at one stage setting himself up as a rival pope (or anti-pope), before dying as a martyr in Sardinia. There are many question marks over the age, accuracy and authenticity of this document, as indeed there are over the shadowy figure of Hippolytus himself, but he writes of Aristobulus as one of the seventy-two unnamed disciples referred to in the Gospel of Luke.[13] In this passage, Jesus sends them out as evangelists, 'like lambs among wolves', to prepare the way for him. Hippolytus suggests that Aristobulus travelled all the way to Britannia and so became known as the first 'Bishop of the Britons'.

His legend was subsequently taken up with much more gusto by Eastern Christians than by those in the West, where he remains little venerated. In the Orthodox tradition he is revered as a saint, as the brother of the apostle Barnabas, as a sometime companion on the travels of Saint Paul, and as a missionary in his own right who made his way to Britannia via northern Spain. Some Orthodox accounts of his life state that he died peacefully when he reached his destination; others that he was martyred in Wales. This second theory was expanded in the nineteenth century by Anglican cleric and antiquary John Williams, who attempted to show that Aristobulus established churches and even ordained priests and deacons.[14] If he did, no convincing evidence has ever been found, much less any building associated with that mission. Williams' theory is just that.

The same can be said of the tale that Saint Paul made a missionary journey to Wales around 63, an idea that was promoted by Williams' cousin and fellow Anglican cleric, Richard Williams Morgan, in his book *Saint Paul in Britain* in 1861. It speculated about a connection between Paul and a Welsh Druidic chieftain, Caradog ap Bran (a figure based on the first-century British leader, Caratacus). As a preface to meeting Caradog, Paul is said to have travelled to Llantwit Major in the Vale of Glamorgan on the coast of the Bristol Channel. While it was later a centre of Christianity with a monastery most closely associated with the sixth-century saint Illtyd,[15] there is no evidence it existed in the time of Saint Paul (though that did not stop the claim fuelling the burgeoning Celtic revival in Wales, of which Williams Morgan – or Mor Meirion to give him his Bardic name – was a part after he broke with Anglicanism in 1874 and became the first Patriarch of what he termed the Ancient British Church).

With no better footing in any documented fact is a reference to Aristobulus found in a post-Reformation Catholic tradition that takes us back over the border once more to Glastonbury. The source this time is the seventeenth-century Benedictine monk and historian, Serenus de Cressy, who had been allowed to return to England at a time of ongoing persecution of Catholics because he was chaplain to King Charles II's Portuguese wife, Catherine of Braganza. He suggested in his account of Christianity's origins in Britain that Aristobulus' life had ended in 99 at Glastonbury.[16] He quoted various secondary sources to back up his contention, including *English Martyrologe*, a sixteenth-century text:

Artistobulus dyed at Glastonbury, a place far enough removed from the Trinobantes [the ruling tribe in modern-day Essex, including Colchester, before 43] where the Romans exercised their power. Probable it is, that having spent so many years in the laborious exercise of his Apostolick Office, he in his old age retired himself into that place of solitude and Recollection, there quietly disposing himself for his leaving the world.[17]

This appears to be a case of Aristobulus being recruited to another longer-established Glastonbury legend. Had Serenus consulted medieval texts, including amended later versions of William of Malmesbury's history of the town, he would have found plenty of references to the ancient church there, and its association with Joseph of Arimathea. Some of them even claimed that Joseph, as well as Aristobulus, was one of the seventy-two disciples mentioned in Luke's Gospel. How tempting, then, to picture Aristobulus presiding in the church that Joseph built, the first Bishop of the Britons inheriting the building provided by the man who was the first Christian in Britannia.

There was and remains to this day something about Glastonbury that encourages such speculation. This is a town, after all, conflated with the mythical Avalon at the heart of the legends of Arthur and his Knights of the Round Table. It is also regularly cited in discussion about the Grail – the chalice used by Jesus at the Last Supper. In many accounts, Joseph of Arimathea buried it in the ground of Glastonbury, causing a spring to bubble up whose red-tinted water contained traces of Jesus' blood, shed on the cross, and therefore had the power to heal. Long cherished by pilgrims who to this day visit the site of the Chalice Well, this 'blush' has been shown to be a result of the presence in the water of tiny quantities of iron.

Yet so very popular did those stories of Joseph of Arimathea prove in Glastonbury's medieval heyday that in the late fifteenth/ early sixteenth century a chapel in the Abbey was dedicated to him. The Reformation may have destroyed the Abbey, but it couldn't eclipse the legend. Such tales are dancers to the music of time, and by the nineteenth century this particular one had segued into regional folklore in the south west of England. It was told that Joseph – now described as a merchant and trader – had brought a young Jesus, presented as his great nephew, to Glastonbury as part of a commercial trip connected with the tin mines in Cornwall. The idea of a young Jesus, in those years before he started his public ministry, coming to Glastonbury and walking up its landmark Tor, inspired the mystic and artist, William Blake, to add another layer to the legends that shape the town with an 1808 poem,[18] later set to music by Sir Hubert Parry as 'Jerusalem'.

And did those feet in ancient time
Walk upon England's mountains green:
And was the holy Lamb of God,
On England's pleasant pastures seen!

All of this leaves me, in my search for a tangible remnant of first-century Christianity, standing in the grounds of the ruined Glastonbury Abbey in front of a small thorn tree. It is tucked away behind the visitor centre, one of a number of 'holy thorns' dotted about Glastonbury, all claiming a common link to the rumoured visit of Joseph of Arimathea. He reputedly arrived at Glastonbury by boat – the surrounding lowlands at the time often being covered by sea water – and moored on Wearyall Island, better known as Wearyall Hill since subsequent draining of the area. As he climbed out, Joseph rested briefly upon his wooden stick, pressing it into the ground. It is reported to have miracu-lously taken root in the soil.

A succession of thorn trees, including this one in the Abbey, planted in 1992 to replace its eighty-year-old predecessor, claim descent from that original. Until 2019, one stood proudly in splendid isolation on Wearyall Hill itself, bent by the wind and attracting pilgrims who brought garlands for the branches. This seems to have annoyed someone so much that under cover of darkness they hacked it down.

The thorn tree in the Abbey grounds may not be on such prominent display, but at least it enjoys the protection of locked gates at night. If the stones of church buildings can speak across the ages, so too, in this town where the boundary between the physical and the metaphysical is unusually thin, can the branches of an ancient tree, though its prickles would deter anyone tempted to hug it to tune in better.

One variation of the legend suggests that Joseph brought with him one of the thorns from the crown placed on Jesus' head at the crucifixion, and that is what gave rise to this succession of thorn trees. Records down the ages refer to them blossoming, with great liturgical sensibility, at Easter and at Christmas. As, more or less, do their successors now. All fun, fancy and invention? To add in a dash of science, the trees in question come from a species that is unknown anywhere elsewhere in Britain. Its natural home is . . . yes, the Middle East.

The Reformation's attack on monasteries fortunately didn't stretch to holy trees, which explains why the cult of the Glastonbury thorn as the oldest physical manifestation of Christianity in Britain and Ireland continues to this day. It is, at best, a tenuous link in gnarled wood to the first century. Over the next hundred years, however, Britannia changed to become a land that the early Church Father Tertullian (born in 160) describes as 'conquered by Christ'. And that conquest did leave behind something in stone.

ALSO WITH A STORY TO TELL . . .

ST JUST IN ROSELAND in Cornwall is a thirteenth-century church, built on the site of an earlier sixth-century Saxon foundation. If you wander along bamboo-lined paths that lead through sub-tropical gardens down to a tidal creek on the River Fal, you are, according to local legend, walking in Jesus' footsteps. When accompanying Joseph of Arimathea on one of his folklorish expeditions to the tin mines of Cornwall, the ship carrying the young Jesus sought shelter from a storm in this very creek. For centuries, a stone on the shoreline, marked with a cross, identified the exact spot where the Son of God stepped onto England's pleasant pastures.

CHAPTER 2
The Second Century

Saint Alban's Shrine: The First Home-grown Martyr

By embracing the faith of the Gospel, the Christians incurred
the supposed guilt of an unnatural and unpardonable offence.
Edward Gibbon, *The History of the Decline*
and Fall of the Roman Empire (1776–88)[1]

THE MEDIEVAL CATHEDRAL housing Saint Alban's shrine in the Hertfordshire commuter city to the north of London that bears his name is vague about the year of his martyrdom. The display boards in the user-friendly modern visitor centre, added on to this mighty Norman cross-shaped church that was reputedly built on the spot where Alban died, hedge their bets with talk of his death happening 'around' 300. In the north aisle, however, an older, Gothic-style framed timeline, in elaborate black-and-red calligraphy, places it firmly almost 100 years earlier, in 209.[2]

The gap between the two highlights the degree of flexibility necessary in any telling of how Christianity spread through Britain and Ireland. The cache of details that we possess from this period is so much more meagre than that from later centuries, while most of what we do have is subject to fierce scholarly debate about provenance and dating. The picture that emerges, therefore, doesn't always conform to a neat series of 100-year parcels. Instead, what works better is to regard the killing of Alban – wherever we place it on the spectrum of possible dates – as instructive about the next distinctive stage of Christian development after a first century spent in the shadows of Roman rule. It was an age of martyrs, with sporadic persecution of Christians shaping the second and third centuries as the Church took its first hesitant steps out of the private and into the public domain.

While Aristobulus has a prior (though historically flimsy) claim to be Britain's first Christian martyr, Alban has long held this honour, largely unchallenged by dint of the endorsement of the Venerable Bede in his enduringly influential *Ecclesiastical History of the English People*, written around 731 and still one of the earliest and best sources we have on Christianity in the Roman outpost of Britannia. The circumstances that this scholarly monk describes for the martyrdom of 'noble Alban' took place against a backdrop of an increasingly widespread and active suspicion of those early British Christians. Actual repression of the new Church, though, waxed and waned. Much of what is routinely referred to as Roman persecution of Christians throughout its Empire in this period was localised, sporadic and sometimes mob led, or else carried out in bursts by over-zealous individual officials on the spot rather than as a systematic programme directed from the imperial capital.

'Being yet a pagan,' Bede writes of Alban, 'when at the bidding of unbelieving rulers all manner of cruelty was practised against the Christians, [Alban] gave entertainment in his house to a certain clerk [priest], flying from his persecutors.'[3] Witnessing how diligently his guest (first given a name, Amphibalus, in accounts that date from the twelfth century[4]) prayed to his Christian Lord, Alban was moved to join in with him and so, Bede continues, 'cast off the darkness of idolatry [to] become a Christian in all sincerity of heart'.[5] When soldiers came to arrest his house guest, Alban insisted that the two men should swap cloaks, allowing Amphibalus to escape. Alban surrendered himself into custody, dressed as a priest.

The detail is instructive and perhaps even anachronistic. Alban's guest was unlikely to have been going about in public dressed a Christian priest. That, in Britannia, would have been to draw attention to himself and invite trouble – though, of course, his sartorial misjudgement may have been precisely what brought the soldiers knocking on Alban's door. Christianity elsewhere was by this stage developing a leadership structure that separated clergy and laity – a distinction unknown in its earliest decades – and introduced dress codes to demarcate the two.

Slowly taken before a judge, Alban refused to recant his new-found faith, (Emperor Septimius Severus in 209 had decreed that all converts to Christianity should be executed). 'If you desire to hear the truth of my religion,' he declared defiantly, 'be it known to you that I am now a Christian'.[6] Torture (the favoured Roman tactic to strong-arm captured Christians into apostasy) failed to break his resolve. Indeed, so oblivious did Alban appear to the prospect of losing either his limbs or his life that, at the last minute, his executioner couldn't bring himself to carry out the beheading, as ordered, and instead fell to his knees in front of Alban and declared himself 'a companion in faith and truth'.[7] A stand-in was summoned and did manage to complete the job, but as Alban's head tumbled to the ground, Bede reports, so too did the eyes of the man who had decapitated him. Even the judge was not immune to the spectacle; he urged an end to the persecution of Christians and became one himself.

Bede tells a well-formed, dramatic and – for those of faith, open to the intervention of the miraculous hand of God – persuasive story, but those same qualities have led some modern scholars to question whether it might have been deliberately fashioned that way by early Christians so as to strengthen their resolve that God was with them, as with Alban, when they encountered the full force of Roman wrath. There are various theories as to how this shaping of the narrative about Alban that came down to Bede might have been achieved. Some suggest a borrowing of details from the cults of gods worshipped by pagans, others that Alban's death was subsequently embellished with elements taken from the cult of Saint Ailbe of Emly, popular in Ireland in the fifth century. And yet another has it that Alban's martyrdom was created as a saintly human manifestation of the spirit of 'Albion', a word originally used by the Greeks in the third and fourth century BC to refer to what we now know as Great Britain. While none has become the orthodox explanation, what is certainly agreed, concludes the ancient historian, Robin Lane Fox, is that the 'date and historicity' of Alban 'are highly disputable'.[8]

As Christianity won over ever more converts, what is known is that it grew ever more skilled, often in particular regional contexts, at what is referred to as 'baptising the customs' – taking on board the narratives of those religions it sought to replace, then rearranging and repeopling them to make them its own, but keeping sufficient of the heart of the original story to win round those who had once taken them as an article of faith.[9] One well-known example from Britain and Ireland (and elsewhere) is how pagan shrines to water deities were subsumed into Christianity by rebranding them as holy wells and attaching saints' stories to them.

Bede, of course, insisted on the literal truth of what he wrote about Alban. Quite what sources he used are unknown, which leaves his account open to question. The earliest description of Alban's martyrdom came in *Vita Germani* (*Life of Germanus*), a hagiography written many years later, between 460 and 480, which told how the sainted Christian Bishop Germanus of Auxerre in Burgundy had visited Britain to help put down a revolt against the Church. '[He] went to the tomb of the blessed martyr Alban,' it reports, 'to give thanks through him to God'.[10] That night, the *Life* recounts, Alban appeared to Germanus in a dream and shared with him the details of his martyrdom. When he awoke, the bishop wrote them down and, on his return to Auxerre, put what he had recorded on display in a basilica he had built that was dedicated to Alban.

So a shrine to Alban did exist in Britannia in the latter half of the fifth century, but no mention is made in the *Life* of where it was. For that sort of precision we have to wait almost another century, until 547, when the Welsh monk and chronicler, Gildas, listed among the British martyrs of Roman persecution 'Alban of

Verulamium' – the Roman name for modern-day St Albans. His name appears alongside those of 'Aaron and Julius, citizens of Caerleon' (sometimes called 'the City of Legions', on the River Usk in Wales, one of three permanent Roman legionary bases in the later stages of its occupation of Britannia, along with York and Chester) and 'others of both sexes who stood and fought courageously for Christ'.[11]

Bede is believed to have relied in several passages in his *Ecclesiastical History of the English People* on details found in Gildas, but it is Bede's own version of Alban's story that has been re-enacted down the ages in St Albans, revived in recent years as a colourful procession of life-size puppets through the main streets to the west front of the cathedral on Alban's feast day, 22 June. Bede is careful in his writings, though, to make it plain that the tale of Alban had long been famous not just in one place but throughout Britain. That process had been under way since 'peaceable Christian times were restored', with pilgrims making their way to a church 'of wonderful workmanship, altogether worthy to commemorate his martyrdom' in the place of the execution. It was, Bede says, somewhere 'the cure of sick persons and the frequent working of wonders cease not to this day'.[12]

That reference to when 'peaceable Christian times were restored' could mean once the Roman Empire officially ended the persecution of Christians with the Edict of Milan in February 313. Or once imperial forces started leaving Britannia later in the final decades of the fourth century. Or when the so-called 'golden age' of Anglo-Saxon Christianity dawned much closer to Bede's own times. The one thing that is sure is that a shrine to Alban had existed for some considerable time before the early decades of the eighth century.

On the day of my visit, I have the Shrine of Saint Alban to myself. Not a single other pilgrim is present to mitigate the experience, nor a cathedral usher in sight to keep a watchful eye on me. Once there was no hour of the day or night when, given its fame, the shrine could be left unsupervised. No ordinary pilgrim could be trusted to be alone with Alban's relics. To the north side of the central shrine monument is a free-standing medieval structure, known as the Watching Loft. Two storeys high, in mellow, pinkish-red wood, it contains a steep staircase that leads up from the pillared lower floor to an upper tier, fronted by a delicately carved viewing gallery. Here, from 1400 onwards, the resident monks of Saint Alban's Abbey would keep a vigil over what was then a jewel-encrusted structure. Their twenty-four-hour wakefulness sprang not only out of concern that thieves might creep into the Abbey under cover of darkness to steal the precious stones that had been given to honour Alban's memory, but also that they might desecrate this sacred precinct by removing his bones from inside the shrine's casing. Relics were, in medieval times, a commodity almost as valuable as gold. It was known for them to be stolen and sold on to another abbey or cathedral, or to a pious prince to be added to his collection and then put on display to boost a thriving pilgrim trade that could bring up to 100,000 visitors to the major shrines during the Church's great festivals.[13]

For pilgrims, there was a much greater attraction than the prestige or monetary value attached to saints' relics. 'Surviving body parts and clothes of a dead saint would retain a residue of supernatural and efficacious essence,' writes the expert on medieval manuscripts, Christopher de Hamel, in his account of the shrine of Thomas Becket in Canterbury Cathedral that in those times rivalled Saint Alban's as a destination. 'Devotion at a saint's tomb or reliquary brings the pilgrim into almost tangible proximity to actual godly presence still on earth.'[14]

Such intensity of faith is hard to imagine in our secular, sceptical age, but there is nowhere better to come within touching distance of it than where I am standing. The shrine itself is a curious-looking thing, like a tall, thin scale-model of a Gothic chapel, held up by similarly miniature, slender buttresses. Stranger still, on top of it sits what looks like a tiny, ornate, deep-red tent, more suitable as the desert residence of a small-in-stature Eastern potentate. On closer examination, though, the main plinth, in greyish marble, is a richly carved pedestal, on two levels: a lower tomb-like structure with diamond-shaped recesses, and above it a series of alcoves that are adorned with angels, the outline of their wings worn away by time, and still just-about discernible details of Alban's martyrdom. This is where pilgrims would rest their heads against the shrine as they knelt beside it to pray, or where they could leave their gifts. Today there are rails and kneelers, to keep visitors at a distance, but they don't stop some carrying on time-honoured traditions. One niche is filled with long-stemmed red roses to match the almost claret colour of the silk cloth above.

That tented upper section, trimmed in the 1990s with fresh gold and silver embroidery that is based on medieval sketches of the shrine, would originally have housed the casket containing Alban's relics. It still has the desired effect of inexorably lifting my eyes upwards to what symbolises Alban's eternal presence at the heart of the cathedral and the city named after him. The design once allowed, too, for this elevated final resting place to be peri-odically uncovered, and the casket of Alban's relics to be lifted down and then processed around the building on high days and holy days, as one might lift a coffin off a bier.

One effect of being all alone in this space is to imagine myself as the latest, insignificant link in an endless human chain of pilgrims drawn to this spot that may even stretch back to the age of martyrs in the second and third centuries of Roman Britain and Alban's death. Such thoughts are augmented by details on the walls that surround the shrine with, in one corner, a carving of a severed head, presumably Alban's, as if in full flight down to the ground, red markings representing the blood spilling from his severed arteries. Yet reason intervenes to remind me that what is here today does not date back to those earliest centuries of Christianity, or even to the time of the pilgrim visits that Bede records. The church 'of wonderful workmanship' to which he refers in his 731 text was replaced at the end of the eighth century.

Of all the different kingdoms that made up England at the time, the Christian gospel was particularly late in reaching Mercia, which covered much of central England down as far south as the River Thames. Not until 653 did its pagan king, Penda, allow Christian priests to enter his territories. By 757, when Offa ascended the Mercian throne, he enthusiastically established new Christian monasteries. Among their number was one at Verulamium, where Offa made it his business to recover the remains of Alban and place them at the heart of a community of Benedictine monks.

Matthew Paris, the most celebrated scholar to have graced the resulting monastery, tells in his *The Lives of the Two Offas* how in 793 Offa the King was guided by a beam of light shining down from heaven to the precise spot where the bones of Alban were subsequently unearthed. It suggests that they had been either hidden or misplaced despite Bede's confident talk of pilgrims coming to a church.[15] In building a monastery, church and shrine to Alban in which to house his remains, Offa was undeniably motivated by faith, but it was only one of his considerations. He could also see the value of associating himself, and his claim to hegemony over his rivals as the first English king, with the man who was Britain's first martyr. For succeeding generations of monks who lived in this monument to Alban, the combination of a much-visited shrine and royal patronage allowed them to thrive.

Quite what form was taken by the original shrine built by Offa to hold the relics is lost in the mists of time. What is in front of me now dates to the rebuilding of the Abbey in 1077 under Paul de Caen, following the Norman Conquest. It may have replicated the existing shrine, but that seems unlikely. In church design, each age seems to try to outdo what was there before. More plausible is that it was constructed in the same place as its predecessor, such continuity being the medieval practice, responding to the need to reassure pilgrims (however questionable the evidence) of an enduring direct and tangible line back to the saint. A casket containing Alban's remains was therefore positioned near the main altar of the new Norman abbey.

A century later it was placed in a feretory, an elaborate outer housing-cum-platform, and relocated directly behind the main altar so that when the priest was saying Mass he could look up and be inspired by Alban's example.

The next stage in the shrine's evolution began in 1484, when the building of a great stone screen separated it off, and split the abbey in two. The impetus for its construction seems to have been to divide the space where Mass would be celebrated from where pilgrims would come, allowing the monks peace and contemplation at one end, removed from the noisy visitors. That arrangement, however, came to an abrupt end in December 1539 when, as part of Henry VIII's Reformation, the dissolution of the monastery of Saint Alban took place, one of the last to surrender to the King. Its treasures were stripped out and taken to the royal treasury, including those associated with the shrine. The pedestal on which it stood was broken up and the relics removed. From 1553, the abbey served as a parish church to St Albans, later its cathedral.

The fate of Alban's relics is unknown. It may have been that they were burnt or ground down, as was the fate of those of Thomas Becket at Canterbury. They have not, though, been completely lost. At the end of the tenth century, some portion of them had been sent by the monastery to Germany, to the Church of Saint Pantaleon in Cologne, where they survived every religious and military upheaval that followed.[16] In 2002, symbolically laying to rest the ghosts of the Reformation, the Catholic authorities in Cologne agreed to return one of the relics preserved in

Saint Pantaleon's – said to be part of Alban's shoulder blade – to St Albans. There is therefore, in religious tradition at least, once again something physical of Alban in the cathedral that today carries his name and celebrates his role in British Christianity down the centuries.

Destroyed during the Reformation, the shrine structure has also returned from oblivion. During an 1872 renovation of the cathedral, a stash of 2,000 fragments of Purbeck marble, some painted and gilded, was unearthed behind the blocked arches of what would have been, pre-1539, the east wall of the medieval shrine. Experts painstakingly pieced them together to bring the shrine back to life. In 1990 those Victorian efforts were updated by the insertion of an invisible stainless steel frame. It now holds the shrine up, for the dramas and reverses of many centuries have visibly taken their toll.

Close up, the stone of the pedestal has a coarser texture than the word marble might suggest, but it only adds to the sense of quiet, dignified antiquity the shrine exudes, befitting of the status of this particular spot (despite all the necessary caveats) in the Christian history of these islands.

Of the many dates proposed for Alban's martyrdom, Bede opts for 304, linking it (though not explicitly in his text) with what proved to be the final, bloody spasm under Emperor Diocletian (284–305) of persecution of what was an ever-expanding and ultimately – despite his efforts and those, intermittently, of his predecessors – uncrushable Christian Church. Diocletian's edicts, removing Christians' rights and requiring them to offer sacrifice to pagan gods, were brutally imposed, with much loss of life, especially in the eastern parts of his domains, including Thessalonica, Caesarea and Nicodemia. Churches were razed to the ground, Scriptures destroyed, and those who resisted burned. In Britain, as with much of the western section of the Empire, however, there is little evidence that this, or previous purges, reached anything near such intensity.

The first reliable reference to Christianity's rapid spread in the British Isles in the second century comes from a far-removed source, the Christian convert, theologian and polemicist Tertullian, who was based in Carthage in north Africa, now on the outskirts of modern-day Tunis but in its day the second city of the Empire. In a tract entitled *Adversus Judaeos* (*Against Jews*) from around 200, which demonstrates how early antisemitism had taken hold of Christian thought, Tertullian writes of 'the place of the Britons not reached by the Romans but subject to Christ'. In such a location, he adds, 'Christ's name reigns'. It is a fleeting reference made, sceptics note, in a document that is more polemic and prejudice than history or reportage, and by an individual who had never been to Britannia, or anywhere just beyond its borders.

His suggestion that there were Christians thriving just beyond Britannia's border seems to be referring to the lands north of Hadrian's Wall, named after the Emperor who commissioned it in 122 as a stone defensive and customs barrier from the River Tyne in the east, to the Solway Firth in the west. But Tertullian's remarks are not backed up by any other contemporary text. Significantly, there is no mention at all of Britannia in a list of places where Christianity is thriving in the second century compiled by Irenaeus, Bishop of Lyon, in *Adversus Hareeses* (*Against Heresies*), dated just twenty years before Tertullian's tract. The omission may have a benign explanation. Irenaeus – unsurprisingly, given his office – was keen on the establishment of a hierarchical structure throughout Christendom, led by bishops and ultimately the Bishop of Rome. His decision to leave out Britannia may simply have meant that, at the time, it had no bishop-leader and so was unworthy of consideration.

Easier to discard in trying to establish the truth is a story that circulated from the seventh century onwards (in *Books of Popes*, and later in Bede) of how, in 167, a British king called Lucius had written to Pope Eleutherius in Rome asking to be accepted into the Christian faith, and for the dispatch of missionaries to help him spread the good news in his lands. Few modern historians believe that Lucius ever existed.[17] Bede, in his account, does, and he embellishes the legend by claiming that Lucius' conversion had, indeed, prompted his people to follow in his footsteps. The response of the Roman authorities was, he writes, to cast a tolerant eye on such developments until the Diocletian persecution at the start of the fourth century wiped out a British church of 130 years' standing. No archaeological find of a church or meeting place has ever pointed to this period of grace which Bede writes of as having taken place.

That didn't stop Geoffrey of Monmouth in 1135, in his colourful *Historia Regum Britanniae* (*History of the Kings of Britain*), creating a whole new narrative whereby Eleutherius actually sent two missionaries to help Lucius, variously referred to in subsequent copies of his text as Fuganus or Fagan and Duvianus, Deruvian or Damian. These two, he told, made converts, built churches and established dioceses. Again, nothing has subsequently been turned up to substantiate this account, though Fagan is recalled as a saint in Welsh Christianity and has churches dedicated to him.

While Diocletian was targeting Christians in other areas of his Empire, he subdivided oversight in the rest of his lands between four 'tetrarchs'. Of this quartet, Britannia fell under Constantius Chlorus. It was his son, Constantine, who succeeded Diocletian in 305, and within eight years had declared an end to imperial persecution of Christians. It was to transform their lives and see the institutional Church start to take shape. First, though, there were more hard times for them to endure, in Britannia as elsewhere in the Empire.

ALSO WITH A STORY TO TELL . . .

At the excavated Roman settlement of Calleva Atrebatum, near SILCHESTER IN HAMPSHIRE, the layout of this once important centre of imperial rule in Britannia after 43 includes public baths, an amphitheatre, a monument to nymphs and several temples. Close to the forum is what some believe may be the footprint of a very early Christian church, shaped like a basilica with an apse (semicircular recess, usually behind the altar).

CHAPTER 3
The Third Century

Lullingstone Villa: Worshipping at Home

The scattered Christians of the third century had by now organised themselves into a definite church.

J. R. H. Moorman, *A History of the Church in England*[1]

To GRASP IN one place the evolution of Christianity in Britain and Ireland from the private sphere to the public, and from being one cult among many accommodated in a largely pragmatic polytheistic pantheon by the colonial authorities to becoming the prestigious religion of the Roman Empire, head for Lullingstone Villa. In the shadow of a tall, nine-arched, red-brick railway viaduct, a long, thin, green valley extends beside the River Darent in Kent. In the mid 1930s, this peaceful corridor was earmarked for the building of London's first international airport, but after the Second World War that cup passed to Heathrow, west of the city. Lullingstone was left to the archaeologists, who in 1949 started to unearth the remains of a remarkable Roman villa dating back to the early decades of their occupation of Britannia. Now looked after by English Heritage, its unearthed foundations and recovered mosaic floors are housed inside a vast and anonymous structure that ironically looks like an aircraft hangar.

A walkway takes me inside above what would have been the villa's east-facing veranda. One room immediately stands out. Among the intersecting low stone walls that map out the floor plan of this once grand residence is what the curators refer to as the 'deep room'. Sunken further into the earth than any of the others around it – even the sub-floors nearby that were added in 275 to provide the rooms above with heating – this cellar had been part of the first, modest, stone-built house that was put up around 80 following the conquest of Britannia. Back then, the villa would have been a utilitarian block of rooms, with a wing at either end, as part of a working farm on a slope running eastwards down to the river. The identity of its first owner is unknown, but historians speculate that it could have been a Briton, who had prospered by working with the new colonial overlords and was now keen to cosy up further by adopting the Roman style of living. The site is part of a group of seven other similar villas in this area of north Kent, located close to Watling Street, the major trading route that the Romans built to connect Durovernum (Canterbury) on the coast with Londinium (London) and, beyond it, Verulamium (St Albans).

Over the next three centuries, the villa regularly changed owners and size, shape and decoration, to match the status and ambitions of its occupiers. So while this 'deep room' may originally have been used as basement storage, according to Lieutenant Colonel Geoffrey Meates, one of that first team of archaeologists who excavated the villa, by the second century it had become a sacred place for worshipping various indigenous British deities. Another hundred years later, it had switched to being a space for ritual observance of the imperial cult that regarded dead emperors as gods. And as the third century became the fourth, Christianity made its presence felt in this part of the villa, leading ultimately to the addition on top of the existing subterranean structure of an upper room, or house church.

The tell-tale signs of the second-century usage of the 'deep room' are in front of me. In the centre of its dirt floor is a well, and cut into one of its sides is a niche containing a wall painting of three nymphs. This was, at that time, the place in the villa dedicated to a pagan water cult. These were common during the Roman conquest of Britannia, including that to the Celtic goddess Sulis at the thermal spring in present-day Bath. In the context of a farm, such a cult would more likely have been one way of imploring the gods to provide a regular and adequate supply of rainfall to sustain the crops. Less obvious to this modern visitor's eye, but attested by archaeologists, are other wall painting decorations in this 'deep room', which include illustrations of date palms. A set of four marble pots made in the eastern Mediterranean in around 150 was also found buried in the floor. They may once have contained offerings to the gods.

By the start of the third century, though, the water nymphs had been covered up and the niche filled in, reflecting a change in the focus of rituals to fall into line with the official variety of Roman religion. This made gods out of deceased emperors and attributed to them the power in death to bequeath eternal prosperity and unity on the domains they had ruled in life. What appeared to give a clue to such usage was the discovery during excavations of the villa in the 1950s of two battered, late-second-century marble portrait busts at the foot of the steps leading into the sacred space. They are not on view today in situ (they now reside in the British Museum in London), but one of them bears a striking resemblance to other images of Pertinax, governor of Britannia from 185–86, who later rose to be Roman Emperor in 193, albeit only for a few months before he was murdered by the Praetorian Guard in what is known to history as the Year of the Five Emperors. A ring found at the villa also carried his personal seal. Together, the presence of these items has been used to argue that Lullingstone could have been his country retreat when governor, perhaps even a grace-and-favour property that went with the job.

With so little evidence to pick over of life in Britain in Roman times, there can be a temptation, as here, to jump to conclusions. The classicist and well-known broadcaster, Mary Beard, sounded a note of caution after her own visit to Lullingstone shortly before mine: 'Finds such as these [portrait busts] are rare in a Roman-British villa, but they also illustrate quite how hard it can be to make sense of material from even the best documented excavations, and how eager we can be to tell stories about the people of the past that honestly don't quite add up.'[2]

One attraction of making a link between Lullingstone and Pertinax is that his presence in the villa would account for why it had been so enlarged and adorned in this period. And extended it certainly continued to be. By the middle decades of the fourth century, the central section of the villa had been rebuilt to incorporate a new dining room (*triclinium*) with an adjoining audience chamber to greet grand guests with its ostentatious display of mosaic floors. These offer an ambiguous clue in the search for evidence of the growing influence of Christianity in Britannia.

The main panel in the audience chamber is of the story of the Greek hero, Bellerophon, prince of Corinth. He rides on the winged horse, Pegasus, as he kills the chimera, a fire-breathing monster. Such a tale would have been uncontroversial in the Roman pantheon, which seamlessly assimilated such Greek myths. But might the choice of design in the mosaic before me carry a coded message for Christians who could not yet be as open as they might like about their beliefs in what may well have been a government house? For the ostensibly perfectly acceptable Greek reference in the mosaics could also have been a less obvious allegory for the triumph of good (i.e. Christianity) over evil, in the shape of Roman persecution of the Church.

The first decades of the third century saw long settled spells without any great spasm of violence and scapegoating directed at Christians in the Empire. This despite Emperor Septimius Severus, as we have seen already, having in 209 ordered the death penalty for converts to the new religion. Yet the description of Septimius Severus as a persecutor of Christians is based, in large measure, on writings in the 320s by the early Christian bishop Eusebius in his celebrated *History of the Church*.[3] Other evidence suggests Eusebius may have been doing him an injustice, and that the Emperor not only employed a Christian as his personal doctor (another believer in high places), but also saved several others

42

from the mob who targeted them as different, and therefore as their enemy.

The same Septimius Severus had headed north from Rome in 208 to subdue that part of Britannia that was not under Roman rule. He ordered the strengthening of the 116-kilometre-long wall – from the River Tyne in the east to Solway Firth in the west – built in the 120s during the reign of the Emperor Hadrian to mark the northern border of the Roman Empire and to keep out the northern Britons. A subsequent emperor, Antoninus Pius, had tried in the 140s to establish a second defensive barrier (the Antonine Wall) about 160 kilometres further north, between the Firths of Clyde and Forth in what is today the Central Belt of Scotland, but that plan had failed. The Romans had subsequently fallen back to Hadrian's Wall. Septimius Severus, with his army of 50,000 men – an indication of how seriously Rome took this local difficulty – was intent on re-establishing the Antonine Wall as the northern boundary, but once again the might of Rome was frustrated by its wily opponents. In mid conflict, the emperor was taken ill and died in Eboracum (York) early in 211. His forces retreated back behind Hadrian's Wall and peace once more returned to Britannia. That enabled Christianity, here as elsewhere, to continue becoming more widespread and slowly, slowly, moving out of the shadows.

In Rome itself, Christians were elected as senators in these decades of the third century and were appointed to senior roles in the army. Yet Christianity, like Judaism from which it sprang, proved curiously tricky to integrate into the Romans' vast and diverse pantheon of acceptable gods, even when efforts were being made in that direction during the rule of benign rulers. Unlike other deities that could exist without modifying their core beliefs alongside those officially promoted by the Roman state, Christianity and Judaism were monotheistic – they believed in one god, not many. 'You shall bow down to no other god, for

Yahweh's name is the Jealous One,' it is written in the Book of Exodus.[4] And so many of the new Christians refused in conscience to go through the motions of offering public sacrifice to the Roman gods for the sake of a peaceful life.

Such principled dissent, inevitably, rankled with less-tolerant or harder-pressed emperors. Decius (249–51) shattered the relative peace over such matters in the mid third century when he unleashed an official pogrom against Christian communities to compel then to bow down to Rome's gods. Some accounts say his persecution cost 3,000 lives, with Pope Fabian dying of his brutal treatment in prison after refusing to submit. And, soon afterwards, in 257, one of Decius' successors, Valerian, was busy scapegoating Christians for a general malaise across the Empire. The spilt blood of the martyrs, however, only strengthened Christian resolve to resist, whatever the personal cost.

Their witness was one challenge in the decades of growing turmoil across the Empire in the middle of the third century. From the assassination of Emperor Severus Alexander in 235 through to the reign of Aurelian in the 270s and Diocletian a decade later, Rome was in a constant state of unrest and discord, characterised by political instability, recurrent plagues, confidence-sapping invasions by Goths, Vandals and Sassanids, and the breakdown of Empire-wide trading patterns when the western provinces of Gaul, Hispania and Britannia briefly broke away as a separate entity. In looking for someone to blame for these misfortunes, there were emperors who fell back once again on pointing a finger at Christians for chipping away at the cement of the state religion. Valerian, for example, purged the Christian members of the Roman Senate (as well as putting to death another pope, Sixtus II, who was summarily beheaded along with his deacons after being caught presiding over worship in one of the funerary chapels in the catacombs).

The pressure wasn't relentless. In 260, Emperor Gallienus, son and sometime co-ruler with his father Valerian, issued an edict that decriminalised Christianity and allowed the Church to own property as a corporate body. That reform proved short-lived. As emperor succeeded emperor, twenty-five in forty-seven years, of whom only one died in his bed, the dominant theme was hostility to the Church. Diocletian, who ruled from 284, is thought to have had a Christian wife and daughters, but he nevertheless picked off Christians in the upper ranks of the imperial army. He even forced Pope Marcellinus to cave in and perform a public act of worship to the Roman gods as part of another bout of persecution in the early 300s, the last sustained imperial attack on Christianity.

If, then, the first three decades of the third century saw Christianity grow in Britannia in what were generally more tolerant times, the rest of the century largely saw them retreat once more into private spaces to avoid being targeted and blamed. At Lullingstone, the resulting nervousness may have delayed, as part of the wider upgrading of the villa, the building of the upstairs house church until well into the next century. The green light came with Emperor Constantine's Edict of Milan in February 313. It finally and definitively gave Christianity legal status and freedom from persecution. Some accounts suggest Constantine was inspired to do so on the eve of a battle after seeing a vision of Jesus promising him victory if he fought under the banner of the cross. This prophecy came true at Milvian Bridge in 312. Others see a more strategic purpose behind the Emperor's change of heart. After centuries of trying and failing to wipe it out, he had realised that the resilience and energy of Christianity would be much better harnessed to the imperial cause.

Just over a year later, in August 314, three bishops from Britannia are recorded as attending the Council of Arles in southern Gaul (France) to discuss imposition of doctrine across the newly legal Church. The presence of Eborius of York, Restitutus of London and Adelphius of Colchester (or perhaps Lincoln), all three centres of the Roman colonial government, suggests that a diocesan structure and possibly even churches had been in place and operating for longer than a few months.

At Lullingstone, flint and mortar piers were built against the north and south walls of the 'deep room' to support a new structure being added above. When completed, its decorations looked very much like what is seen today in many Christian churches. As part of the site was being excavated in the 1950s, thousands of fragments of painted plaster walls were unearthed. Painstakingly pieced together, they revealed that someone who lived in this villa had not only commissioned the building of a house church, but had also decorated its west wall with six near-life-size male figures in long tunics with beaded sashes who were probably clerics. Their arms were outstretched, the 'Orans' position still adopted by Christian priests when standing at the altar during Mass and joining the congregation in prayer.

On the east and south walls were two Chi-Rho symbols, the unmistakable mark of the early Christians. Made up of the first two letters of Christ's name in Greek – *chi* (X) and *rho* (P), they were superimposed one on top of the other to make a cross-like shape and invoke Jesus's death on Calvary. The example on the south wall is particularly ornate, its letters red on a white background, its roundel formed by a wreath of leaves and flowers, and the whole flanked by two painted columns. So ornate, indeed, that it has been judged too precious to leave on display in an aircraft hangar in Kent. Like the painting from the west wall and other pieces found here of the earliest-known evidence of Christianity in the British Isles, it can be seen in the British Museum thirty miles away in central London.

There it shares the Roman Britain Room with a near-contemporary exhibit, the Hinton St Mary Mosaic. While the Lullingstone Chi-Rho provides no image of Christ himself, this neighbour does. There is no historical record of what Jesus looked like. The Gospels do not deal in such details, and the Jewish tradition from which he emerged did not as a rule depict God. Yet the influence of Roman worship was being felt here in Britannia among these early Christians. For the Romans liked nothing better than to be surrounded by images of their deities. So while the well-off, well-educated owners of Lullingstone may have resisted imagining a face of Christ, in the floor of their villa at Hinton St Mary in what is today Dorset, another wealthy Roman-British family, drawn in some measure to the new religion, did include a shoulder-length portrait of a clean-shaven, fair-skinned Jesus as well as the Chi-Rho.

If this was the first attempt to put a face to God's Son in British Christianity, it was a modest one. Perhaps to avoid drawing too much attention to itself, he is presented in the typical toga that a man of power and influence would have worn in that age. The one symbol that does discreetly stand out in the mosaic is the pomegranates. In Greek mythology, pomegranates feature prominently in the story of Persephone, as symbols of the cycle of death and rebirth into the light of spring. Like the use of the tale of Bellerophon at Lullingstone, these pomegranates may have been a subtler message for those with eyes to see it – namely the Christian belief that Jesus rose from the dead and ascended into the light of heaven.

Back in the giant shed in Lullingstone, where the archaeologists' spades once dug, what is apparent is that this early house church served more than one dwelling. On the floor plans that line the raised walkways to inform visitors, next to the house church is an antechamber, or what early Christians called a narthex, and modern churchgoers refer to as the porch. Here, those not yet baptised but drawn to Christianity (possibly in preference to the rituals going on in the room below) would have been able to observe services but not participate in them. Those who hedge their bets and stand at the back of Catholic churches rather than take their place in the pews are sometimes called 'ghost Catholics', and here it seems that 1,700 years ago there was an earlier group of 'ghost Christians', not yet sure whether they were in or out, or whether it was safe to make that commitment after so long a history of persecution.

The antechamber, too, had painted plaster walls, and a third Chi-Rho symbol to concentrate minds, though this one also incorporated the alpha and omega letters. They echo the words of Revelation, the final apocalyptic book of the Bible, believed to have been written in a period of persecution of Christians, where Jesus describes himself as 'the Alpha and Omega, the First and the Last, the Beginning and the End'.[5]

Of the structure of the upper room, though, nothing is left. The whole upper portion of Lullingstone Villa did not survive the centuries of neglect that followed after the Romans pulled out of Britannia in the early fifth century. And so the house church crumbled back into the 'deep room' that is so clearly delineated in the excavations. Yet for a period in the fourth century, both levels could have been in operation in this large property. As the religious practices of the various occupiers of the villa evolved, different members of what would have been a large household would have been at different stages in their beliefs. Upstairs and downstairs may even have functioned simultaneously – Christian and pagan, above and below – for this was a time of transition. The rare and revealing rich decorations that have survived the caving in of the house church suggest that it was the Christian God who became progressively more dominant, both in the private life of those who lived there and in the public life of the colonial administration.

CHAPTER 4

The Fourth Century

Ninian's Whithorn: The Shining Place

The parish has a saint's name time cannot unfrock.

R. S. Thomas, 'The Moon in Lleyn'[2]

THE SMALL TOWN of Whithorn in Galloway in the far south west of Scotland – more like a large village, a local friend advises me – was home to one of the earliest Christian communities in Britain and Ireland. That much is for certain. The Latinus Stone, unearthed locally and now on display in Whithorn's Priory Museum, dates back to around 450. Thought to have originally stood in an early Christian graveyard (and later in Whithorn's now ruined medieval priory), its well-worn inscription in Latin reads: 'We praise you, the Lord! Latinus, descendant of Barravados, aged 35, and his daughter, aged 4, made a sign here'. Above the lettering are faint traces of the Chi-Rho symbol, making Latinus the first Christian in Scotland whose name is known for a fact.

Long-standing tradition, however, carries the story of this cradle of Christianity further back still, to the closing years of the fourth century, and to another named but elusive individual, Saint Ninian. He arrived by sea at Whithorn in 397, his biography tells us (unlike Latinus, Ninian comes with a fully formed story), where he set about building a stone church, painting it white. It became known as the Candida Casa – the Shining House/Hut – and thereby gave Whithorn ('White Hut') its name. He was a vigorous and fearless evangelist, winning converts among the pagan Picts, 'the painted ones', as the Romans had called the hostile Britons who lived north of Hadrian's Wall, and went into battle naked and covered in tattoos.

So enduring has Ninian's reputation proved as one of the founders of British Christianity that Whithorn has been a place of pilgrimage in his memory as far back as the seventh century, when visitors would make their way there, often by boat, to seek miraculous cures by praying at his shrine. Down the ages, those who came to pay him homage included Scottish royalty – Robert the Bruce, James IV (who, it is said, much preferred Ninian to Scotland's official patron saint, Andrew), and Mary, Queen of Scots – before the Scottish Reformation interrupted, but did not end, the practice.

Pilgrims have kept coming right up to the present day, some of them walking the recently established (or re-established) 143-mile Whithorn Way from Glasgow down to the west coast of Scotland. In late August, as close as the often-inclement weather allows to Ninian's feast day of 16 September, they gather in the open air on a stony beach in front of the cave where Ninian reputedly retreated as a hermit between his missionary journeys so as to draw closer to God through immersion in nature in the raw.

This particular aspect of his legend places Ninian in a line that leads back to the Desert Fathers, groups of monks who, a century earlier, had gone out into the unforgiving landscape of the Egyptian wilderness to live solitary, ascetic lives. They, in their turn, had inspired one of the most celebrated of fourth-century saints, Martin of Tours. Originally a soldier in Gaul, his conversion came when he recognised Christ in a naked beggar and gave him his cloak. He went on to found his first monastery in Gaul, around 360. When he was made Bishop of Tours ten years later, he chose, when not on the road, to live as a hermit in a remote hut. In some versions of Ninian's life, it is Martin who sent him from France on the sea journey that ended up at Whithorn, and therefore the date that has traditionally been given for his arrival coincides with Martin's death in 397.

These are the influences that predate Ninian seeking spiritual solace in a cave. Facing forward, his choice of this spot puts him in the vanguard of those now loosely referred to as Celtic saints

– Columba, Aidan, Patrick and David among them – who came after him, and whose labours in Ireland, Scotland and Wales from the fifth to the seventh century in making converts and setting an example of rugged, prophetic holiness were lauded by subsequent writers such as Bede. In his eighth-century *Ecclesiastical History of the English People*, Bede describes Ninian as 'a most reverend and holy man of the British nation who had been regularly instructed at Rome in the mysteries of the truth'.[3]

These maverick ascetics, operating in the furthest extremes of the British Isles as far as the expanding Church in continental Europe was concerned, had in common a preference for remote locations, usually close to the sea. They have come down to us today in hagiographies that show them more interested in practical living-out of belief than in doctrine and dogma, and therefore have developed in recent decades a popularity among those who chafe under the authority claimed by the Church of Rome, and who are drawn instead to the parallels (real or over-stated) between the concerns of these early saints and current ecological, gender and anti-authoritarian preoccupations. Academics who have studied their stories, however, suggest that the men in question – if they existed at all – might struggle to recognise themselves in the descriptions given of them nowadays.[4]

In the case of Ninian, beyond a host of stories of him written down between Bede's first telling of his tale and the celebrated account by James Ussher, Anglican Primate of Ireland in 1639 (which gave him a Spanish princess as a mother, and a grave in Ireland), there is no hard evidence. What circumstantial proof exists comes from the fact that Whithorn and this corner of south west Scotland was a key location in the Christian story of Britain and Ireland. As well as the Latinus Stone, thirty miles to the west of Whithorn, in a porch attached to a disused church at Kirkmadrine, are two sixth-century gravestones, both with

Chi-Rho symbols, one recalling the 'holy and outstanding priests' Viventius and Mavorius.

The stories of Ninian and Whithorn, though, have become inextricably intertwined. Real or imagined, Ninian is now the face (though there is, of course, no record of what he looked like) of those early Christians from the end of the fourth century onwards who lived in and around Whithorn. It is a conflation that frustrates scholarly opinion that Ninian was most likely a composite of other nameless but intrepid early Christian monks who at this time began the task of bringing the gospel to those Britons who had never heard it, and who were moreover fiercely and sometimes violently reluctant (especially in the case of the Picts, thought to have been based largely in northern and eastern Scotland) even to entertain it.

Whithorn, then, is one of those crossroads places where the followers of Jesus were working to change the local and regional religious landscape. The triangular peninsula of rolling hills and the occasional loch – known as the Machars – on which Whithorn stands is just twenty-two miles away by sea from the north east of Ireland, which made it a focal point for the interchange of ideas and personnel between the two. In various probably fanciful accounts of the origins of the Picts, notably found in Bede, it is said that they came from eastern Europe, had landed first in Ireland, but then had been redirected to Scotland. And there was traffic in the other direction, too. The fifth-century Saint Patrick, patron of the Irish, to whom we will come in a later chapter, is described in some accounts as having been born in what is today Cumbria, between Carlisle and Hadrian's Wall.

Whithorn also straddled another border, this time economic and geographical, between the Roman Empire and what lay beyond its northern-most boundary at Hadrian's Wall, placing the Latinus of the gravestone in Whithorn in the category identified by Tertullian as early as 200 of 'Britons not reached by the

Romans but subject to Christ'. The design of Latinus' memorial is certainly in the Roman style, fittingly since Whithorn was a prosperous trading town during the age of Empire, its natural harbour to the south of the town at the Isle of Whithorn giving rise to close links with Roman Britannia. These happened both on a local level – across the waters of the Solway Firth to the Roman garrison at Luguvalium (Carlisle) – and further afield. The names Viventius and Mavorius on those stones at Kirkmadrine are thought to be of Gaullish origin, where Christianity was already better established. Beyond that, Whithorn was on the sea routes that 1,700 years ago linked it with the very centre of Empire in Rome, as well as with the eastern Mediterranean. Traces of ancient glass from such far-flung places have been unearthed in Whithorn during recent archaeological digs.

One of the earliest accounts to have survived of the expansion of Christianity throughout Britain and Ireland once it was no longer a persecuted faith is Gildas' *On the Ruin and Conquest of Britain*,[5] dating from the 540s, or possibly earlier. Its author, a monk born to the north of Whithorn on the banks of the River Clyde and who later founded a monastery in Brittany, paints a dismal picture of the twilight years of Roman Britannia. Imperial control was crumbling as the legionaries who enforced it were redeployed elsewhere in Europe to deal with more immediate threats to the Empire. In 383, Maximus Magnus, the general posted to Britannia to uphold the Emperor's authority, had seized power for himself, combining it with Gaul to the south to create his own fiefdom. Though his rebellion was eventually defeated, by 401 the attacks elsewhere, especially from Germanic tribes, caused the imperial troops to be withdrawn from Hadrian's Wall for the last time. By 410, the Roman army had departed from Britannia for good.

Gildas describes what followed not as missionary growth; neither does he write – as later found in Bede – of inspired and saintly missionaries like Ninian, but rather of chaos descending amid the competing claims of marauding warlords. On a visit from Gaul to newly liberated Britannia in 429 on the instructions of Pope Celestine I,[6] Bishop Germanus, as well as recording pilgrims at Saint Alban's shrine as already described, noted his surprise at the sheer number of Christians who were worshipping outdoors under trees, though whether that was a result of the lack of a church building (compared to his native Gaul) or of a desire to carry out rituals close to nature, as part of a revival of pagan practices, is not specified.[7] As late as the sixth century, Adomnán, biographer of Columba, reports that Communion was often celebrated outdoors in the bracing Atlantic breeze at the monastery Columba had founded on the island of Iona.

Seen in such a context, British and Irish Christianity was still in its infancy. As already reported, within one year of the Edict of Milan in 313, signalling the end of persecution of the Christian Church throughout the Empire, three British bishops from three different English cities had set off for Arles in France to take part in a council of the whole Church. That suggests some sort of structure was being established, even if patchily. The next great gathering, at Nicaea in 325, was billed as a meeting of representatives from every part of Christendom. It was convened by Emperor Constantine who was now busy funding out of the imperial treasury the building of Christian basilicas in Rome. The wider Church was operating in a whole new world, and representatives from Britannia were there among the estimated 300 who responded to the 1,800 invitations sent out to attend the gathering at Nicaea. We do not know their names, or whether they met the Emperor as he presided over some of its sessions, but the leading theologian and Church Father, Athanasius of Alexandria, wrote in his report on the meeting to his fellow African bishops that the British were among those who signed up to a common position on the dating of Easter, on the first (canon) laws to bind all Christians, and on the text for the first part of the Nicene Creed, designed to be a single statement of beliefs that was repeated by all believers in acts of worship.[8]

In Britain, though, away from such a glittering gathering, the reality on the ground, especially outside the strongholds of Roman colonial power in southern England, was rather different. It seems unlikely that the British attendees, once they got home, had any means at their disposal of enforcing conformity with the decisions made at Nicaea. And while British representatives were once again recorded as attending the Council of Rimini in 359, so too is the detail that three of the bishops in the party could only afford to come because the Emperor covered their costs. Prelates from other provinces had turned down the offer of expenses from him lest it compromise their independence, but the British Church, it seems, was in no position to refuse.[9]

Yet, if it was young and poor in comparison to longer- and better-established Churches in other parts of the Roman Empire, British Christianity was in the fourth century at least producing theologians who made their influence felt in the most elevated Church circles. Like Pelagius, a Romanised Briton, possibly from Wales (though some say he was Irish[10]). To make his voice heard, he had in 380, when in his mid twenties, left his home on the fringes of the Christian world and relocated to the capital of the Empire and the Church. He never made it back, dying in Palestine in 420.

Pelagius became a stern critic of moral laxity when in Rome, and lived austerely as an ascetic. His concern with the sinfulness of what he saw around him prompted him to re-examine the workings of God's grace in the world, as set out by Augustine of Hippo, the dominant theologian of the time (and since, especially in Catholicism). Humanity was fundamentally flawed, Augustine had taught (his own life having been rackety before he saw the light and converted to Christianity), and its weakness was revealed by the 'original sin' of Adam and Eve in the Garden of Eden. Their failure to resist doing wrong showed an intrinsic characteristic of the human condition. God's grace was required to help them overcome it, and to allow any chance of eternal salvation. Pelagius found all of this far too pessimistic and disempowering. Instead, he suggested that humankind had been created by God so as to be able to make the right moral choices without his constant intervention in their lives. This counter-argument proved popular, especially when seen in the context of Pelagius' own frugal lifestyle – something of which Ninian would have approved. With bishops and priests in Rome already reaping the benefit of imperial largesse, the theologian from the far end of the Empire touched a raw nerve and was accused by the authorities in Rome of heresy.

Fear that Pelagius' views held some sway in the land of his birth, even after his death in 418, prompted the visitation in 429 by Germanus of Auxerre (already mentioned in the context of the cult of Saint Alban) and Lupus of Troyes. Some accounts have Germanus coming twice. British Christians, it seems, were already gaining a reputation in Rome for being troubled and troublesome.

One interpretation of what that meant in daily life involves a struggle between a free-spirited Church (sometimes called Celtic) in the west and north of the country, successfully reaching out to those who followed existing pagan religions, and those in more southerly parts who were more attentive to Rome's – like the nameless bishops who attended great Church gatherings in Europe, known as synods and councils. The free spirits founded monasteries – at Whithorn and later Iona, Llantwit Major, Clonmacnoise and Lindisfarne – while the bishops sought to impose rules and hierarchies.

Once again, the evidence for such an attractively clear narrative is thin. As Ian Bradley wrote in his study of Celtic Christianity,

'the early Christians were probably too much involved in missionary work and setting up churches, and too preoccupied with
thoughts of imminent judgement to reflect on their times or leave
records for posterity'.[11] Any buildings they did put up in this age
of itinerant preachers – with the exception of Ninian's Candida
Casa (of which no trace has been found at Whithorn, though a
thirteenth-century building claiming to be on the site of his first
chapel does exist) – would have initially been of wood or wattle
and daub and haven't therefore survived to bear witness.

There was, according to the *Miracula Niniae Episcopi*, a poem
written by a monk at Whithorn in the eighth century, an elaborately carved sarcophagus that stood next to the main altar of the
church in Whithorn, but many now regard the text as fanciful
hagiography of doubtful origin and date. On firmer ground
historically are accounts from the early 1500s, inspired by his
regular pilgrimages to Whithorn, that James IV of Scotland had
bones, believed to be from Ninian's arm, placed in a silver reliquary, made by the royal goldsmith. Following the Reformation,
these relics of a flesh-and-blood Ninian were taken for safekeeping by Catholics to the Scots Seminary at Douai in France – where
priests were being trained to bring the faith back to their now
Protestant native land. During the period of turmoil after the
French Revolution of 1789, however, the reliquary was reportedly
seized. This last tantalising trace of Ninian has been lost ever
since.

What remains, then, is a legend, and a chain of churches named
after Ninian, and not just in Scotland. None, though, has anything
to match the power of his cave to reach back more than sixteen
centuries. It is a modest trek to get to it, from a car park near a
lonely farmhouse, along a track through the wooded Physgill
Glen, flanked by streams, and out onto a stony beach. Once at the
shoreline, the only modern amenity that gives away that this is

not the fourth century but the twenty-first is a small notice board near the entrance to the otherwise unremarkable cave that stands at the northern end.

A natural cleft in cliffs that are sometimes steely grey, others a soft sandy colour, it is small inside, no more than seven metres deep and three metres high. This was no fourth-century church built in, rather than of, stone. Instead, the legend tells that it was a place for Ninian's use alone. Nothing suggests it ever contained an altar or the sort of decorations that might grace a place of worship. Only the graffiti of pilgrims over the centuries, who have carved crosses (one incorporating a Chi-Rho), their initials and dates into the rock inside, gives the visitor anything to go on beyond an inexplicable but insistent sense of standing on holy ground.

More recent pilgrims have left behind small individual stones, some with markings, from veins of silica that look like rough crosses to inscriptions with names. That was another early Christian habit that has been revived in recent times.

During excavations of the cave at the end of nineteenth and in the middle years of the twentieth centuries, following rock-slides and collapses, something older and more monumental was found. A series of large carved crosses, dating from the tenth and eleventh centuries, were recovered from the cave and put on display in the museum in the town. What they attest to is the existence of a local Whithorn 'school' of stone-carving. These monolithic crosses, some now in pieces, feature similar intricate, interlaced, repeated and sinuous patterns on their shafts. Whether they had been placed in the cave for religious or ritual purposes, or were stored there at some stage, is unknown. In the Scottish Reformation, Whithorn developed a strong Presbyterian tradition, with its dislike of ornament and decoration. Perhaps they were put in the cave to prevent them being destroyed.

Now removed to the safety of the museum, their absence means the timelessness and other-worldliness of the cave is uninterrupted. From this V-shaped recess the view of the beach is as it was when Ninian may have sat watching seals and the occasional dolphin in the sea beyond. To be here – and outside the peak pilgrim season in July and August, the chances are high that it will be a solitary vigil – is to come as close as can be to both this enigmatic saint and the untamed fourth-century world inhabited by him or by other missionaries whose names are now forgotten.

ALSO WITH A STORY TO TELL . . .

ST NINIAN'S CHURCH AT TYNET, near Buckie on the Moray Firth, reveals the honoured place that the saint has in Scottish Christianity. This mid-eighteenth-century building, named after him, was the first Catholic church to be built in Scotland following its Reformation. Designed to look like a long, low barn, it operated for years as a clandestine place of worship, in defiance of penal laws.

The ruined ST REGULUS' CHURCH, with its tall tower, stands in the precincts of ST ANDREW'S CATHEDRAL in Fife. It was built in the eleventh century to celebrate the apostle who became Scotland's patron in preference to Ninian because he had appeared to the Pictish King Angus in 832 before he won a decisive battle with the Northumbrians. In the vision, Andrew was being martyred on a diagonal cross (or 'saltaire'), having refused to be crucified in the same way as Jesus because he was unworthy. The diagonal cross of St Andrew is the flag of Scotland.

CHAPTER 5
The Fifth Century

St Martin's, Canterbury: Britain's Oldest Church

Saint Martin's Church reflects in tangible form the reintroduction of Christianity to southern Britain.
                                        UNESCO World Heritage Listing

THE EARLY DECADES of the fifth century saw the Roman Empire in the West fighting for survival. Wave after wave of invaders not only menaced its borders, as the Picts had long been doing along Hadrian's Wall, but also struck at its very heart. A mass incursion across the River Rhine in 405 brought chaos to Roman Gaul, while Alaric's Goths headed out of what is modern-day Germany to cause havoc down the boot of Italy before slowly starving the imperial capital into surrender in 410. It was the first time Rome had fallen in eight centuries.

The conquerors spent the next three days pillaging the city, but Alaric was a Christian nobleman and largely spared the recently built churches and basilicas, instead ransacking the pagan temples with exceptional venom. When his forces departed, the citizens of Rome were left traumatised. The authorities sent out an emergency call to army units across the Empire to return to base to help stem the next wave of the barbarian tide. As a result, garrisons in Britannia rapidly emptied, leaving behind Britons ill prepared to manage their own security. That failure was felt especially in the south, the heartland of the Roman imperial set-up. Thinly populated, but for the most part civilised, prosperous and blessed with decent roads and sturdy walls, it was suddenly defenceless.

In their desperation, the Britons turned to the Angles, Frisians, Jutes and Saxons, all hailing from the other side of the North Sea in what are now Germany, Denmark and the Netherlands. They had pre-existing connections with Roman Britannia, sometimes as settlers coming over to farm, occasionally as traders, but most often as raiders attacking and plundering the rich pickings to be found close to its long and vulnerable coastline. The Romans had built forts to repel them but, with the imperial forces gone, the Britons were now inviting the very people who had proved the biggest threat to their security to come over as mercenaries to provide security.

Unsurprisingly, it didn't work. In his sixth-century writings, Gildas points a finger of blame at one of the British kings, the hapless and naïve Vortigern, for allowing these Germanic warlords to establish camps on the Isle of Thanet in Kent that housed not only their fighting men but also vast numbers of their followers. Such assembled military might was used against Britannia.[1] The treacherous interlopers swept all before them, with the Angles installed in East Anglia, and the Saxons in those kingdoms whose names made plain that they were now in control – Wessex, Sussex, Essex and Middlesex.

In Gildas' account, the worst part of the takeover by these pagan usurpers was the desecration of whatever Christian places of worship established in the years since the Roman colonisers had permitted it. 'All the columns were levelled with the ground by the frequent strokes of the battering-ram, all the husband-men routed, together with their bishops, priests and people, whilst the sword gleamed, and the flames crackled around them on every side.'[2] Disdain for Christianity was common among the new Anglo-Saxon ruling class, whose beliefs were older and polytheistic.

If the Britons were ill equipped to resist their conquerors, a still fragile Church was utterly powerless. It had yet to put down strong-enough roots with its converts to cause them to rally to its defence. Many simply reverted to the practice of older nature rituals to ensure an easy life for themselves, or life at all, while those reluctant to abandon their Christian beliefs for the most part headed west and north to get out of the way of the new Anglo-Saxon rulers. Their writ did not yet reach into such parts of the country where Christianity, thanks to the monk-missionaries like Ninian, had started to make inroads.

Among those at risk in what was effectively a purging of Christianity from the soil of southern England may well have been those who had hitherto worshipped in the declining years of imperial rule at a small chapel built of reclaimed Roman brick in Durovernum Cantiacorum (Canterbury). It stood, in the fifth century, on Watling Street, the paved Roman road that linked the port at Richborough, entry point from the continent, through Canterbury to London and beyond.

Quite who had built the chapel is a matter of dispute. It may have originally been part of a cemetery standing on the outskirts of the city (excavations in the surrounding area have shown this to have been an area full of burial plots from the Roman era). Or it could have been a different sort of public building, once used by the imperial administration, fallen into disuse once the garrisons had emptied. What is not in dispute, however, is that this structure, its Roman walls still standing, went on to become St Martin's Church, the oldest in Britain, and the oldest in continuous use in the English-speaking world. Or as Bede put it, imprecisely, '[a] church built in ancient times'.[3]

The most ancient part of today's St Martin's is the section of its chancel – the area around the altar – that is closest to the nave (main body of the church). Unlike Lullingstone Villa, all carefully preserved behind barriers and seen only from afar, here there is plenty of opportunity to touch and feel whole sections of the long, flat, reddish, fourth-century Roman bricks used in the original building.

Even more authentic, I discover, gently guided by its current vicar, Mark Griffin, is to go back outside, through the graveyard and round the exterior to the south wall of the chancel. Here he points out a flat-topped, red-brick-flanked, filled-in Roman door-way (of which only the lower portion can be seen on the inside of the church). Archaeological excavations carried out in 1896 revealed that once this fifth- or sixth-century entrance took visitors into a small room, of which only the foundations now remain. If, as seems possible, even probable, Christian worship went on in that room, now disappeared and incorporated in to the chancel, then this easy-to-miss doorway – though no longer leading anywhere – is frustratingly the closest I am going to get to stepping into the life of the early English Christian Church.

A little further along the same south wall is the rounded arch of another now redundant doorway. This one, though, is of later vintage, from towards the end of sixth century. It links the Roman-era origins of St Martin's to its starring role in the return of 'official' Christianity to these islands in the person of the monk Augustine (not to be confused with Augustine of Hippo, the north-African theologian mentioned previously), who was despatched by Pope Gregory the Great from Rome and arrived on the Isle of Thanet in 597. This modest church of recycled fourth-century bricks, whose outlines can so clearly be discerned now I have eyes to see the layers inside and out that are part of its south wall, was the first home for Augustine's party of – according to Bede – 'nearly 40' who came to bring the erstwhile Britannia back into the wider Christian fold.[4]

What is not known is whether worship had continued in the building between the triumph of the Anglo-Saxons and Augustine's arrival. By the mid fifth century, Roman rule had been replaced in Kent by a Jutish king. *The Anglo-Saxon Chronicle*, recorded between the ninth and twelfth centuries and based on the annals of various great monasteries, recounts the story of brothers Hengist and Horsa who initially came in 449 from the other side of the North Sea among the Anglo-Saxon mercenaries recruited by defenceless Britons.[5] Struck on arrival by both the richness of the land and the weakness of their employers, the two brothers turned on and defeated Vortigern's forces in 455. Horsa died in battle, leaving Hengist to install himself as king.[6] His domain grew geographically and economically, allowing his successors to achieve overlordship among the neighbouring Anglo-Saxon kingdoms as they spread further and further west, dominating southern England.

In his *Ecclesiastical History of the English People*, Bede describes Hengist as the great-great-grandson of Woden, the principal god in Germanic mythology. He goes on to tell how one of Hengist's descendants, Eormenric, had a son, Ethelbert, who in around 580 married a young Frankish princess, Bertha. Her father, by then dead, had been King of Paris, while her grandfather had ruled the whole Frankish kingdom. She was quite a catch, the match providing the ambitious Kentish ruling family with a strategic alliance with the powerful Merovingian dynasty on the other side of the English Channel.

There was, however, a hitch in the betrothal. Like his ancestors, Ethelbert worshipped many gods, while Bertha came from a Christian family who worshipped only one. A compromise was reached, by which she would be permitted to practise her religion in peace and was even allowed to take with her on her journey to Kent her own chaplain, Bishop Liudhard. On arrival, they were allocated St Martin's as a church in which to follow their beliefs. Indeed, it may well have been thanks to Bertha that it was named after Saint Martin, since she had been raised near Tours and was devoted to the memory of the hermit bishop, Martin of Tours, who had been, in some accounts, Ninian's mentor.

Every day, Bertha would walk from her royal quarters in the centre of Canterbury to St Martin's to pray, her route taking her through what became known as the Queningate – or Queen's Gate – a Roman postern gate. Its outline in flintwork can still be seen in the old city walls (overlooking a car park). The apartness of the church from the rest of the city was probably judged a plus when Bertha arrived. Her religion, regarded as a threat by some, could be kept out of sight. Not, though, from Ethelbert, who succeeded his father around 589. Bertha's quiet piety and devotion caused him to become ever more favourably disposed to Christianity. In some accounts, he converted to his wife's religion even before the arrival of Augustine. Whenever his baptism happened, it was believed for centuries that it took place in the ancient stone font that still stands in St Martin's today.

However, more recent research suggests that is impossible, since the font was originally a wellhead from around 1100 in the cathedral cloisters and only came to the church much later. According to the customs of the time, Ethelbert's baptism would anyway have more likely involved him stepping into a late Roman style hexagonal brick font (of which the only known example surviving in Britain is in the ruins of the Roman shore fort at nearby Richborough) and having water poured over his head with a shell.

Whether that baptism came before or after Augustine's arrival is, like much in these distant and ill-recorded times, debated, but the majority suggest it came after. Whatever the truth, however, the arrival of Bertha at St Martin's does seem to have started something. The building was extended into what is today the nave, the original cramped space presumably no longer regarded as suitable for a queen. Nineteenth-century restoration work saw the plaster on the walls of the nave stripped away to reveal more recycled fourth-century Roman bricks as well as blocks of Caen limestone dating back to the sixth century.

The expansion of St Martin's continued when Augustine landed on English shores at the end of the century. If the great cathedral that lies in plain sight from the steps of today's St Martin's tells of what happened after his arrival, it is this modest church that bridges a crucial period in which Christianity finally established a secure footing in southern England. It is the mother church of the mother church of English Christianity.

Catholicism teaches of an apostolic succession that connects every pope from the current incumbent all the way back to Peter, the humble fisherman, chosen by Jesus in the Gospel accounts as head of his Church.[7] Yet the papacy that existed in these early centuries of Christianity had little of the status and authority of the all-powerful office that evolved in the medieval period. A widespread belief in the precedence of the Bishop of Rome over local churches only emerged in Christian writings in the second century, and it took much longer to enforce the idea on the ground. It wasn't until the fall of the child Romulus Augustulus, the last Roman emperor in the West in 476, that the bishops of Rome were sufficiently powerful and respected to step into the vacuum in a fragmented and troubled Europe as temporal as well as spiritual leaders. Of them all, Gregory the Great (590–604) was arguably the most accomplished and influential. That is certainly true of his interest, bordering on obsession, with reviving the English Church.

Gregory had held high secular office in Rome until, in 575, he changed course in his life and became a monk. He established a monastery at his family home on the Caelian Hill, one of the seven hills of Rome. His stated intention was to retreat thereafter into prayer and contemplation, but he was too able an organiser and communicator to leave the world behind. Having been drafted in as a papal emissary and sent to Constantinople, capital of the eastern and surviving half of the Roman Empire, he returned after several years to find Rome in the grip of plague. His innate gift for leadership in a crisis saw him elected to succeed Pope Pelagius, who had been one of the plague's earliest victims. Gregory set out at once to bring order to the chaotic administration of the Church and propriety to its clergy, demanding obedience and conformity from priests and bishops everywhere, while simultaneously cultivating friendly relations with rulers across the European continent so as to increase his own and the Church's influence.

His mission to Anglo-Saxon England was, writes the historian Eamon Duffy, 'to have the most momentous consequences for the papacy. No other pope had ever before thought in terms of missionary outreach to the world beyond the empire.'[8] Quite why he picked out the beleaguered rump of Christians in England for special attention has never been satisfactorily explained. In one of his surviving letters, Gregory says that news had reached him that the English were anxious to embrace – or re-embrace – Christianity. Quite who his informant might have been wasn't made clear – perhaps Bishop Liudhard who had accompanied Queen Bertha to Kent at the time of her marriage? Or even Ethelbert, impressed by his wife's faith and calculating that he would need missionaries from Rome if he were to persuade his subjects to follow the lead of his own conversion?

A cheesy anecdote is often put forward to explain Gregory's special interest in England. While still a deacon, he had seen strikingly fair-haired Anglo-Saxon boys among a sea of dark heads in a market in Rome. When told they were Angles, he corrected his informant. These were angels, not Angles. In that moment, he is meant to have determined to evangelise the country from which they had come.

More realistically, there had already been contact between the centre of the Church and the former Britannia over the centuries, with British bishops at synods and even, potentially, a papal hand at play in encouraging the betrothal of Bertha to the pagan Ethelbert (long before Gregory ever became Bishop of Rome), with a view to reChristianising a province that seemed, in part at least, lost to the Church. Whatever his motivations, Gregory demonstrated a strong commitment to the fate of a people who were, as his earliest biographer would incorrectly put it, 'worshipping stocks and stones . . . at the edge of the world'.[9]

In 596 he despatched a party to England, led by Augustine, his successor as head of the monastery on the Caelian Hill. Augustine was not by nature a risk-taker, and seems to have been unenthused by his mission, undertaking it only out of obedience to his superior. Halfway through Gaul, hearing stories from his hosts of how savage were their neighbours on the other side of the English Channel, Augustine even wrote to Gregory asking to be allowed to return to Rome. The Pope would have none of it. And so, in May 597, Augustine's unarmed and anxious party landed at Ebbsfleet on the Isle of Thanet, the most easterly point of Kent, then divided from Canterbury and the mainland by the Wantsum Channel.

If he wasn't immediately murdered by the 'savages', as he had feared, Augustine still had to go through agonies waiting to find out his fate. 'Some days later,' writes Bede, 'the King came to the island.' Ethelbert insisted on meeting Augustine outdoors – for fear, Bede suggests, of witchcraft if they were indoors. Both sides appeared to suspect the worst of the other, though that may be a product of the telling of the tale in order to build up to a miraculous happy ending. Ethelbert's actions certainly don't sound much like those of a king already converted to Christianity, or indeed of one who might even have sought the despatch of such a mission from the Pope. Maybe, though, Ethelbert had to appear as surprised as his subjects by the new arrivals in order to retain their trust and any chance of a successful outcome.

The party from Rome approached the King 'bearing as their standard a silver cross and the image of Our Lord and Saviour painted on a panel. They chanted litanies and uttered prayers to the Lord for the eternal salvation both of themselves and those to whom they had come.'[10] For his part, Ethelbert declared Augustine's words 'fair', Bede tells, and pronounced that, while he understood the monk's motives for making the journey, he was not ready to set aside the long-standing beliefs to which his people were attached. Instead, he gave the missionaries his permission and his protection to travel to Canterbury. There, they were to make their base in Bertha's church, St Martin's, and began to evangelise.

As always, caution is required when reading Bede's accounts – they were written more than a hundred years after the events they describe, at a time when the English Church was experiencing tensions between the different claims of, on the one hand, the missionary monks who had come in the wake of Ninian in the areas beyond Anglo-Saxon control and, on the other, the expanding 'official' structure that developed following Augustine's arrival. Bede was anxious to bolster the official 'Roman' line and so paints a vivid picture of what went on within these walls of St Martin's.

'In this church,' writes Bede, 'they first began to meet to chant the psalms, to pray, to say Mass, to preach, to baptise, until the King had been converted to the faith [when] they received greater liberty to preach everywhere and to build or restore churches.'[11]

They would have been hard pressed to do all of this in the original area in the chancel identified by its Roman bricks, or even in the extended nave if Bertha had had works done prior to 597. Yet here it was, in the place where I am now standing, that Augustine gathered with his closest companions on that initial missionary journey, including Laurence, who was later to become his successor as Archbishop of Canterbury, to give thanks to God for their safe arrival, for a warmer reception than they had been led to expect, and for the courage necessary to move forward with the next stage of their work.

The cramped quarters at St Martin's were soon to become redundant. Ethelbert made Augustine a grant of land to its west on which to build a monastery, at first dedicated to Saints Peter and Paul, but after Augustine's death in 604, named after this Italian monk who had taken the first crucial steps in bringing Christianity back to southern England. As well as the monastery, Ethelbert in 602 gave Augustine the site of his palace in Canterbury, having moved with Bertha to a new home he had built at Reculver on the Thames estuary, ten miles east of the city. Augustine began work on the first cathedral in Britain and Ireland.

In 601, a party of reinforcements arrived from Rome, bringing with them from Gregory the pallium – an ecclesiastical vestment shaped like a loose scarf or tie and worn round the neck. It was the symbol of a bishop – in this case of Augustine as Archbishop of Canterbury – and a reward for a job well done.

In another of his letters – this time to the Patriarch of Alexandria – Gregory boasts of Augustine baptising 10,000 converts on Christmas Day 598 in Canterbury. It seems unlikely that such a public spectacle could have taken place without the blessing of the King, and so Ethelbert may well himself have been baptised by that point.

Also handed over by the party from Rome were instructions from Gregory on how Augustine was to consolidate his early positive results and continue the missionary push:

> Upon mature deliberation of the affair of the English, I determined upon, viz., that the temples of the idols in those nations ought not to be destroyed; but let the idols that are in them be destroyed; let holy water be made and sprinkled in the said temples, let altars be erected, and relics placed. For if those temples are well built, it is requisite that they be converted from the worship of devils to the service of the true God; that the nation, seeing that their temples are not destroyed . . . may the more familiarly resort to the places to which they are accustomed.[12]

As well as this repurposing, Augustine was told by Gregory to send a bishop to York, in the north, to establish twin provinces based there and in London (rather than Canterbury) as part of the Roman Church. Once that had been achieved, Pope Gregory set out, Augustine was to appoint twelve bishops to assist the two primates in York and London.

In an age when communication took as long as the fastest horse could cover the distance between two points, Augustine had considerable flexibility in implementing Gregory's orders. There were practical problems with the Pope's vision from afar of the future of English Christianity. For a start, London was not under Ethelbert's control. It was ruled by his nephew, the East Saxon king, Saebert. In 604, when Saebert converted to Christianity, Augustine named Mellitus, one of the relief party of monks who had arrived from Rome three years earlier, as Bishop of London, but he retained Canterbury as the seat of himself as archbishop. In 619 Mellitus was to become the third Archbishop of Canterbury.

Another of that second party, Justus, was appointed by Augustine as the first Bishop of the West Saxons in Rochester. In 624, he ascended the ecclesiastical ladder to become the fourth Archbishop of Canterbury. It took longer still, long after Augustine and Gregory had both died, for the final part of the Pope's scheme to be completed, when another Italian monk, Paulinus, headed north in 625 to accompany Ethelbert and Bertha's daughter, Ethelburga, on her way to become the second wife of King Edwin of Northumbria. At Easter in 627, Edwin, all his nobles and the pagan high priest, Coifi, who sat on the king's council, were baptised by Paulinus in a newly built wooden church in York. Pope Honorius I marked the occasion by naming Paulinus the first Bishop of York.

Though formal links with Rome had been disrupted in the decades after the Roman withdrawal from Britannia, there were still those, at the time of Augustine's arrival, who held the title of bishop serving in Wales and the south-western kingdom of Dumnonia, both of which had largely remained free from Anglo-Saxon influence. Gregory had given Augustine authority over these men who had laboured to keep the flame of faith alive in a time of trial, and so, in 603, a gathering was arranged, according to Bede. Augustine was keen to enlist the support in the work of evangelisation of these bishops who knew the local language and customs so much better than he did. Proceedings got off on the wrong foot, however, when he clumsily refused to stand to greet them when they arrived. In their eyes, he was being presumptuous and overbearing. Such a bad start did little to smooth the task of finding agreement on how to bring into line with Roman practice the rituals and customs these bishops had developed in their years of isolation. The meeting ended in failure.

The tensions it revealed for an expanding Christian Church were to dog the century to come.

ALSO WITH A STORY TO TELL . . .

On the site where the CHURCH OF ST PAUL IN THE BAIL once stood in LINCOLN, excavations in the 1970s found the remains of what are believed to have been two much earlier churches: the first, considerably smaller, from the fourth century, and the second large enough to hold 100 worshippers, made from timber, dating to the fifth or perhaps the sixth century. They would have stood at the centre of what was in colonial times the Roman Forum in Lincoln (or Lindum). The outline of the second church is picked out on the ground, while just to the east is a well that may have been used for baptisms by early churchgoers.

CHAPTER 6
The Sixth Century

Clonmacnoise: Celtic Powerhouse

Therefore, let God never permit me to lose the people that He has won in the end of the earth.

Saint Patrick, *Confession*[1]

IRELAND IS SHAPED like a saucer. Within the broad dip in the centre where the teacup would nestle stands Clonmacnoise, to the south of the town of Athlone. Its name in Gaelic means 'the meadow of the sons of Nos', a character who, the eleventh-century *Annals of Inisfallen* tell, was swineherd to the King of Connacht. The royal domains included the spot where this great monastery was founded in 548. The key figure in Clonmacnoise's story, however, is not Nos, or any king. Instead, it is the lowly born Ciarán, son of a carpenter from what is today County Roscommon, who founded the monastery.

The early decades of the sixth century were a time when a group of high-born sons of Ireland's various tribal kings decided to dedicate their lives to the Christian God. For each it was an individual calling, but they are now clustered together as the Twelve Apostles of Ireland. Despite his own modest beginnings, Ciarán ranks among them, his achievement at Clonmacnoise in terms of reach and influence in missionary and intellectual pursuits, nationally and internationally, second to none. This was arguably the greatest of all Ireland's early monasteries.

Like others among the Twelve, he had been drawn to study under pioneers such as Saint Finian. His solitary monk's cell at Clonard in County Meath was already a renowned centre of learning. Having served their apprenticeship, the devout, deter-mined young men who came to Clonard moved on to establish new monasteries, all the time rooting Christianity in Irish soil that had for centuries been the home to polytheistic beliefs in nature spirits. Many of them were not tied to a single place, but travelled where the Spirit took them, planting monasteries as they went.

Ciarán's story is told in the many versions of his life that feature in the annals of those monasteries, compiled by their scholar-monks from the late eighth century onwards in gloriously illus-trated manuscripts. First he spent time at Clonard – now all but disappeared from the map – and then at Arranmore, a barren island in the mouth of Galway Bay, where under another of the pioneers, Saint Enda, young monks learnt the essential practices of private prayer and fasting. They lived austerely in nature facing out on to the Atlantic Ocean in individual, rough-built cells, coming together for communal worship and the hard manual labour required to feed themselves.

Ciarán would, it is said, have stayed at Arranmore, but Enda sent him on his way to find the right place for him to do God's work. Galway was at one end of the *Slighe Mhór* ('Great Highway'), the main west–east route across Ireland at the time, a raised pathway, or *Esker Riada*, crossing the boggy land of the centre of the country, made of sand and gravel left behind after the last Ice Age. It carried him east to the banks of the River Shannon and Clonmacnoise.

Expanses of water – inland as well as coastal – had special significance for these early generations of Christians, and in particular for the wandering monks who evangelised Ireland, Scotland and Wales. It was an attachment that owed something to the influence of existing beliefs in the gods of nature. The great Welsh monk Beuno, for example, is said in tales of his ceaseless missionary activity to have been happiest when pray-ing up to his neck in cold water on the shoreline, subduing his flesh by numbing it so as to bring his soul closer to God, a habit shared with other monks sometimes collectively referred to as 'the watermen'.[2]

It was not, though, just the volume of the water in the Shannon stretching out before him that caused Ciarán to pause at this spot. He felt he had reached a destination he had already glimpsed in his dreams. And he could see, too, from a practical point of view, that this was a natural crossroads where the *Slighe Mhór* met the north–south thoroughfare along the river's valley. Such a central location would serve his missionary purposes. So he stayed.

First there was a short period on Hare Island, further up the Shannon, in a monastic community. Then, in 548, Ciarán moved, with ten companions, to where the ruins of Clonmacnoise stand to this day, on a green bank that slopes gently down to the river. Together, they set about building in wood their monks' huts and a church. Within a year of arriving, though, Ciarán was struck down by 'yellow' plague and died (like half of Ireland at the time, according to some estimates). He was still only in his early thirties. Some accounts of his life emphasise that he died at thirty-three, the age at which tradition holds that Jesus was crucified. Fact, legend and symbolism merge seamlessly in such monastic texts.

That parallel with Christ was certainly one aspect of the cult of Ciarán that quickly grew up at his grave. It helped his original group of followers, and those attracted subsequently to Clonmacnoise, to develop it into one of the principal centres of Christian devotion, learning and craftsmanship in Ireland until the thirteenth century. As was the case elsewhere in emerging Christianity, first with martyrs like Alban and subsequently with charismatic and fearless monk leaders such as Ninian, pilgrims started arriving at Clonmacnoise from the seventh century onwards in search of miracle cures wrought by proximity to a relic of his hand. Another draw was the hide of the cow that, Ciarán's legend told, he had brought with him when he arrived at Clonmacnoise, and which miraculously provided enough milk each day to satisfy not just the growing number of monks there, but also the many others in the community that at its peak is estimated to have numbered 2,000.

In these early centuries of Christianity in Britain and Ireland, monasteries as centres of the faith established the first loose Church network. Their elevated status rested, in particular, on the status of their dead founders. 'The graves of the saints,' writes Professor Peter Brown of Princeton, 'had become centres of the ecclesiastical life of their region.'[3] And monasteries, too, conveyed to those who made pilgrimages to visit them a sense of endurance and permanence at a time when the social, political and economic context of their lives was regularly being turned upside down. 'The cult of saints,' Brown concludes, 'emerged as one of the few institutions of western Christendom that passed, like the magnificent span of a long bridge, across the many chasms that opened up in Europe after the fall of Rome to join the ancient with the medieval world.'[4]

Clonmacnoise is sometimes referred to as the 'seminary of Ireland' on account of its role in sending out clergy to all parts of the island of Ireland, regardless of which local or regional king ruled that area. Beyond providing the priests who gave Ireland a kind of spiritual unity, Clonmacnoise prepared and dispatched missionaries to evangelise in Scotland, England, Wales and later continental Europe.

Alongside Ciarán in the Twelve Apostles of Ireland is Saint Columba – or Colmcille ('Church Dove') – from Donegal in the far north west, the great-great-grandson of the fifth-century Irish high king, Niall of the Nine Hostages. Before setting off in 563 from Irish shores to establish a new monastery at Iona off the west coast of Scotland, Columba came to Clonmacnoise to consult one of Ciarán's immediate successors, Ailithir.[5]

It is Ciarán that I am seeking out on a bright, blue, summer's day as I walk around the site of Clonmacnoise, the river a quiet but powerful presence just beyond the boundary walls. After a period of steep decline from the 1200s, the monastery's buildings were laid to waste in 1552 by the English colonial garrison at Athlone. 'There was not left,' it was written at the time, 'a bell small or large, an image, or an altar, or a book, or a gem, or even glass in a window, from the wall of the church out, which was not carried off.'

There is nonetheless still plenty of history to feast on for me and the school party who are the only other visitors to the site: the shells of the various churches (one of them once a cathedral) that stood here from the tenth century; an eye-catchingly tall, thin, tapering round tower from the twelfth century that is closest to the wide waters of the Shannon; and, most captivating of all, three magnificent free-standing stone crosses. They are, on closer examination, replicas, the originals on display in the adjoining museum, in rooms designed to look like the original monks' beehive cells. This trio of crosses dates from the eighth to the eleventh century. In their intricate carvings, each provides a pictorial sermon in what was an age of illiteracy. For today's generation they vividly tell how over those years the pre-existing pagan pantheon was slowly subsumed into Christianity by the inclusion, alongside images associated with the one God who died on the cross of Calvary, of depictions of animal and nature spirits.

There is something utterly beguiling about these crosses, as if watching centuries pass in front of your eyes, and faith traditions blend into one. Next to such an experience, Clonmacnoise's Temple Ciarán is all too easy to overlook or dismiss. Tiny and tumbledown – just four metres by three inside – it has no roof. If it did, I would be ducking my head when I squash inside, while its higgledy-piggledy stone walls appear set to collapse in on me with any sudden movement. Yet it was on this modest spot, today overshadowed by its more rugged, ruined neighbours, that Ciarán was buried. The current structure – if it merits the word – dates back only to the tenth century. Before that, there would have been a series of wooden churches.

When Ciarán was laid to rest right here by his grieving companions, it was done in the original church they had put up with their own hands so recently. Wooden buildings, though, are both quick to build and quick to burn down. That proved to be the case, especially in the eighth and ninth centuries, when Clonmacnoise's accessibility to the major routes crossing the country was more curse than blessing. Viking raiders headed up the Shannon from the sea, intent in Ireland as in England, Scotland and Wales at the same time, on looting and destruction, but they were not the main culprits. Most of the damage to Clonmacnoise was done by rival Irish clans who, on no fewer than three occasions in the eighth century, descended on the monastery (which stood on the boundary between the kingdoms Connacht and Meath) carrying torches, intent on obliterating its influence.

Nothing, then, survives of those earliest buildings, save minute traces of blackened wood that have been found during recent excavations. Such cycles of wanton destruction prompted the first stone buildings in the ninth and tenth centuries, but the monastery at Clonmacnoise was always more settlement than cloister. Traders and craftsmen made their homes in what, in its medieval heyday, would have felt like a town, the religious and the commercial, the seminarian and the artisan, living side by side.

My eyes light on what could be a final tenuous link with the still elusive Ciarán as I leave via the museum. On display is the Ogham Stone, unearthed in May 1990 when workmen were digging a new grave in the more recent cemeteries that now surround the Clonmacnoise site (along with a primary school). This rectangular piece of sandstone has been dated back to the sixth century, possibly earlier, and may just have been in place, in some unknown capacity, around the time of Ciarán's death. Its unearthing has revealed an earlier use of stone than previous evidence had indicated. However, what it is and what its inscription conveys remain a mystery.

The characters are written in the Ogham alphabet, based on Latin and used in Ireland at the time (also seen on stone monuments near the Welsh coast, emphasising the close links between the two). Scholars suggest they equate to 'nadav', but can offer no suggestion as to what or who 'nadav' was, their efforts hampered because other characters were lost back in the mists of time when the stone was damaged from being used for sharpening iron implements. The story of Clonmacnoise and its place in the development of Christianity in Ireland and Britain may rise up from this holy ground, but the founding abbot remains tantalisingly out of reach.

Unlike Britannia, Ireland was never colonised by the Romans, though it certainly had trading links with the Empire since Roman coins have been found by archaeologists buried in its soil in plentiful numbers. The Romans referred to it as Hibernia, and sometimes Scotia, conflating Ireland with Scotland as areas that bordered their Empire, and suggesting once again close connection between them. More widely, the extent to which Britain and Ireland were perceived as one entity in imperial and post-imperial eyes can be judged by passages in *Almagest*, written by the celebrated second-century geographer Ptolemy of Alexandria, where he refers to them, respectively, as 'Great Britain' and 'Little Britain'.

Two individuals in particular are associated with the arrival of Christianity in Ireland. Less familiar is Palladius, the 'Bishop of the Irish'. Sent by Pope Celestine, his mission was to bring Ireland within the Christian fold. Prosper of Aquitaine, a former papal secretary, wrote in 447 in his *Chronicles* of Palladius as a highborn 'deacon' from Gaul who landed in what is now County Wicklow in the south east in 431.[6] The given date is significant since it was also the year of the Council of Ephesus that condemned the heresy that carries the name of the British-born theologian Pelagius. Palladius' immediate task may have been to ensure that the infection of Pelagianism hadn't spread from Great Britain to Little Britain.

As for bringing Ireland into line with Rome and the wider Church, his work would have been complicated, some modern researchers have argued, by the presence of Christian missionaries who had already arrived there on the coat-tails of Roman traders.[7] They could have resented his intrusion; though if they did exist it could only have been as a tiny minority in the tribal kingdoms. And, as a rural society based on working the land, there were no large urban trading centres of any consequence until later.

The dominant religion that Palladius found in still largely preChristian Ireland is nowadays referred to as Celtic. There are references in Greek and Roman writers from around 700 BC to *keltoi* or *celtae* as a collection of associated tribes with related languages and cultures who lived in central Europe around the Danube and north of the Alps. Over time, these peoples migrated both westwards and eastwards, possibly under duress from Roman forces. Those in the west gathered in significant numbers in northern Spain, along the Atlantic coast of France (including Brittany), and up into Cornwall, Wales, Scotland, the Isle of Man and Ireland. Whether there was ever a Celtic 'invasion' of Ireland is disputed. The process of assimilation of the Celts' language, written in the Ogham alphabet, seems to have been more of a gradual process. Their own pantheon, too, slowly gained a wider following.

As expressed on the earliest of the stone crosses at Clonmacnoise, it was heavily based on nature deities. The eighth-century North Cross, of which only the shaft survives, shows interlaced animals, including a lion with a protruding tongue, what is thought to be

Cernunnos, the antler-wearing god of wild beasts and fertility, and human figures, one in a seated Buddha-like position.

Palladius' instructions, as later with Augustine in Kent when briefed by Pope Gregory, were to find a way of blending and then subsuming existing customs, beliefs and rituals into Christianity. The three crosses at Clonmacnoise graphically illustrate that process, but Palladius can claim none of the credit. Within a year of his arrival, by most accounts, he was sent packing by the King of Leinster, and took the sea route between the north east of Ireland and Scotland. On arrival, he continued his work of evangelisation, culminating in his reported martyrdom near Auchenblae in present-day Aberdeenshire. A thirteenth-century chapel there, known locally as Paldy's Chapel, is dedicated to him and became a place of pilgrimage, possibly even containing his relics.

The better-known of the two names credited with introducing Christianity to Ireland is that of Patrick, who, as we have already seen, was born the son of an official in Roman Britannia, possibly near Carlisle. His biography, the *Confession*, tells how he was kidnapped as a teenager by raiders who regularly plundered coastal areas, and sold into slavery in Ireland (as a swineherd, like Nos, according to some accounts). He escaped after seven years but was to return as early 432 (or more likely the 460s, depending on which version of his story you read) in pursuit of a mandate from God to evangelise what became for the next three decades his adopted home. Some versions have him embarking on his return trip to Ireland from Whitesands Bay in Pembrokeshire, where the remains in sand dunes of an ancient chapel and sixth-century cemetery named after him were excavated in the 1970s.

While the historical reality of Patrick has been repeatedly questioned in modern times, his legend as Ireland's patron saint remains. Some scholars have even gone so far as to suggest that Palladius and Patrick might have been one and the same person.

The early twentieth-century scholar Heinrich Zimmer argued that the confusion arose because of a simple mix-up by the Irish in pronouncing the name of Palladius. The corruption 'Patricius' evidently rolled more easily off their tongues.[8]

His thesis is not widely accepted. The most obvious flaw is that the consensus among historians points to the Romano-Briton Patrick arriving up to three decades after the Gaulish Palladius and staying for a good deal longer. Any confusion between the two may rest on their shared connection with Gaul. After his liberation from captivity – thanks to God's intervention as he relates in the *Confession*[9] – Patrick trained for the priesthood in Gaul, where he was another inspired by the example set by the bishop-monk Martin of Tours. His return to Ireland was, Patrick relates, again at God's behest. 'I Patrick, a sinner, am the most ignorant and of least account among the faithful, despised by the many,' he writes. 'I owe it to God's grace that so many people through me should be born again to him'.[10]

Where Palladius had failed to win round the King of Leinster, Patrick did much better with Lóegaire Mac Néill when he met this fierce, pagan Irish king, sometimes described as ruler of Tara, at others as High King of Ireland. At first, Lóegaire had wanted to kill Patrick and banish Christianity from Ireland, but the various chronicles tell how Patrick persuaded him otherwise, whether by his words, by his courage or by his faith in God, to whom, as he was being ambushed by the king's forces, he successfully addressed a 'prayer of protection', known today as 'Saint Patrick's Breastplate'.

While Lóegaire may or may not have agreed to be baptised, depending on which account you read, in his *Confession* Patrick tells how the sons and daughters of the rulers of Ireland became the most enthusiastic promoters of Christianity in the years that followed. 'Never before did they know of God except to serve idols and unclean things. But now, they have become the people of the Lord, and are called children of God. The sons and daughters of the leaders of the Irish are seen to be monks and virgins of Christ!'[11]

While both his autobiographical *Confession* and his *Letter to the Soldiers of Coroticus* ostensibly provide a clear insight into the fifth-century events they describe, the earliest versions of both are found in the early ninth-century Book of Armagh. That gap of 400 years seems to have allowed the narrative to be shaped by subsequent developments. The Book of Armagh was produced at a time when the Irish Church had a system of dioceses that divided the country into areas, each one under the control of a bishop. The most significant of these was the Archbishop of Armagh. In seeking to impose episcopal authority on the independently minded abbots who still led the great monasteries and wielded considerable power and influence, this new leadership class of bishops may well have recruited Saint Patrick to their cause, describing him in these ninth-century texts as the founder and first head of the Archdiocese of Armagh.

Such a claim is a stretch. Patrick's own methods, in so far as they can be discerned at such a distance, appear to have been more like those of Ninian, forever travelling, preaching to those he met, converting and baptising them. Existing gods were repurposed as Christian saints. For example, Gobnet, held in high esteem by ironworkers before the arrival of Christianity, gave rise to the medieval cult of the female Saint Gobnait from County Cork, whose patronages included watching over blacksmiths. Yet, just as Ninian's legend tells of a base at Whithorn, so too does Patrick's, at Armagh.

Of all those to have emerged from these sixth-century Irish monasteries, none had a bigger impact on Christianity in Britain than Columba. He was not, his legend suggests, a particularly easy man to be around. There are, for example, plenty of references to his loud, insistent voice, though perhaps he needed it to compete with the ever-present roar and swell of the Atlantic around Iona, to which he travelled in 563 with twelve companions. As with others so far described, there is an element of the *seanachaidh*, or storyteller, in every version of Columba's life, and the number twelve may be just too neat a reference to Jesus' twelve apostles.

In his younger days, Columba was, these accounts tell, both the product of violent circumstances, as his own royal dynasty fought it out for hegemony in Ireland with others, and a driven, passionate man. The standard tale is that a petty dispute he instigated over a manuscript in 560 escalated into a mighty battle that cost thousands of lives and caused him to be banished to Iona. That, though, neglects his reported interactions with Finian, Enda and Ciarán's successor at Clonmacnoise, and does not mention how he travelled round Ireland founding monasteries at Durrow and up to twenty-five other sites. There were, then, other motives beyond exile that carried him across the narrowest stretch of the Irish Sea, to wash up at the Bay of the Coracle on Iona.

What greeted Columba and his companions were tough-looking, stumpy, stony hills, and bleached white sand beaches that slide into the sea. As well as their attraction for expanses of water and coastline, these first Christian monk-missionaries from Ireland inherited from pre-existing Celtic belief systems a passion for nature in the raw. Iona certainly catered for that, as Columba established his community on the tried and tested pattern of individual prayer and a life of austerity and hard graft, carried out from individual beehive cells collected around a wooden church.

From its earliest days, Iona was a community skilled in writing things down. The literary and library culture that developed on the island, reputed to have produced the Book of Kells, also brought, just a century after Columba's death, the first hagiography of him by Adomnán, a member of the community. The picture it paints is of a charismatic and compelling man who carried God with him, as if in his shadow, in his every act and pronouncement – 'fair, face ruddy, broad, radiant, body white, fame without falsehood, eyes grey, luminous'.[12]

To this list must be added tenacious, for from their tiny island off the coast of Mull – not quite so remote since it allowed access to the sea routes around Scotland, which were to prove less perilous than overland treks – Columba and his companions headed off 'to wander for God' on missions to bring Christianity to the Picts. How much of that work had already been begun by Ninian, and others who trod in his footsteps, is unclear. There is evidence of already established Christian pockets in Scotland, thanks to the close links it enjoyed with both Ireland and the emerging Christian Church elsewhere in Britain. But these 'island soldiers' from Iona, as Adomnán refers to them, had great successes, none more so than the conversion of the Pict King Bridei at Inverness in the mid 580s, apparently because he had been so impressed by Columba's ability to drive away snakes, frogs and other monsters.

As he grew old, Columba spent more and more time on Iona, leaving a coming generation to continue his missionary journeys and preferring – by some accounts – the company of angels before his death in 597. His achievement, though, is crucial to the story of Christianity in Britain and Ireland. For, if the faith was advancing in his native land, on the other side of the Irish Sea the year of his death also marked the arrival of the Pope's representative, Augustine, in Kent. As the missionaries from Iona travelled ever further south into England, they came face to face with those sent out by Augustine from Canterbury. The amalgam of their efforts made the first version of a truly British Christianity.

ALSO WITH A STORY TO TELL . . .

EILEACH-AN-NAOIMH – or Holy Isle – stands in the GARVELLACHS, islands in the Inner Hebrides to the south of Mull, and therefore close enough to Iona to claim some link with Columba. While there is almost nothing left of the saint's original buildings on Iona, Eileach-an-Naoimh is home to the remains of a monastery said to have been founded by Saint Brendan the Navigator in 542.

SAINT GOVAN'S CHAPEL, NEAR BOSHERSTON on the south coast of Pembrokeshire, clings to the cliffs, wedged between huge lime-stone boulders, and is accessed by fifty-two stone steps. Here, in the late sixth century, an Irish monk, Govan, came to live as a hermit as part of the regular interchange between Ireland and Wales.

The GALLARUS ORATORY stands at the western tip of the DINGLE PENINSULA in County Kerry. Built in stone, without mortar, using similar techniques to those seen in Neolithic tombs, it is shaped like an upturned boat with sloping side walls that meet in the middle. It is the only intact building of its kind in Ireland.

CHAPTER 7
The Seventh Century

All Saints', Brixworth: The Expanding Saxon Church

Have no communion with those who depart from the unity of the Catholic peace, either in not celebrating Easter at the proper time or in evil living.

Saint Cuthbert, Abbot and Bishop
of Lindisfarne (634–87)[1]

THOUGH IT STANDS well away from the main street that runs through the Northamptonshire village of Brixworth, there is not a chance of missing All Saints', even if I keep my eyes firmly on the road and don't raise them up to search the horizon for its spire. A large, bright-green roadside sign adorned with golden letters reads, 'Saxon Church AD 680'. It points me up a gentle hill from the high street, between rows of tiny cottages, and round a sharp bend, to where it presides on gently rising ground, framed by open farmland, tall, wide and majestic in honey-coloured stone.

The Poet Laureate Sir John Betjeman described All Saints' in the 1950s as 'probably the most impressive early Saxon building in the country'.[2] Those keener on calibration refer to it as 'the largest surviving church of Saxon origins in Britain'.[3] And the public face that this eccentrically large – and once even larger – church presents to the visitor is undeniably, solidly and beguilingly Saxon. There is the Saxon lower half of its tower, with what remains of its original two-tier porch, tiny windows and an impossibly low south door (the upper reaches are a fourteenth-century addition, and the unusual round external stair turret was appended in the eleventh). Down at the other end, a remarkable Saxon ring-crypt, one of only three surviving in the country, provides an outdoor, subterranean passageway (known as an ambulatory) behind the main altar at crypt level. Once pilgrims would have walked round it to see relics displayed on the exterior of the building, including possibly a throat bone from Saint

Boniface who had led the Anglo-Saxon mission to convert Germany in the eighth century. Most striking of all, though, are the four monumental, round-headed, Saxon arches, made of reused Roman red bricks (possibly from an abandoned colonial-era Roman villa nearby), that line each side of the nave. Matching sets of three delicate Saxon clerestory windows above them let extra light into the interior.

If other locations I have visited so far have required searching out the individual features so as to roll back the centuries and get in touch with their origins, here at Brixworth is a church that in its fundamentals is all about the century of its foundation. Once inside, that powerful sense of being transported back 1,300 years becomes, if anything, even stronger. The mighty brickwork arches, seen from the nave, may have lost some of their distinctive red colouring in various renovations over the centuries, but they speak of a muscular purposefulness in rapidly expanding seventh-century Saxon Christianity. They are marching triumphantly in two columns towards the chancel (the area in front of the altar). The back wall of the church boasts three more equally ancient arches, two smaller on either side, above Saxon plain glass with delicate inlaid red-trim windows, and the third more substantial, holding up the opening onto the apse behind the altar.

As a statement of intent about permanence after centuries of insecurity, it is hard to imagine how the message could be better conveyed. Why, though, is this vast, remarkable building here, in the middle of the English countryside? Who built in rural Northamptonshire something that, in its mighty arches, white walls and flood of light from above, echoes the early Christian basilicas found in Rome, and none more, for me, than the peerless fifth-century Santa Sabina on the Aventine Hill?

Well, that connection with Rome is important, for the impetus for All Saints' at the end of the seventh century lay in the expansion from Canterbury in the south, up through the various English king-doms, of the Roman template of Christianity that Saint Augustine had brought with him at the end of the sixth century. A former abbot himself, he regarded (as the Irish did at the same time) the establishment of monasteries as one important way to provide Christianity with an on-the-ground presence and structure. These, though, were monasteries that followed a single rule, or way of life shared with other linked foundations, rather than the more inde-pendent, fluid set-up that had characterised Clonmacnoise and Iona.

Among these new monasteries, inspired by Augustine's arrival, was Medeshamstede (modern-day Peterborough), founded in the middle of the seventh century. Its first abbot, Seaxwulf, is said by later chroniclers to have come from the ruling family of the Gyrwas clan, whose kingdom covered the Fenlands of eastern England. It may be that Seaxwulf used his own wealth to endow Medeshamstede – as other family members had done at Ely – but as a monastic house it was certainly eager to expand its influence. And so, in the 680s, it opened a sister house at Brixworth, build-ing the Saxon church that remains to this day. The site seems to have been chosen for its central location in England, one more advance in an ongoing roll-out.

Those twin sets of four powerful Saxon arches that run down the sides of the nave are today filled in by later brickwork and windows. Originally, though, they were arcades that opened onto eight chambers (*porticus*) or side chapels. All Saints' may be vast in proportion to the village it now serves, but 1,300 years ago it was even larger: as wide as it was long. One intriguing explana-tion for such a scale was because it was intended as a gathering place for councils – the regular meetings of the expanding English Church – that started to take place in the seventh century under the auspices of Augustine's successors as Archbishops of Canterbury.

In various chronicles, some regarded as more reliable than others, reference is made to assemblies at Clofesho in 673, 716, 742, 747, 794, 803, 824 and 825.[4] Records of each assembly over this 150-year span vary in detail and credibility, but no one has ever been quite able to work out where exactly Clofesho was. In Old English, the word roughly translates as 'a hill spur in a valley'. There are plenty of churches that fit such a description. Examples near Rochester in Kent, Abingdon in Oxfordshire, Tewkesbury in Gloucestershire and Mildenhall in Suffolk have been championed as the original Clofesho, but since the 1960s there has been a persuasive school of thought that adds together All Saints' unwieldy size and its easy-to-reach location and favours it as the answer to the mystery of the lost Clofesho.[5]

Certainly, the physical geography of the Brixworth site can be plausibly stretched to fit it being a hill spur in a valley, but, for enthusiasts, it is its location in the ancient Midlands kingdom of Mercia that is most telling. Repeatedly in the various records of councils at Clofesho – where attendees include kings as well as bishops, abbots and nobles – there are references to kings of Mercia either presiding (742, 824 and 825) or being in attendance. The host, at a time when England was a patchwork of rival kingdoms, was most likely to be the ruler within whose realm Clofesho stood. And in Mercia, All Saints' is regarded as the best candidate.

Mercia had been the last of the larger kingdoms of England to follow Ethelbert in Kent in embracing Christianity, though in some others formal acceptance of the new religion may not have gone more than skin deep. Sutton Hoo near Woodbridge in Suffolk, an Anglo-Saxon ship-burial site, is believed to be the last resting place of Raedwald, King of the East Angles at the start of the seventh century. He became a Christian, and ten silver bowls, each divided into four with an ornamented cross, among his 'grave goods' seem to speak of the sincerity of his conversion. But

Bede records that in life he also allowed an altar to what are referred to as devils, more likely the pagan deities that predated the arrival of Christianity and remained part of the religious landscape.[6]

Augustine's mission had initially spread north, as we have seen, through the marriage of Ethelbert's daughter Ethelburga to the Northumbrian King Edwin in 627. However, Mercia's king, Penda – 'a most warlike man of the royal race of Mercians', as Bede refers to him[7] – held out against the new religion. And since he was so successful on the battlefield in the wars he fought with the Christian kings of both Northumbria to the north and Wessex to the south, his lands represented a substantial obstacle across the midriff of England to the spread of the faith. In 653, Penda came to an arrangement with Oswiu, the Northumbrian king, to end hostilities. As part of it, he agreed to allow four priests to enter his realm. Led by the monk Cedd, this tiny group began the conversion of the Mercians. 'Arriving in the province, [they] preached the Word, and were willingly listened to,' writes Bede, 'many, as well of the nobility as the common sort, renouncing the abominations of idolatry, were baptised daily.'[8] When Penda was killed in battle in 655 by Oswiu, his son and successor, Peada, was already a Christian who, according to *The Anglo-Saxon Chronicle*, had played a part in founding the monastery at Medeshamstede.

The expansion to Brixworth was, then, also part of rooting Christianity in hitherto hostile Mercian soil. Seaxwulf, who founded Medeshamstede, went on to become Bishop of Lindsey,[9] covering the present-day county of Lincolnshire as well as parts of the Fenlands. It was part of a new episcopal structure in Mercia that elevated Lichfield as a centre of Christianity to rival Canterbury and York. Seaxwulf personifies the connection between the various strands that were driving the growth of the faith in Saxon England – the high-born prince who established a monastery and went on to be a bishop. In him, royal authority, the status of the abbot and the powers of a bishop were combined in one.

The conversion of Edwin in Northumbria in 627 had given the missionary push that had begun in Kent under Augustine its first great success. As a king, his influence was far reaching over northern England and into Scotland. As the seventh century progressed, Christianity continued its spread in similar fashion through the patronage of kings. In East Anglia, it was the arrival on the throne of Sigeberht, who had been baptised as a young boy, Bede reports, while visiting Augustine's protector, King Ethelbert, in Kent. The new Christian king then recruited the Burgundian monk Felix to convert what had, under his father, been a polytheistic kingdom. And so Felix became the first Bishop of Dunwich, the Suffolk port town which he seems to have made his base in the diocese. (Its prosperity was later ruined by coastal erosion, with large portions of it swept into the sea in the thirteenth and fourteenth centuries, including eight churches, whose bells, local legend still holds, can still at certain tides be heard chiming from beneath the water.) Felix is credited by Bede with enlisting Sigeberht's support for opening one of the very first Christian schools, 'where boys could be taught letters'.[10]

Monastic schools were to go on to ground Christianity in English life, but the more immediate priority was to revive efforts to bring all of southern England and Wales under the authority of the Archbishop of Canterbury. In Augustine's time these had stalled, partly because of his mishandling of the existing bishops there, who had long been serving those believers displaced to the south west and Wales by the earlier Anglo-Saxon invasions. The Welsh monk and chronicler Gildas, writing in the 540s, was scathing in his judgement of this quasi-independent branch of Christianity, characterising it as run by 'unworthy wretches, wallowing, after the fashion of their swine, in their old and unhappy puddle of intolerable wickedness'.[11] Yet, as Augustine's unhappy encounter with the bishops suggests, it was not without some sort of cohesion, and had developed its own distinctive culture, albeit insular and largely cut off from the mainstream of Christendom.

The sixth century had seen the Church in Wales, in particular, sharing the growing enthusiasm in Ireland (with which it shared sea-links) for monasteries founded by saintly, ascetic and independent-minded leaders. Most notable among these was the high-born Dewi (David), who refused to allow his communities to eat meat, drink alcohol or use animals to till the fields, but instead made monks place yokes on their own shoulders. It was how you lived your life that mattered for Christians, Dewi taught those drawn to him. Though he respected the faraway Pope as the leader of Christianity, his worldview was local and regional. In his last sermon, Dewi urged, 'do the little things, the small things you've seen me doing'.

As in Ireland, many of these rugged, zealous, charismatic monks in Wales, still-revered figures such as Dyfrig, Illtyd, Teilo, Padarn and Beuno, were, by nature and by religious inclination, travellers. Monastery begat monastery. Between 550 and 650, some thirty-six *clasau* – *clas* in Welsh being a major church, headed by an abbot, consisting of a community of monks living in individual cells – are reported to have been established throughout Wales, spreading out from Dewi's foundation in Pembrokeshire to Penmon in Anglesey in the north, Caerwent in Gwent in the south and Bangor-is-y-Coed, near Wrexham, in the east.[12]

Given such vibrancy, Rome was anxious to make its authority felt in this flourishing branch of Christianity. In 633, Pope Honorius I sent Birinius on a mission to, in Bede's words, 'the most inland and remote regions of the English, where no other teacher had been before him'.[13] As well as being a bishop, Birinius was a Benedictine monk, part of the order founded by Benedict of Nursia in Italy in the sixth century at Monte Cassino. Benedict's 'Rule' directed monks' lives and gave a shared identity to the Benedictine monasteries that were spreading rapidly, with papal encouragement, across Europe, but not yet in Britain and Ireland.

Birinius is thought to have landed at what is now Southampton. From there, he journeyed inland to the region ruled by Cyngelis, King of the West Saxons, where he encountered a population that was, Bede writes, 'completely heathen'.[14] His initial plans for venturing further afield towards Wales were delayed while Birinius tackled what greeted him. He persuaded Cyngelis to be baptised in 635, and in return was given land to establish a monastery at Dorchester-on-Thames, south of modern-day Oxford. He remained there until his death in 650.

The task of bringing order to Christians further west had to wait until the end of the century, when, as Ine, the new King of Wessex, expanded his realm, he also extended the reach of the 'official' Church. He ordered an abbey to be built at Glastonbury in Somerset – 'in a sequestered marsh,' one chronicler reported, 'intending that the more confined the monks' view on earth, the more eagerly they would hold to heavenly things'.[15] And in 705, the ecclesiastical heart of his kingdom was moved away from Dorchester, with new bishops installed in Winchester and Sherborne.

Elsewhere, the growth and development of Christianity did not always proceed smoothly. In Kent, Ethelbert's son, and successor on the King's death in 616, had refused for the first years of his reign to be baptised. He finally succumbed only when he was married to a Christian Frankish princess, as once his father had been to Bertha. In Northumbria, after Edwin's death in battle in 632, the succession was disputed. Those who came immediately after him abandoned Christianity, causing Bishop Paulinus of York and the widowed Queen Ethelburga to flee back to Kent. Not all was lost, however, and James the Deacon, a member of the second group of missionaries to arrive in Kent in 601, stayed put, basing himself in Lincoln in a church that Paulinus had built, and continuing his missionary work into old age.

The office of deacon, as held by James, was one of six grades of ministry below priesthood (doorkeeper, reader, exorcist, acolyte, subdeacon, deacon). For some they were the steps to eventual priesthood, a state to be reached ideally by the age of thirty, according to papal directives of the time. Others stopped at the diaconate but were nonetheless regarded as senior figures in the Church. And, while shut out of the priesthood on account of their gender (despite there being well-attested evidence of female priests in the earliest centuries of Christianity in southern Italy), women could still become deaconesses, and in some cases heads of 'double' monasteries. These included separate male and female houses, but all ultimately answered to abbesses. One such was Hilda, great-niece of Edwin of Northumbria, who had been baptised alongside him in 627 by Bishop Paulinus in York, and in the 650s established Whitby Abbey.

She had survived the turbulent years following Edwin's death, when a chaotic and bloody battle ensued for the Northumbrian throne in what Bede refers to as the '*annus infaustus*' or 'disastrous year'.[16] The conflict was resolved when the young Oswald, one of the claimants who had been sent to study at Iona as a young man so as to escape court intrigues, raised an army and returned to reclaim the kingdom for himself and Christianity. The following year he requested that the Iona community provide him with a missionary to assist in his efforts to restore Christianity to his lands. The first despatched was Corman, but he decided quickly that his evangelising was falling on deaf ears. He returned to western Scotland with horror stories of being confronted by barbarians.

Undeterred by such reports, another member of the Iona community, Aidan, stepped into the breach, promising to offer Oswald's subjects, Bede writes, 'the milk of simpler teaching'.[17] Arriving around 635, he was named a bishop by Oswald and offered his pick of sites on which to build a new monastery. He opted for an uninhabited island known as Lindisfarne – literally 'retreat' (*farne*) from or in the Lindis, the small tidal river that emptied into the sea around it. From the ramparts of Oswald's castle at Bamburgh, Aidan could see Lindisfarne sitting a few miles off the coast to the north, amid 5,000 acres of tidal mud. He made his choice, the chroniclers later reported, because monks liked islands, and Lindisfarne in particular reminded him of Iona.

There may have been more pragmatic reasons. The island was close, but not too close, to Bamburgh. The political and the spiritual in Anglo-Saxon Britain co-existed, with those with temporal power key to the success of the evanglising mission, but it wasn't a seamless garment. Disputes and misunderstandings could arise, so the limited tidal access – the six-mile route from Bamburgh to Lindisfarne was notoriously treacherous and required local fishermen as guides – represented a boundary Aidan was keen to maintain, not to mention a deterrent if the King or his successors became too insistent on their own agenda.

He built a wooden church on an elevated site at the south end of Lindisfarne at a spot that is today known as the Heugh. As the monastery's reputation grew, it was repeatedly enlarged.

The most celebrated of the abbots to follow Aidan was Cuthbert. As Lindisfarne's bishop in the last third of the seventh century, his reputation as a scholar, preacher and healer drew crowds of pilgrims who braved the tides to reach the island. Following Cuthbert's death in 687, his stone coffin, containing his perfectly preserved body, became one of the wonders of the age, reputed to have the power to effect miraculous cures. As such, it proved a more powerful magnet than the Lindisfarne Gospels, peerless late-seventh-century illuminated manuscripts produced by the island's monks which are now in the British Museum.

By the end of the seventh century, the position of clergy within Christianity was more clearly defined and accepted, notably around their responsibility for the sacraments of baptism and Eucharist. Ordination made these their preserve, and so marked them off from the laity. That gap was now tangibly demarcated not just by clothing but also by tonsure – a shaved patch on the middle of the head done in boyhood on those who opted to study for the priesthood. It should have been a simple matter of choice and custom as to where exactly that tonsure was carried out on each head. Yet it proved anything but, and is the best known of the disputes in British Christianity that were settled at the land-mark Synod of Whitby in 664.

Abbess Hilda played host, but it was her relative, King Oswiu of Northumbria, who summoned the gathering. Clergy in those parts brought to the faith by Augustine and his successors took a modest approach to tonsure – removing hair in a circle on the top of their heads. Meanwhile, those whose principal influence came from Iona and before that Ireland (what is sometimes labelled the Celtic rather than the Roman approach), went much further with the blade and shaved the whole of the front of their heads in what was intended to be, and was, an eye-catching detail to mark them out.

The geography of tonsure was not, though, the main business of the Synod. This included the wearing of crowns by bishops, the introduction of feet-washing at baptism, and 'joint consecration' of the Eucharist by two priests as was the custom on Iona. The most contentious issue at Whitby concerned the dating of Easter. The 'Celtic' tradition used a different method for calculating it from the 'Roman' group, with both claiming Gospel authority for their way. King Oswiu regarded the problem as practical rather than scriptural. He had been raised on Iona while his wife had grown up in Kent, and so, he pointed out, while his Queen was still observing Palm Sunday (Jesus' triumphant entry into Jerusalem), he was already on Easter Sunday, by which time Jesus had died on the cross and risen from the dead.

Great set-piece debates took place at the Synod, with on one side Cedd, the Lindisfarne monk who had converted the Mercians, and Colman, the Bishop of Lindisfarne. On the other stood James the Deacon, by now a very old man but a living link back to Augustine, and Wilfrid, Abbot of Ripon. The latter claimed no less an authority than Saint Peter, the first pope, for the Roman method of dating Easter, and carried the day with King Oswiu. He reportedly remarked that he would rather be on good terms with the keeper of the gates of heaven (Saint Peter's traditional role) than Columba, founder of Iona. For Wilfrid it was a triumph that saw him soon afterwards elevated to be Bishop of York. For Colman, it was a bitter blow that caused him to leave Lindisfarne, taking with him the relics of the founder, Aidan, and return to Iona, and eventually to Ireland. There he founded a monastery in Mayo.

In the wake of Whitby, Lindisfarne itself was much reduced in influence. Soon it no longer had a resident bishop. Its status as the principal base of Church power in the north had passed to York.

It is easy to regard the Synod of Whitby as the crushing of the 'Celtic' Church by the 'Roman' Church, with its independence, quirkiness and concentration on the small things, nature and inner life replaced by a centralised bureaucracy keen on rules, conformity, hierarchies and papal power that reached out across Christendom. Indeed, in recent times, with an exodus of believers from institutional Christianity in all its forms because of their perception of the Church's inflexibility around doctrine, the appeal of what is presented as a free-wheeling, open-minded Celtic approach has won many converts. But such a characterisation distorts a complex reality.

Professor David Rollason of Durham University writes:

Misconceived is the often repeated view that the Synod of Whitby marked the victory of the 'Roman' Church over the 'Celtic' Church, for the terms themselves are misleading. There was no homogeneous 'Celtic' Church, for there were substantial differences in the organisation and practices of the Churches of Ireland, Wales, the south-west of England and Pictland [Scotland].[18]

Even the division into different camps of the voices raised at the Synod can be oversimplistic. Wilfrid, for example, was a monk of Lindisfarne who had also travelled to Rome and spent three years in Gaul, where Church practices had been heavily influenced by the Irish monk Columbanus. As Bishop of York, Wilfrid worked through a network of monasteries that he founded not only in the north but also in Mercia, Sussex and Kent in what seems to have had strong parallels to the Irish model.

Neither did the role of the Archbishop of Canterbury suddenly expand greatly after Whitby. In part this was because a plague swept through the land, causing chaos and a four-year hiatus in replacing Archbishop Deusdedit, the first native-born primate, who had died in 664 of the pestilence. In seeking out a successor, Rome chose to revert to recruiting from abroad, with the appointment in 668 of Theodore, an already elderly monk from Tarsus in Asia Minor. Its hands may have been tied since Theodore found on his arrival only one bishop in post, south of the River Humber, and just two to its north – Chad, younger brother of Cedd, and Wilfrid. Fortunately, he was a man of ability and determination. In his twenty-two years in office, Theodore introduced discipline and resilience into the Church, calling the first General Synod of the Church in England in 672, carefully implementing the decisions of Whitby, dividing dioceses, appointing new bishops and even reining in the ambitious Wilfrid in York.

Such an outcome did not mean the monasteries of Wales and Scotland suddenly lost their independence, or that they had to fall into line with busybody bishops doing Rome's bidding. In north west Wales, the island monastery on Bardsey was still following its own distinctive path well into the twelfth century, travellers reported, while at Iona, Easter continued to be dated in its traditional way into the eighth century. Yet there was, undeniably, a greater unity and sense of shared purpose in the Church than ever before as it went into the next century – far greater, it should be added, than in the jigsaw of rival kingdoms that made up Britain. It was, arguably, such Church cohesion that allowed the cultural and spiritual flourishing of the Anglo-Saxon 'golden age' of the eighth century, along with its towering figure, Bede, whose moment has come.

ALSO WITH A STORY TO TELL . . .

ST JOHN AT ESCOMB in County Durham is one of only three complete Saxon churches in Britain. Tall and narrow, it was built from 650, using large recycled Roman stones from nearby Vinovium – or Binchester Fort – part of the military infrastructure close to Hadrian's Wall.

ST PETER-ON-THE-WALL, standing next to mudflats at BRADWELL-ON-SEA on the Dengie Peninsula in Essex, is perched on the edge of what looks like an unchanging natural world. Built around 653 by Saint Cedd, using the stone from a derelict fourth-century Roman fort (including one of its walls – hence the name), only the nave remains of what was a thriving monastery until the ninth century, and a church into the sixteenth.

YORK MINSTER is the successor to the first wooden church where King Edwin of Northumbria was baptised by Paulinus in 627. A stone church came a decade later, and in 670 it was renewed by Wilfrid soon after his elevation. His creation was destroyed by fire in 741 and what replaced it went through several incarnations until the current-day Minster was largely completed in the fifteenth century.

CHAPTER 8

The Eighth Century

Jarrow Abbey: Bede and the Golden Age

Anglo-Saxon and Celtic Christians between them made the Atlantic Isles in the seventh and eighth centuries a prodigious powerhouse of Christian activity. Their energies flowed together.
Diarmaid MacCulloch, *A History of Christianity*[1]

IT IS THE oldest foundation stone in a church anywhere in the British Isles. Laid in 685 close to the south bank of the River Tyne, it stands in St Paul's, Jarrow, and reads in Latin, 'The dedication of the Church of St Paul on 23rd April in the fifteenth year of King Ecgfrith and the fourth year of Ceolfrith Abbot and under God's guidance founder of this same church'.

It is not for either Ecgfrith – though he was King of Northumbria, the mightiest power in the land, with extensive territories that stretched from the River Humber in the south to the Firth of Forth in the north – or even for Ceolfrith, later declared a saint, that visitors today come to this ancient church in a post-industrial city-scape. Rather it is to walk in the footsteps of the Venerable Bede, referred to as the 'father of English history', who lived and worshipped here all of his adult life, and whose writings shape our view of the early centuries of English Christianity.

As a young boy of probably no more than seven, Bede was sent, as was increasingly the way with the sons of noble families, to be educated by the monks who were establishing St Peter's Abbey on the River Wear, often referred to as Monkwearmouth. A few years later, at ten, he accompanied a group of monks to Jarrow, eight miles north, to start St Paul's as a twin abbey to St Peter's. He would most likely have stood in front of this foundation stone as it was unveiled.

Not all who studied with monks went on to take vows, but Bede did. His writings at what is usually referred to as Jarrow Abbey made its name as well as his own renowned throughout

Europe and down through history. Between around 700 and his death in 735, he produced more than sixty works. Even the distinctive script he used – 'pointed minuscule', a variation of the 'insular' style developed in Irish monasteries from the seventh century, and in those in Britain influenced by them – was much admired and imitated. The subjects he covered were many and varied, from texts on the grammar to be used by teachers in the new abbey schools to biblical commentaries, vernacular poetry, music and science, including promoting the dating BC/AD system that pivots on the life of Jesus Christ.

It is, though, his *Ecclesiastical History of the English People* that has endured, its contents all the more remarkable because he seldom left the monastery during his life in Jarrow, though he did receive visitors (including Columba's biographer, Adomnán, from Iona) and maintained a wide correspondence. What the abbey offered in abundance, besides time and a desk, were books. There were some 250 of them in its library, said to rival any other collection this side of Rome, amassed on five trips to the capital of Christianity by Benedict Biscop, the founding abbot of the twin institutions of St Peter's and St Paul's.

A Northumbrian by origin, high-born and at one stage a thegn (or attendant) at the court of King Oswiu, Biscop had travelled extensively in Europe, including two years spent at Lérins, the Benedictine monastery on an island in the south of France, where he took vows. He returned home when accompanying Theodore of Tarsus on his arrival in England as the new Archbishop of Canterbury in 669.

Biscop intended his twin abbeys to be models of best practice in the British Isles as to how a monastic community should live, enabling it to catch up with developing practices in Europe. There the disciplined life of the Benedictine monastery had spread far and wide. In England, it propelled St Peter's and St Paul's in the north-east of England to a leadership role in a golden age in the

Saxon Church whose glow extended far and wide at home and across the continent. Biscop summoned a cantor from St Peter's Basilica in Rome to teach his monks to chant. He shunned local craftsmen and instead imported the expert masons and glaziers he had come across in Gaul to introduce the Pre-Romanesque style of church building into England. The result was that simple, tall, narrow chapels were superseded by wide-aisled churches lit by stained-glass windows.

Biscop's was a truly European vision – in terms of upholding papal authority and the ecclesiastical structures that Theodore imposed from Canterbury, as well as the integration of religious and cultural life. His impact, even before his death in 690, cannot be underestimated.

In the eighth century that followed, his 'one monastery in two places' became the cradle for early English art, producing three fine and delicately illustrated copies of the whole Bible, one each for the abbey churches at St Peter's and St Paul's, and a third to be hand-delivered by Ceolfrith to Pope Gregory II. Jarrow was no longer to be part of what Rome regarded as a satellite Church in Britain and Ireland. It joined the mainstream.

Abbot Ceolfrith died en route to Rome in 716, but the treasure he bore did reach its destination. It survives as the *Codex Amiatus* in Florence's Laurentian Library, the earliest manuscript of the Vulgate[2] version of the Christian Bible. From a tenuous fringe Church in those early centuries of Roman occupation, on life-support following the tumult of decolonisation and the invasion that followed, Britain began in the eighth century to send more and more monks to the continent, including Boniface, born in the Devon town of Crediton, and a leading figure in the Anglo-Saxon mission to convert the Germanic parts of the Frankish Empire to Christianity.

One section of Benedict Biscop's monastery at Jarrow survives as part of the present-day church of St Paul's. It stands amid the ruins of subsequent pre-Reformation ecclesiastical buildings on the same site. Divided into two parts by a tower, on one side is a longer, wider, neater church, where the monastery church once was, rebuilt in the 1860s by George Gilbert Scott. It is the smaller of the two halves, though, that has most to contribute to this story, for the chancel of the present-day St Paul's Abbey Church is what remains from those Saxon glory days.

Originally, archaeologists suggest, in addition to terraced vegetable gardens, metal- and glass-working workshops, a communal hall with a stone central seat for the abbot and a refectory (where food debris including fish bones has been unearthed), the eighth-century monastery would have had not one but two churches. One was where local people could join the monks, the other exclusively for members of the monastery community. Positioned end to end, there was a narrow passageway between them, filled in at the start of the ninth century with what later became a tower, its original lower portions remaining, with sturdy vaulting to its ceiling.

The current-day chancel, the smaller of those two churches, is a typically plain, tall, thin Saxon structure, built in what are thought to be stones reused from a Roman-era building. Big Gothic windows were added in the thirteenth century to brighten the darkness, but three Saxon originals halfway up the south wall are as small as they are precious – so small that from the outside they are easy to miss. The openings that house them are no more than thirty centimetres wide and seventy-five centimetres high, with more stonemasonry surrounding them than glass itself. Inside, they are set in deep recesses in the Saxon walls. None survived intact the troubled post eighth-century history of St Paul's, but the middle one of this trinity has been pieced together in a lead-and-iron frame using fragments of original Saxon glass found during late twentieth century excavations on the site.[3]

A mosaic of yellows, greens, blues, pinks and oranges, it is billed as the oldest stained-glass window in the British Isles, which may be stretching things a little since so many centuries went by between destruction and reassembly. Nevertheless, it fires the imagination when standing in the chancel and considering how the light from these three tiny openings (the other two now filled with complementary but modern works by John Piper and Leonard Evetts) would have played 1,200 years ago in the dark interior of the original church, unlit as it was by any other opening. There is evidence of plain glazed windows in Roman Britannia, while the first painted ornamental glass on the continent is found in the last days of the western Roman Empire in the Church of St Vitale in Ravenna. Here in the monastery, those shafts of colour would surely have seemed both miraculous and a sign of God's presence. Light is, in his own words in the gospels, a symbol of Jesus: 'As long as I am in the world,' he says in John's Gospel, 'I am the light of the world.'⁴

As Archbishop of Canterbury for twenty-one years until his death in 690, Theodore's legacy to the eighth century was a more robust system of dioceses and synods than ever before. In 735, the model that Pope Gregory the Great had entrusted to Augustine so many years earlier on his mission to Kent, of establishing twin northern and southern provinces, was finally realised when York was upgraded from bishopric to archbishopric. As its first head, Ecgbert, taught by Bede and brother of a subsequent King of Northumbria, was given authority over the whole of the north by Pope Gregory III – though not over Monkwearmouth and Jarrow Abbeys, which had been exempted by a previous pope from any diocesan control. Ecgbert built up his cathedral school and library to the point where it was said, towards the end of his thirty-year tenure, even to have eclipsed Benedict Biscop's collection of books.⁵ He also sought to impose rules over personal conduct and how to lead a liturgy on clergy in his province, in the interests of discipline and uniformity.

These were to be concerns for many centuries to come, and they had already engaged Theodore at Canterbury. In his lifetime, he had enjoyed a reputation for great wisdom and so had been asked to rule on a whole range of questions around the proper behaviour of priests, and the right and wrong way to conduct the sacraments. After his death, some of his close associates combined his various judgements into a collection of decrees, the *Paenitentiale*. Their influence was felt throughout the country in the eighth century, and not only among bishops, priests and monks. They included measures to embed the settlement reached at the Synod of Whitby. Those who had been ordained by 'Scottish or British bishops, who are not Catholics in the keeping of Easter and in the matter of tonsure,' it stated, 'are not united to the [Roman] Church but must be confirmed by the laying-on of hands by a Catholic bishop'.[6] While enforcement was by no means immediate, especially the further away from Canterbury those who demurred were located, the claim to authority as Archbishop of Canterbury and the Pope's representative was plain to see.

Likewise in the matter of more general clergy discipline: 'If anyone who is a bishop or an ordained man shall be a habitual drunkard, let him either cease to be so or be deposed. If a monk makes himself sick through drinking, let him do penance for 30 days.'[7]

And the *Paenitentiale* also had wider ambitions to lay down social mores for a society that lived under a variety of different kings. 'If a woman leaves her husband, despising him, and will not return nor be reconciled to him, after five years and with the bishop's consent it shall be lawful for him to take another wife.'[8] Remaining pagan superstitions and rituals were dismissed: 'Anyone burning corn where there is a dead man, for the benefit of the living and of the house, shall do penance for five years.'[9]

An ambitious and expanding Church was growing more confident of its role in broader society, with the pronouncements of popes, archbishops and bishops promoted in the local realm by a new army of priests sent out from central cathedral towns to evangelise over large rural areas. Necessity saw the creation of a second level of centres, with Minster churches and, below them, though still patchily spread by the end of the century, parishes with their own church and resident priest. Usually these were endowed and controlled by a local landlord as part of the growth of the manorial system, a Europe-wide development, built on serfdom, which gave those who owned the land extensive rights over every aspect of the lives of those who resided on it.

For his part, the priest stood somewhere between the upper and lower tiers of Anglo-Saxon society, as well as between God (and his representative, the local bishop) and the lord of the manor. If it was God who had called the priest to ministry, it was the lord of the manor who had granted him his church and his living, in the form of the 'glebe' land attached to the church to support it, and the 'tithe' – from the Old English word for a 'tenth' – a share of all produce in the parish, whether of the fields or the animals in them. Payment was made obligatory in the tenth century.

Then there were the monasteries, where the Benedictine Rule introduced by Biscop at Monkwearmouth and Jarrow (though some claim Wilfrid of York pre-dated him in this) became the norm, sometimes in versions customised to particular settings. They were the real backbone of religious life in Anglo-Saxon England, but there were tensions between abbots and bishops, especially in areas where monasteries held great swathes of land. Who was ultimately in charge? At a gathering of Church leaders in 747 (at the mysterious Clofesho), summoned by the then Archbishop of Canterbury, Cuthbert, it was agreed that bishops had to be more diligent in visiting monasteries to check that the Rule supposed to shape their daily life and rhythms was being followed, right down to dressing as prescribed and 'not in fashionable gartering of their legs'.[10]

That same pull and push was seen, too, between monasteries and cathedrals, especially over who should lead the prominent role the Church was increasingly taking on in the promotion of learning. Alcuin of York belonged to the generation after Bede, born in the kingdom of Northumbria five years after the latter died. He was sent by his family of lower-ranking nobility, probably from the area around Holderness on the coast of what is today East Yorkshire, to be educated at the school attached to York Minster. There he became the favoured pupil of the hands-on archbishop, Ecgbert, who was determined that a broad education should be offered not just to trainee monks and clergy, but also to young lay men.

With Alcuin at its head in the second half of the eighth century, York developed into a pre-eminent centre of learning in western Christendom, building on and eclipsing the reputation of Jarrow. Archbishop Ecgbert believed the more each individual knew, the greater their insight into divine reason and God's creative purpose in the world. And in his turn, Alcuin moved away from teaching in the vernacular to using Latin, and promoted the full range of subjects: grammar, rhetoric, logic, arithmetic, astronomy and music. York was one of the few places in Europe where the literature of classical Rome and Greece was studied. No longer was the purpose of education to be about saving souls, or arithmetic a means of calculating the days of Easter.

The breadth of the curriculum at York attracted not just locals who felt no call to monastic or priestly vocation, but also students from across Europe, who saw in the cathedral school somewhere more outward-looking than those attached to monasteries (which were, by their nature, at least partly prone to be introspective). As a result, York, then a port city, saw a constant flow in and out of those with new ways of thinking.

In the 780s, on one of his journeys to the continent, Alcuin was asked by the then King Charles of Francia to join the group of the brightest and best scholars he was assembling at his court in Aachen to celebrate knowledge and change education for good. Together, the King and his advisors, of whom Alcuin was the most prominent, worked to promote a revival in learning throughout the European Church that is referred to by history as the Carolingian Renaissance, its scope extending to raising standards in both the clergy and monasteries.

For all the evidence of a golden age, Bede's last letters to Ecgbert include laments about the downsides that came with the rapid expansion of the Church in the British Isles: negligent bishops, ignorant clergy who overlooked the Eucharist, and 'sham' monasteries founded by wealthy families as havens where 'poets, harpers, musicians and buffoons' retreated to the cloister to avoid being co-opted to fight alongside their king.[11] While the 'great monasteries' like St Peter's and St Paul's had blossomed, others had been established for more dubious motives.

The special and protected status that monasteries held in Anglo-Saxon England meant that members were exempt from the demands of royal military service. Some noble families saw this as an open invitation to spare their sons the battlefield. But without anything approaching a vocation, the behaviour of the young men hardly matched their official status as monks. Appointing a family member as abbot or abbess (in the case of smaller female communities now being established) of a new foundation could ensure control of the land on which it stood, since whatever property had been given to a religious house could not be alienated from it. Dynastic calculation displaced spiritual discipline.

Alcuin spoke out forcibly against such corruption, even when writing to the monks of St Peter's and St Paul's:

Consider the splendour of your churches, the beauty of your buildings, your way of life according to the [Benedictine] rule. Let the boys [in the abbeys' schools] be present with praises of the heavenly king, and not by digging foxes out of holes or following the fleeting courses of hares ... he who does not learn when he is young, does not teach when he is old.[12]

His passion for reform extended to the standard Roman rite – the words and accompanying actions used when celebrating the Mass. In the revised version he produced, Alcuin included the custom of singing the *Credo* ('I Believe'), which had been part of the liturgies in the Irish-influenced monasteries of the Northumbria of his youth. Again, it is evidence that the 'Celtic' had not been eclipsed by the 'Roman'. What he proposed in this case became the preferred option everywhere in Europe.

Alcuin's retreat from the Aachen court appears to have happened in stages. He returned briefly to his native England but then headed for France to be Abbot of Tours, where he died in 796. He did not, therefore, witness events four years later when King Charles was, as Charlemagne ('Charles the Great'), crowned Holy Roman Emperor in St Peter's in Rome on Christmas Day of 800 by Pope Leo III. It was a recognition of the King's achievements in reuniting much of Western and Central Europe under one ruler and one set of ideas for the first time since the collapse of the Roman Empire three centuries earlier. That intimate connection of Church and State that this represented was to resonate widely around the continent in the centuries to come, including throughout Britain and Ireland.

Strains in this core relationship between kings and bishops were already being experienced in the second half of the eighth century, with the rise to prominence of the central kingdom of Mercia under King Offa, who made the provocative claim that he was 'King of All the English'. Offa was a great benefactor of monasteries, but his motives were earthy. He wanted the Church in his kingdom to reflect his own ambitions and status, and therefore resented any interference in his affairs by the Archbishop of

Canterbury, in whose province Mercia fell in terms of Church governance. Matters were complicated since, in temporal terms, the Archbishop lived in the territory of a king in Kent whom Offa was aiming to defeat and replace.

Pressure was therefore put on Rome to agree to 'free' Mercia from the authority of Canterbury by carving out a third province on Mercian territory at Lichfield, to sit alongside (and rival) Canterbury and York. In 787, two papal legates came to England to force the measure through, placing the dioceses of Worcester, Hereford, Leicester, Sherborne, Elmham and Dunwich under Hygeberht (or Higbert), whom Offa handpicked as a tame first Archbishop of Lichfield. As it turned out, he was also the last. After Offa's death, Canterbury's authority over these dioceses was restored, but the dispute signalled that the matter of who made Church appointments, king or pope, was getting ever more difficult.

The divisions and rivalries among the English kings had another downside. Embroiled in their domestic struggles, they had paid too little attention to external threats and left the door open for outsiders to strike. The golden age ended in 793 with Viking raids on the monastery at Lindisfarne. Alcuin wrote, his agony obvious, of 'pagans desecrating the sanctuaries of God, [and] pouring out the blood of saints around the altar, laying waste the house of our hope'.[13] The following year, the same attackers pitched up at St Peter's and St Paul's in the north east, doing such damage that they caused both eventually to be abandoned. The same fate was to befall many other coastal churches and monastic foundations in the century ahead. A dark age was dawning.

ALSO WITH A STORY TO TELL...

LICHFIELD CATHEDRAL in Staffordshire, with its three medieval spires, is the third building to stand on this spot, which some believe was where early Christians were martyred during the Roman occupation. On Christmas Day, 700, a first cathedral in wood was started, the adjoining monastery producing the celebrated eighth-century Lichfield Gospels.

ST LAURENCE'S in the Wiltshire town of BRADFORD-ON-AVON shares the Saxon taste for chapels that are taller than they are long. The traditional view is that it was built by the monk Aldhelm around 700, as part of his expansion plans from nearby Malmesbury. More recently, though, it has been dated to the tenth century, possibly as a place where Aldhelm's relics were placed.

ST MARY'S, DEERHURST in Gloucestershire was originally part of a Saxon monastery, close to the River Severn. Started around 790, St Mary's nave is typically Saxon, narrow and high, with arcades and aisles added later. This church has a carved angel, outside as part of the ruined apse, with curly hair that suggests an Irish influence, as well as one of the Virgin Mary.

CHAPTER 9
The Ninth Century

Sherborne Abbey: Alfred and the Vikings

Alone among the rulers of his times, [he] realised the vital importance of the spiritual issue and devoted no less energy to the recovery of the tradition of Christian culture than to the defence of national existence.

Christopher Dawson on King Alfred,
Religion and the Rise of Western Culture[1]

*T*HE *ANGLO-SAXON CHRONICLE* refers to the Viking raiders who harried the British coastline in the first half of the ninth century, and then in the second half sought to conquer and colonise the land, as 'the heathen army'. It would, of course, use such pejorative language since it was compiled from the writings of Christian monks at Winchester, Canterbury, Peterborough, Abingdon and Worcester, who were keen above all to portray the struggle that dominated the century as one between God's light and pagan darkness. There can, however, be no mistaking the shock waves sent through a complacent Anglo-Saxon Church by that first hit-and-run raid by the Norsemen on Lindisfarne in 793. There had been other seaborne attacks before in Kent by the Vikings, but the assault on Cuthbert's monastery on Lindisfarne by warriors intent on 'ravaging through rapine and slaughter'[2] was the prelude for a battle for the very survival of British and Irish Christianity.

The Norsemen had concentrated first on the eastern coast, closest by sea to their own homeland in modern-day Norway, Sweden and Denmark. Soon they were ranging further afield in their insatiable appetite to plunder rich and largely undefended pickings. Lambay, off the coast of County Dublin, was in 795 the first of what subsequently became many targets in Ireland, its well-endowed abbey founded by Saint Columba in the 530s. The celebrated Iona, off the west coast of Scotland, was attacked repeatedly – in 795, 802 and 806 – its buildings ransacked and its monks slaughtered. Its greatest treasure, what became known as the Book of Kells, was spirited away to County Meath early on for safekeeping. The Vikings had little interest in the craftsmanship and learning that had been poured into such manuscripts. What attracted them much more were the jewels and gold on their covers. Once those had been removed, the texts were of use only as fuel for the fires the raiders left behind when they departed.

Their smash-and-grab attacks became ever bolder as the new century got under way. By the 830s, the arrival on the horizon of the Vikings' slender, shallow-bottomed, fast and flexible longboats was an almost annual ordeal in many blighted coastal spots. Those who stood in their way were often brutally despatched, and others were taken away to be traded as slaves.

The cause of such unprovoked aggression is a matter of dispute. The Vikings' motives do not seem to have been strongly religious. There was certainly no overarching plan to return Britain from Christianity to the pagan Norse gods that the raiders continued to worship (and who are the origins of the names in our calendar for the middle days of our weeks from Tuesday to Thursday). Greed for portable wealth appears to be the greatest stimulus, and in particular for the silver found so abundantly in churches' chalices and adornments. The metal used in the coinage – some of it from Islamic Spain – had started to reach Scandinavia via its trading routes in the 790s. Having no silver mines of their own, the Vikings came to regard Britain and Ireland as the next best source of a ready supply.

Those who organised the raids were the younger sons of noble families, planning to use what they plundered to buy land and livestock of their own once back home. And there may have been, too, a connection between these latest invaders and some of the Anglo-Saxons who had come four centuries earlier, especially among those from Frisia, whose eastern border lay in today's Denmark. Old Norse and Old English were still sufficiently similar for any landing party to believe it could make its demands understood by locals with words as well as swords.

Yet it wasn't only Britain and Ireland that attracted the Vikings. Their curiosity, avarice and seamanship took them to France, Spain, Italy, Constantinople, and even to Greenland and North America. Moreover, the crisis in Christianity in the British Isles that resulted (Wales, too, suffered raids from the 850s onwards) should be seen as part of a bigger emergency that threatened the future of Christendom. There was the continuing advance of Islam on the Iberian Peninsula in the ninth century, after its initial incursion after 711, while in the east the Magyars in the 860s grew bolder in attacking the outlying areas of the Christian Frankish Empire in modern-day Germany.

In the second half of the century, the Vikings' tactics changed. Already some raiders had started to stay around for longer than it took to make off with anything of value they could grab. They would spend winters in Britain before returning to Scandinavia with their booty. Then, in 865, a 'great army' of several thousand warriors landed on the east coast with a new ambition – to conquer and colonise. In this, they rapidly proved remarkably successful. Northumbria fell in 867, with a puppet king installed to rule its territories that spread from York in the south across to Scotland in the north. East Anglia followed in 869, when its ruler, Edmund, defeated in battle, was martyred by Danish arrows – according to legend because he refused to renounce his Christian faith. Even mighty Mercia could not resist the invaders, its king Burgred fleeing to Rome in 874 after the Vikings had sacked his stronghold at Tamworth and replaced him (according to *The Anglo-Saxon Chronicle*) with a 'foolish' royal relative, Ceolwulf.[3]

That left only one of the four major Anglo-Saxon kingdoms standing. Wessex covered southern and south-western England, had expanded into Kent and, in partnership with Mercia, into South Wales. Its good fortune in the face of a threat so potent that it had overwhelmed all others was to be led from the spring of 871 by the remarkable Alfred, just twenty when he inherited the crown from his brother, Ethelred, who had died a month after confronting the Vikings in battle near Reading.

It is Alfred who brings me to Sherborne on a bright, crisp December morning. The honey-coloured silhouette of its abbey dominates the skyline of this Dorset town. In 705, Sherborne had been established as the western diocese of the kingdom of Wessex, complementing Winchester in the east. Its first bishop had been the aged Aldhelm, scholar, renowned poet and founding abbot of Malmesbury, as well as its brother houses at Frome and Bradford-on-Avon. His statue greets me over the south-west porch of today's abbey, which is successor to the first Saxon cathedral he built. Of that original, only two doorways remain in the west end, both with the tell-tale rounded arches favoured in that period.

Behind one, hidden from public view in a storage cupboard, a guide shows me a section of ancient, pink-coloured decoration of unknown vintage, between door and arch, perhaps motif or script, on a faded white background. No one has yet been able to make head nor tail of it. There is no mystery, though, about the affection in which Sherborne's original cathedral was held by King Alfred and his royal relatives.

The youngest of five brothers, Alfred was the 'spare' never expected to end up on the throne. Then, one by one, those above him with a prior claim to be king died. Two of his deceased siblings, Ethelbald (died 860) and Ethelberht (died 865), who, like Ethelred, had attempted to halt the Viking advance, were buried in the Saxon cathedral. A plaque in the north side of today's abbey commemorates the place (Sherborne ceased to have a resident bishop in the twelfth century, when it was replaced by Salisbury, and was henceforth an abbey not a cathedral).

Alfred was, surviving accounts of his life tell, someone of profound faith, who had made two visits to Rome before he became king, even being anointed by the Pope. As the baby of the family, he had seemed destined to become a priest or an abbot after learning by heart at an early age some of the psalms and the Divine Office, the set of prayers that marks the different stages of the day. Now, though, he found himself with a different calling – to demonstrate his military prowess in the face of the Viking threat and to save English Christianity.

Perhaps, though, religious and military vocations were not so far apart as they may seem today. There is a telling reference (albeit modern, from the 1930s) to Alfred in the abbey that locals in Sherborne still refer to as 'the cathedral of Dorset'. Behind the glorious medieval painted fan-vaulting roofs of the nave and chancel – the earliest of their kind in Europe – lies a Lady Chapel that dates back to the thirteenth century. On its north side is a stained-glass window with two panels that celebrate Alfred's close relationship, politically and spiritually, with the bishops of Sherborne. In one is Alfred, the steely warrior, his hand purposefully clutching the hilt of his sword, as if about to confront the Danish army that was sweeping across England. In the other is Asser, Bishop of Sherborne in the 890s as well as tutor and adviser to the King, in his white-and-blue chasuble, or priestly vestment.

Originally a monk from St David's monastery in the kingdom of Dyfed, Asser is believed to have come to Alfred's court around 885 as the influence of Wessex spread across South Wales. His particular contribution to the reforms that Alfred instigated to revive and renew a Church whose failings had been laid bare by the Viking onslaught came in the field of education – of both the clergy and the laity. Later, he went on to write a *Life of Alfred*, on which we rely for most of what we know about this great English king.

Other ninth-century bishops of Sherborne were more warriors than teachers. According to *The Anglo-Saxon Chronicle*, Bishop Eahlstan spent fifty years in post, a span that saw him in the 820s shoulder to shoulder with Alfred's grandfather King Ecgbert as he defeated first the Mercians and then the Welsh kings. Later,

Eahlstan served alongside Ecgbert's son Ethelwulf in his seizure of the kingdom of Kent. *The Anglo-Saxon Chronicle* tells that this bishop did not just bless the troops, but also went into the fray himself with clerical robes over his armour.[4] So trusted was he by the King on the battlefield that in 845 he was placed, with two earls, at the head of the forces of Wessex as they drove back skirmishing Danes in a set-to on the River Parrett. By 871, in the clash at Reading that precipitated the death of Alfred's brother and his accession to the throne, Eahlstan's successor as Bishop of Sherborne, Heahmund, was again there on the frontline, paying for his courage with his life.

One revealing moment captured in Bishop Asser's biography of the then Prince Alfred occurs at the Battle of Ashdown in 871 – a rare Wessex victory over the Vikings. The day starts with him at Mass, head bowed in prayer, in full military garb. As the final word of the closing prayer is uttered, he unsheathes his sword and hurries straight into the thick of the action, confident that God is on his side.

It must have been hard for Alfred to detect God's hand in his first months as king. They were hardly auspicious. Almost his first act was to pay off the Vikings, who remained as keen as ever to accumulate riches. In return, they agreed to retreat from Wessex's territory to their stronghold in London, which they had seized when they took control of Mercia. It was a temporary solution, as Alfred knew all too well. The Danish army, sensing the weakness of his position, would undoubtedly be back for more.

As indeed they were, but in 878 fortunes changed. At the start of the year, an army of Danes under Guthrum took Alfred by surprise at his royal palace in Chippenham. He escaped by the skin of his teeth, with just a small band of supporters. Other men might have accepted that defeat as a final, fatal blow, but not Alfred. Regrouping in the Somerset Levels, a marshy area he knew well, he copied the tactics of the Danes and launched a series of successful guerrilla attacks on their positions.

It is from this period in his life that perhaps the most enduring story of all about Alfred dates. Sheltering among the local population, it is told that he was asked by the woman of the humble home in which he was staying to watch some cakes – small loaves of bread – that she had placed on the fire to cook. So distracted was he in pondering deeper matters that the cakes were burnt when the woman returned, causing her to scold him.

The story appears in a later edition of Asser's biography that dates from the sixteenth century. Its source, though, is not in Asser's original text but was added subsequently, taken from the now lost twelfth-century Annals of St Neots. The real point that whoever wrote it into the biography was trying to make was that Alfred was a thinker and a holy man, more concerned with pondering the will of God than the fate of some cakes. And since that moment of inattention turned out to be swiftly followed by a mighty victory, it was time well spent.

By May, Alfred had gathered sufficient men – thought to be an army of around four thousand from the south western parts of his kingdom – to head east from Somerset and engage Guthrum's forces at the Battle of Edington on the edge of Salisbury Plain. With the advantage of greater numbers and prior knowledge of the terrain (Edington was part of his royal estates), Alfred drove the Danes back in disarray. When they took refuge in Chippenham, he laid siege for fourteen days until they surrendered.

That Guthrum accepted he had been decisively defeated is clear by the terms of the peace he subsequently agreed at Wedmore. His army was to leave Wessex and offer hostages to Alfred – a gesture that was not reciprocated. Alfred's principal demand, though, was that Guthrum and twenty-nine of his followers should agree to be baptised as Christians. Their submission to this condition resulted in Alfred referring thereafter to Guthrum as his 'spiritual son' and giving him the Christian name Ethelstan, after one of his own deceased royal brothers.

Alfred's intention was not to humiliate his opponent – and risk the conflict resuming as soon as Guthrum was in a position to seek revenge – but rather to give him his blessing as a Christian king. As a tactic, it worked, and greatly reduced the threat to the Christian status of England when both sides agreed to respect a diagonal line running north-west to south-east between London and Chester. Everything to one side was under the control of Wessex, while everything to the other, to be known as the Danelaw, would be ruled by Guthrum.

It was an imperfect but pragmatic arrangement that just about endured until Guthrum's death in 889. In the 880s there had been repeated breaches, including a Danish attack on the cathedral city of Rochester in Kent. For his part, Alfred, in 886, took control from them of the city of London, an event that *The Anglo-Saxon Chronicle* (with the benefit of hindsight) describes as akin to a coronation: 'All the English peoples acknowledged Alfred as their king, except those who were still under the rule of the Danes in the North and the East'.[5]

The traditional picture of Viking rule in the Danelaw is that any hopes Alfred might have nurtured following Guthrum's baptism for some sort of tolerance of Christians there were dashed. Under Danish rule, the dioceses of northern and eastern England – from Hexham through Leicester to Dunwich – were left vacant and abandoned. At Repton in Derbyshire, what had been a major monastery under the patronage of the kings of Mercia, even containing a mausoleum for one branch of the royal family, was seized by the Vikings in 874. Thereafter they made it their camp, scattered its community and recycled its church buildings as fortifications.[6]

Yet the image of Church structures collapsing in the face of Viking rulers hell-bent on destruction of Christianity – as conveyed in *The Anglo-Saxon Chronicle* – sits uneasily with other known details. In York, such a beacon of Christian learning in the previous century, renamed Jorvik by the Vikings who made it their capital, evidence has now been unearthed that points to cooperation between the occupiers and the existing ecclesiastical authorities. Further afield, in the churchyard of St Mary's Church at Gosforth in Cumbria, part of the Danelaw, there stands a celebrated stone cross, erected during Viking rule. Its carvings suggest an accommodation between Christianity and Norse myths, with Jesus' crucifixion featuring alongside an image of the Viking god, Vidar, slaying the wolf that had killed his father, Odin. Both convey the same message – the triumph of good over evil.

Likewise, the Viking burial cross at Middleton in North Yorkshire uses a Christian format but has a deceased Viking warrior in the place Jesus occupied on the cross. He is being saved in death from the corpse-eating dragon, Nidhogg. In both traditions, it is a salvation narrative. And then there are the many villages in the Danelaw given the name Kir-by or Kirk-by – 'village of the church' – which hardly suggests a wish to obliterate churches from the landscape. Other documentary evidence shows small monastic communities and individual churches, away from their grander, richer equivalents, surviving this period of 'heathen' rule largely unscathed.

Such tolerance contributes to a more nuanced picture of the Danelaw. This was not a period of wanton destruction, akin to those early raids, but rather a time when the new rulers, who were keen traders, set about expanding towns such as Lincoln, Leicester and York (the latter by anything up to ten times its size at the time of their arrival). Excavations in the Coppergate area of York have shown evidence of iron and leather works, even textile manufacture, established during these decades of occupation.

There was inward immigration, too, with the families of the invading armies coming from Scandinavia to be reunited with their husbands, sons and fathers, putting down roots and leaving their mark on English place names and language. That adaptation included the newcomers embracing the 'English religion' – namely Christianity. We know that some of these new arrivals must have followed in the footsteps of Guthrum and accepted baptism because by the next century men with surnames that indicate Viking heritage begin to appear in lists of abbots and bishops. In 941, Odo, reportedly the son of a warrior in the 'great army' of 865, was named as Archbishop of Canterbury.

In the twenty-one years of his reign that remained after his famous victory at Edington, Alfred set about the less eye-catching task of addressing within his half of the country the weaknesses in Anglo-Saxon Britain that had made it so vulnerable to the Viking raiders. Some of his solutions were practical. Faced by fleet-footed attackers, the kings of Northumbria, East Anglia, Mercia and even Wessex hadn't been able to respond quickly enough to counter the threat. By the time they realised the danger, it was too late to summon help, and anyway, they had no standing army. So Alfred established a chain of *burhs*, or fortifications, at intervals of twenty miles and linked by roads (*herepaths*), the length and breadth of Wessex. Eventually numbering more than thirty, they ranged in size from the one fashioned in Winchester out of the remains of its Roman walls, to tiny Pilton near Barnstable in north Devon. Some were built on top of preexisting Iron Age forts, others close to royal villas, or at the mouths of major estuaries so as to spot Viking boats, but all had to be both funded and provided with a garrison by local landowners.

Defence of the realm thereby became no longer just a task for the king. Never again would rulers be caught napping by invaders. At the first sight of trouble, a force of men could quickly be summoned from the *burh*, and reinforcements were only as far away as the next one. That sort of security encouraged the beginnings of urbanisation around the *burhs*.

Alfred, though, as the episode with the cakes sought to reveal, was also one whose intellect stretched to instigating change in less obviously measured ways. It wasn't only the absence of a standing army that had caused the Anglo-Saxons to be so vulnerable. For Alfred, their defeat by the Vikings was also a sign of God's displeasure at how faith had been lived out in the eighth century. A handful of monasteries may have been revered at home and abroad, but too many smaller ones, for men and women, were either lax in their daily life or openly corrupt.

The disruption and destruction caused to so much of religious life in the decades of Viking pressure gave Alfred his chance to rebuild in a new way. He wanted to instil a clear sense of Christian identity, purpose and discipline to both the Church and his own court. Among the texts that he encouraged to be used more widely was Pope Gregory the Great's *Pastoral Care*, dating from almost three hundred years earlier. This, of course, was an age of widespread illiteracy, but what Alfred aspired to create was a more-educated leadership class, be it nobles, bishops or royal administrators. Some of these individuals, he judged, might stumble with the Latin of Gregory's original, so he set about translating it into Old English himself, there being, his biographer reports, 'very few men . . . [south] of the Humber who could understand their divine services in Latin, or even translate a single letter from Latin into English'.[7]

For the Church leaders of his day, Alfred echoed Gregory's guidance to the bishops of his own day that 'the art of arts is the guidance of souls'.[8] This was what they should be doing more of, Alfred urged. And for those in positions of power, he took the Pope's words that 'the ruler should be the near neighbour to everyone in sympathy and exalted above all in contemplation',[9] as a clarion call against corruption, complacency and laziness.

By promoting the English language, extolling good governance (including amalgamating the differing legal codes of Wessex, Mercia and Kent into a single definitive document) and emphasising the Christian nature of his whole realm across southern and western England and Wales, Alfred was attempting to give it for the first time a single identity that could bring together its up-to-now different component parts. And that identity, subsequently, was to become the basis of a distinctive Englishness.

When it came to questions of authority in the Church, Alfred had more time for bishops than independent-minded abbots, seeing them – as his experience in Sherborne had demonstrated – as more likely to obey and promote the royal will. His reforms therefore placed a greater emphasis on strengthening the diocesan structures and continuing to build the parish system with the local church rather than the monastery at its heart. He did, though, also endow two new abbeys. Both followed the Benedictine Rule and opened in 888. The first, for men, was situated at Athelney in the Somerset Levels, where the King had planned his comeback. It was a sign of the poor state of Church life that most of its first batch of recruits were drawn from France, while its founding abbot was German. Despite the royal seal of approval, it never thrived, lacking the support of local noble families, and suffered in the shadow of nearby Glastonbury Abbey.

Alfred's foundation for women, at Shaftesbury, initially led by his own daughter, Ethelgifu, fared rather better, achieving a status and pre-eminence unmatched by single female houses until its dissolution by Henry VIII in 1539. It was said, at that time, to be the second richest in terms of income and land in the kingdom.

It may not have been his intention, but with these two foundations Alfred was looking forwards rather than backwards. For, after the Viking threat was finally defeated, the next century was to see a great revival of monasticism under way.

ALSO WITH A STORY TO TELL . . .

ST WYSTAN'S IN REPTON in Derbyshire, with its tall thin spire, is outwardly a handsome medieval church, but it contains a Saxon crypt, complete with beautifully carved stone piers. It is believed this is where relics of the Mercian royal family lay until the Vikings seized Repton in 874.

THE GOSFORTH CROSS, in the churchyard of St Mary's in this Cumbrian village near WHITEHAVEN, once part of the ancient kingdom of Northumbria, tells in its carvings of how the Viking invaders and conquerors of north and east England came to accept Christianity. It shows the victory of Christ over Norse gods, including Loki, Heimdalir and Thor plus the serpent Jörmungandr. Inside the church are two tenth-century Viking 'hogback' tombstones.

ST SEIRIOL, PENMON, on the far south east tip of Anglesey/Ynys Môn, looks back over the strait that separates the island from the mainland. Seiriol, the son of a local king, established a church in the sixth century, but its location made it a target for Viking raiders in the ninth. The current incarnation has a twelfth-century Norman tower, but in the grounds of the adjoining priory are the remains of what may have been Seiriol's cell.

CHAPTER 10

The Tenth Century

St Andrew's, Greensted: Anglo-Saxon Restoration

The Anglo-Saxon Church in the last quarter of the tenth century was well organised, well staffed, and well integrated into the fabric of the nascent kingdom of the English.

Professor Simon Keynes[1]

WHILE THE ABBEYS and cathedrals of the tenth century were built in stone, smaller local churches in an ever-widening parish network continued to be wooden. And so it was that fifty-one vertically placed split oak logs, rounded on the outside but flattened on the inside, were put in place from the 990s onwards to enclose the nave of what is today St Andrew's Church at Greensted-juxta-Ongar in that part of Essex that is far away from the roar of London's orbital motorway. Remarkably, they survive largely intact, and palpably carry those who turn up in this rural location back to Christian life in Britain and Ireland at the end of the first millennium. This is the oldest wooden church in the world, and has survived fire, fashion and furore. What is most endearing about St Andrew's is that it manages to carry this great weight of historical significance with little fanfare or heritage paraphernalia that distract from its continuing daily existence as a modest countryside parish church.

The immediate impression St Andrew's gives is one of playing down quite how remarkable it is. That is helped by the central tree-trunked section of the church on which its claim to a place in history rests being bookended by an eye-catching but hardly unique eighteenth-century weather-boarded tower and spire, and a picture-postcard Tudor brick chancel (built on a Norman shingled base). And the roof of the nave (originally thatched) was given a makeover by the Victorians who installed distractingly large dormer windows in an attempt to throw some light into the atmospheric darkness of the Saxon nave. They succeeded admirably in their aim, but not so much as to lessen a tangible sense indoors of time concertinaing.

There may once have been other openings in St Andrew's to the light – and anyway, Saxon builders favoured high walls and light from above – but the only original one remaining is tiny. Referred to as a 'leper's squint', it is a space carved out between the timbers on the north side of the church so that, legend has it, the priest could bless lepers who gathered outside the building without having to admit them for fear that they would spread infection. It is a tale that brings history vividly alive, but more recent studies favour a more banal explanation of the feature – that it may simply have been a peephole, close to the original entrance, so those within could spot the approach of armies. At the time of its reconstruction, that would have been useful, since the Vikings were once again landing on the coast of Essex away to the south and east. Their threat had not been completely extinguished by Alfred and his successors on the throne of Wessex. At the very end of the tenth century, they came back to terrify the Anglo-Saxons.

That, though, is to skip ahead in our story. Of greater significance in the history of this particular church was the boom in the later decades of the tenth century in the cult of saints in the imagination and religious practices of British Christians. Pilgrimages and processions to sites associated with those who had lived and died saintly lives, and where miraculous healing might as a result take place, had long been a core part of Christianity in these islands, but it was given extra potency by the approach of the millennium. It was a date that provoked widespread fear of 'Last Days' and of the sort of blood-soaked apocalypse described in graphic terms in Revelation, the final chapter of the New Testament.

Millennial anxiety was stoked, too, by graphic representations of God sitting in judgement on humanity on the Last Day, such as the one found at the time on the wall of the main church at Jarrow Abbey. Its purpose was to remind the congregation always to live in fear of the end of the world and of eternal punishment. In his history of the Monkwearmouth–Jarrow twin monasteries, Bede explained the presence of such depictions as being 'so that everyone who entered, even if they could not read, might have . . . the perils of the Last Judgment before their eyes [and] examine their hearts the more closely'.[2] With the year 1000 on the near horizon to concentrate minds, that warning took on for many an immediate and ominous echo.

End-times anxiety was everywhere. Turning to the saints for solace, begging them in prayer to intercede with God to keep believers safe in whatever tribulation lay ahead, was the antidote. So there was a rush to put the relics of saints on display even more prominently in cathedrals and abbeys. Since the sacking of Lindisfarne by the Vikings in 793, when the remains of its great abbot, Saint Cuthbert, had been spirited away by monks, his bones had been moved round various locations in northern England. In 995, though, capturing the mood of the time, they were finally given a permanent home in a shrine in a wooden structure, known as the 'White Church', on a bend in the River Wear. Three years later, pilgrim numbers arriving there were so large that it was rebuilt in stone, and in the next century became Durham Cathedral. Likewise in 896, the relics of Saint Ethelwold, the revered local bishop and a promoter of the revival of Benedictine monasticism, were given a permanent home in Winchester Cathedral.

Such renewed enthusiasm for the cult of saints, then, outlasted the turn of the millennium and spilled into the next century. So it was that, in 1013, the relics of Saint Edmund, the East Anglian king martyred by the Vikings in 869, are reported to have spent time in Greensted Church, perhaps as a temporary shrine to be visited by local pilgrims. This stopover was one stage on their slow and ritual progress towards a final resting place at Bury St Edmunds. The event is recalled in a much later, ghoulish carving on St Andrew's roof beams, where Edmund's decapitated head is shown guarded by a dog. There is even a wooden cover on a Bible kept in the church. According to legend, the wood comes from the tree to which the vanquished Edmund was tied as the Danish arrows rained down to make a martyr of him.

King Alfred of Wessex may have succeeded where Edmund failed in halting the Viking advance, but he had not banished them from the British Isles. Instead, his uneasy truce with Guthrum was made on the basis that neither side believed they could achieve a complete victory over the other. So Alfred contained the invaders, and the settlers who came in their wake from Scandinavia, in the Danelaw to the north and east of the country. The bigger task of fashioning a single kingdom of England, Wales and most of Scotland fell to Alfred's son, Edward the Elder, whose reign covered the first quarter of the tenth century. He was ably abetted by his sister Ethelflaed, married by her father to the senior member of Mercia's royal family and, on his death in 911, titled 'Lady of Mercia', its queen in all but name since Mercia had become part of the expanded Wessex kingdom.

A raid by the siblings into what is now Lincolnshire in 909, ostensibly to rescue the relics of Saint Oswald from the Danelaw, provoked a strong response. A Viking army that contained several kings, *The Anglo-Saxon Chronicle* reports, invaded Mercia but was defeated in 910 at Tettenhall (now part of Wolverhampton) at the cost of 'many thousands' of Danish lives.[3] Edward and Ethelflaed pressed home their advantage by reclaiming territories in the English Midlands and East Anglia, culminating in defeat for the Danes at Maldon in Essex in 917. That forced the Danelaw's surviving leaders to agree terms and submit to Edward as their king. Alfred's son may not have been a match for his father in terms of scholarship, suggests the twelfth-century chronicler William of Malmesbury, but as a military strategist and ruler he was 'incomparably more glorious'.[4]

On account of their willingness to submit, some of the Danish settlers were allowed to keep their lands, and even influence, but Edward's writ now ran all across England. From 920, according to *The Anglo-Saxon Chronicle*, it also stretched to 'all the people of the Scots'.[5] Local kings may have remained, but they accepted the overlordship of Alfred's descendants.

The process wasn't entirely smooth. It took until 954 for the claims of the shadowy figure of the Viking Eric Bloodaxe to the throne of Northumbria to be ended by force, but for the most part there were six decades of relative peace in the middle of the tenth century during which the fabric of the country could be sewn back together under the House of Wessex as kings of England.

Where Alfred had leant heavily on bishops in his ambitions to reform the Church and make it his ally in his expansionist plans, his successors were more inclined to put their faith in a revival of monasticism. Where the one male monastery Alfred had founded had failed to thrive, by the end of the tenth century there had been a flurry of successful creations – including Ramsey (969, by Oswald, later Archbishop of York) and Thorney (early 970s), both in the Fenlands and for men, and at Wherwell in Hampshire in 986 and Chatteris, near Ely, at the end of the century for women. Just as important was the refounding or reform of existing monasteries – for example at Pershore in Worcestershire, in Peterborough and at Abingdon.

All followed the Benedictine Rule, which had first been brought to the British Isles at Monkwearmouth–Jarrow by Benedict Biscop. After the Rule's initial flourishing, however, it had become besmirched amid the chaos of the ninth century. Monks in charge of monasteries had been replaced by secular clergy, who were often married. They owed their appointment to their local lord, and followed his instructions more readily than Benedict's original blueprint for living in religious community. This was not a failing confined only to England. Across Europe, Benedictine monasticism had followed a similar pattern of decline and departure from its ideals. In the tenth century it had started to retrieve some of its lustre as a result of a thoroughgoing reform inspired by Cluny Abbey in France, founded in 910. Its second abbot, Odo, restored the original focus on prayer, silence and solitude, as well as the imperative to pay attention to the needs of the local poor. Soon the 'Cluniac Reform' was spreading across France, Italy, Spain and eventually England.

Among those enthused by it was Dunstan, who in 943 was named by King Edmund as Abbot of Glastonbury. High-born, Dunstan had spent time in his youth as a hermit. He combined piety with worldliness that saw him achieve the rank of chief adviser to the King. His knack for organisation was accompanied by charisma. At Glastonbury, he had translated the continental monastic Reform movement into something that worked in the English context, including founding a celebrated school for local youths. His gifts did not go unnoticed, and he rose steadily up the ecclesiastical ladder to be first Bishop of Worcester, then of London, and finally from 960 to 988 held the position of Archbishop of Canterbury.

Some historians have hailed his arrival at Canterbury and the position of trust in which he was held by King Edgar (959–75) as 'a turning point in history of religion in England'.[6] Certainly his insistence on a cleansed and purposeful monasticism, harnessed to royal power, the Church and State in harmony, found clear expression in the 970 Regularis Concordia, written by his co-reformer, Ethelwold. It laid down a single, shared framework for the life of all Benedictine monasteries across the country. As a sign of its origin, close to the throne, it included the instruction that prayers should be offered each day for the King, and stipulated that the appointment of a new abbot required royal consent.

Where the King's authority was strongest, these reforms had their greatest and most beneficial impact. New foundations and revived monasteries were therefore mostly in southern and central England. Further north, the Wessex kings' claims was more fragile. As a result, local nobles with monasteries on their lands carried on as before, allowing married secular clergy to run them in ways that departed significantly from Benedict's original intentions. Still, where the reform spirit was embraced, new energy was generated among monks for artistic and cultural life, producing peerless illustrated manuscripts and theologians whose reputation spread across Europe.

The model of Church and State proceeding in step gave the kings of the tenth century a significant role not just in the naming of abbots, but also in the appointment of bishops. In theory, this was a matter to be decided in conjunction with the Pope in Rome, but the holders of the throne of Saint Peter in the tenth century were, for the most part, a disreputable and powerless bunch (including, legend has it, a woman called Joan who tricked her way into the office by disguising herself as a man, before being revealed when she gave birth to a child during a procession[7]). The monarch's choice, therefore, went unchallenged. It would take until the next century, when Rome had undergone its own reform and renewal, for settlement of the arguments between popes and kings over who had the final word on senior church appointments.

With the King's wishes paramount, in the sixteen dioceses that now made up the province of Canterbury,[8] as well as the two in the northern province of York (led by Dunstan's close ally, Oswald),[9] monks were appointed as bishops. Moreover, around half of the cathedrals at the heart of these dioceses – including Canterbury, Winchester and Worcester – henceforth became 'cathedral priories', a designation unknown elsewhere in Europe.

Communities of monks were brought in to run them in place of their previous regular clerical guardians, the deans and canons. They were regarded by Dunstan, who believed in celibacy as an essential part of the call of vocation, as far too worldly to carry out such a task on account of them having wives and children. Rome's final ruling that all priests should be celibate was still more than two centuries away – plus several more for it to be enforced – but one result of the monastic reforms across Europe of the tenth century was to give special status in the leadership of the Church to unmarried, chaste men.

That prejudice, though, had yet to make much impact on the parish system that included St Andrew's. The widespread emergence of local parish churches, offering pastoral care to their communities, arguably is the hallmark of the tenth century. The number of new parish churches, though hard to calculate because so little documentation exists, is likely to have been much greater than that of new monasteries and nunneries created or revived, where best estimates suggest a joint figure of thirty-six.

Sometimes referred to in manuscripts of the time as an 'altar thegn', or 'altar attendant', the priest in such parishes relied for his church, his home and his living on the say-so of the local lord of the manor. He would most likely be a local man, with some, but not very much, education, despite the efforts of reformers. The majority were married, though as the reforming wind blew through cathedrals and monasteries and down to the grassroots of the Church, there was from the 960s onwards increased pressure for married men to put aside their wives when they were ordained. Not only would celibate clergy make for better, more attentive, less distracted, more Christlike priests (Jesus, the Gospels tell, was unmarried), they would not, if they followed their ordination vows, leave behind descendants who might otherwise stake a claim to lands and property that the Church insisted were its own.

As with other developments, this realignment was initially seen more widely in the southern province, but overall parish life was becoming more regulated. The 'Lord's Day' increasingly was not marked only on Sunday but began on Saturday evening, with services in church building up to Sunday's Mass. There would be a sermon, music and Communion during the penitential weeks of Lent in the build-up to Easter, but only sporadically at other times of the year. Those who took Communion were expected to follow prescribed periods of fasting in advance to prepare.

In leading and organising parish life, the priest was now serving several masters. As well as input from the local lord, there was much more oversight from bishops than previously, as diocesan structures became more robust. A late tenth-century translation into Old English of the *Capitula* (or *Pastoral Guidance for Priests*), first laid down by the French Bishop Theodulf of Orléans in the eighth century, was one popular source of guidance for what was expected of a faithful priest. It stressed the importance of the clergy doing manual labour. Like monks in reformed abbeys, they were not to imagine themselves as better than their congregations. But at the same time, it urged them also to attend to the basic educational needs of their flocks. 'Mass-priests,' it intoned, 'ought always to have a school of learners in their houses, and if any good man will commit his little ones to them to be taught, they ought gladly to accept them and to teach them at free-cost.'[10]

The death of King Edgar in 975 was followed by a dispute over the succession between his oldest son, Edward, and Ethelred, the son of his third wife, Elfhryth. Both would-be heirs were boys at the time, and most accounts paint Elfhryth's machinations in favour of her boy in unfavourable detail. With the support of Dunstan and Oswald, as the two most senior bishops, it was Edward who prevailed, but it caused a breach with Ethelwold, now Bishop of Winchester, who sided with Ethelred and his mother.

The Anglo-Saxon Chronicle describes the three years of Edward's rein as troubled. The disputed succession had weakened the monarchy vis-à-vis the nobility, who saw the power struggle between different claimants as an opportunity to claw back some of the lands that Edgar had taken from them to give to new monasteries. They were also anxious to reassert the rights of those of their children who had lived comfortably, if not entirely monkishly, as secular clergy before being cast aside by the recent reforms. And there appears to have been unrest in Northumbria, with the King's chief representative there, Oslac, going into exile for unspecified reasons.[11]

Matters came to a head in 978. When Edward visited his step-mother and half-brother at Corfe Castle in Dorset, he was murdered. While the exact circumstances were opaque, the finger of suspicion pointed firmly at Elfhryth, either as mastermind of the assassination or even as the killer. It was her son, aged just twelve, who benefited most, though his assumption of the throne was accompanied by the rapid rise of a cult around 'Edward the Martyr'. The murdered king's body, hastily buried, was disinterred, found to be incorrupt (which was taken as a miracle) and in 979 placed in Shaftesbury Abbey, founded by Alfred the Great. It drew great crowds of pilgrims.

The circumstances of Ethelred's rise to power had already weakened him, but his actions on the throne once he reached adulthood did little to inspire confidence, though he earned his epithet 'the Unready' not on account of incompetence but because in old English the word refers rather more kindly to him simply being poorly advised. The discontent at his rule reached the ears of the Vikings who, after decades of peace, reckoned England was once more in little state to defend itself and so restarted their raids. In 991, a large Viking fleet arrived at Folkestone on the Kent coast and made its way round to the Blackwater Estuary in Essex, where they defeated the English forces at Maldon, gaining revenge for their loss there eighty years previously. Ethelred was forced to pay ransom, under the pretext of buying their protection.

Further raids followed in the years afterwards, and on each occasion Ethelred was forced to pay tribute. Among the targets of the Norsemen, as before, were churches, as well as churchmen. Saint David's on the coastline of what was then the Kingdom of Menevia (now Pembrokeshire) had been a regular target earlier in the century, but in 999 when they came ashore again, not only did the Vikings loot and destroy buildings, but they also murdered the local bishop, Morgenau. His death was seen by churchmen of the time as another sign of God's displeasure at lax discipline, especially since the reforming Morgenau reputedly had let slip the prohibition on eating meat that had been part of the monastic community there ever since David (Dewi) had established it in the sixth century.

Ethelred's vulnerability in the face of the Viking threat left the population at large uneasy. What turned out to be a greater threat to life and limb, however, was a particularly fierce outbreak of a pestilence that had several times already flared up in the latter part of the tenth century. It was fear of it, and the death toll it could exact, rather than the King's army, that saw the Danes head for home in 1005. It was to prove a temporary reprieve.

ALSO WITH A STORY TO TELL . . .

ST CRONAN'S CHURCH IN TUAMGRANEY, Co. Clare, is the oldest in continuous use in Ireland. Originally there was a wooden church on the spot, built by Saint Cronan in the sixth century, but as the Vikings targeted Ireland, it was raided on more than one occasion. The current simple sandstone structure dates back to the aftermath of a Viking raid in 949.

THE MINSTER CHURCH OF ST MARY, STOW-IN-LINDSEY, Lincolnshire, is in an area that took the full force of the Viking raids. It boasts, at the foot of one of its mighty Saxon arches, the earliest example of Viking graffiti in the country, a crude tenth-century scratching of a Viking longboat, complete with oars.

RAMSEY ABBEY, CAMBRIDGESHIRE, was established as a Benedictine community in the 960s by Oswald, then Bishop of Worcester, later Archbishop of York and one of the leaders in the revival of English monasticism in the tenth century. Known in its day as 'Ramsey the Rich', on account of the lavishness of its endowment, it was abandoned in Henry VIII's Reformation. Substantial sections remain, including what is today the Church of St Thomas à Becket.

CHAPTER II

The Eleventh Century

Canterbury Cathedral: The Norman Conquest

[The Normans] came to England at a time when the country was wavering between a closer approach to, or a wider alienation from, the culture and organisation of Latin Europe, and they settled the question in favour of the first alternative for the rest of the Middle Ages.

Sir Richard Southern: *The Making of the Middle Ages*[1]

YOU CAN STILL catch a glimpse of the original Saxon Canterbury Cathedral on a visit to the stately mother church of both English Christianity and the worldwide Anglican Communion. In one of the most prominent niches of its elaborate mid-fifteenth-century choir screen that divides the high altar from the nave is a stone carving of Ethelbert of Kent, the king who welcomed Saint Augustine to these shores at the end of the sixth century. In his left hand, he holds out, as if offering a gift to all who pass by, a model of that earlier cruciform, stone cathedral.

No one can be sure whether its details and dimensions bear any resemblance to what actually once stood on this spot, though it is not unlike an image of the original building found by archaeologists on an early twelfth-century seal.[2] The role of Ethelbert is accurately recorded. As we have seen, once he had embraced the Christian faith of his wife, Bertha, he handed over his palace at the start of the seventh century (having built a new one) to serve as the first cathedral in Britain and Ireland. It was steadily embellished over the centuries that followed. In the ninth, there was the addition of a baptistry and a mausoleum for Augustine's successors as Archbishop of Canterbury.

This Saxon cathedral was destroyed in September 1011 as Viking raiders, led by Thorkell the Tall, swept up the river in their long ships to Canterbury, intent on pillaging and burning the whole city. The pattern of such attacks was well understood by locals. Two years earlier, another Viking assault on Canterbury had only been halted by the payment of a ransom. That time the raiders melted away for a couple years, busy targeting other parts of southern England and even making an unsuccessful attack on London. Now they had returned, and in numbers. When the alarm was raised, the monastic community that had been in residence at the cathedral since Dunstan had taken charge hurriedly sought refuge within its walls as their city was besieged. Archbishop Alphege, a protégé of Dunstan, was in their midst.

They held out for three weeks, but finally the attackers broke their resolve and went on the rampage, setting fire to the whole city, including the cathedral. It was burnt to the ground. Of those inside, only four escaped with their lives, according to *The Anglo-Saxon Chronicle*. One of them, Alphege, was taken prisoner and held for seven months at the Vikings' main camp at Greenwich, close to London. A further ransom was demanded for his release. The Archbishop, though, smuggled out a message instructing that no payment should be made. He would rather die.

And so the ransom requests were turned down, infuriating his captors so much that, one drunken evening in April of the following year, Alphege was tied up, pelted with ox bones left over from their feasting, and then finished off with an axe.[3] The Viking leader, Thorkell, is said to have tried to intervene to stop the murder, but failed. So appalled was he by what took place that he and a group of loyal followers defected to the English forces, taking with them forty-five Viking ships.[4]

The Anglo-Saxon Church, and the country, was once again in crisis. The Danish threat had returned with a vengeance, and in King Ethelred the Unready there was no champion of the stature and resolve of Alfred to face it down. How this weakness and vulnerability ultimately led to the Norman Conquest of Britain, and to the rebuilding of the cathedral by Archbishop Lanfranc in the years immediately following 1066, is what has brought me back to the city. Canterbury's importance in revealing the history of Christianity in Britain and Ireland makes it stand alone in requiring a second visit.

Alphege's final resting place in the cathedral, alongside that of Dunstan, is marked today with a simple floor plaque next to the high altar.[5] A more dramatic image of his fate at the hands of the Vikings is found in stained glass on the north side of the choir. After his death, despite Thorkell's defection, the Viking threat continued to grow, so much so that by 1016 a second full-scale Viking invasion saw Ethelred flee to Normandy, his son Edmund Ironside defeated in battle, and a Danish prince, Cnut, on the English throne. There was, however, one crucial difference from similar events in the ninth century. This time the usurper was not a 'heathen'. Cnut – the same Canute referred to in the popular, though misattributed, story about trying and failing to turn back the tide[6] – had been born and raised a Christian, the product of Saxon missionaries who had travelled to Scandinavia in the previous century. If his faith was not always immediately apparent in his personal and professional conduct – he was a bigamist with a reputation for brutality on the battlefield – then it was undeniably there in the respect he showed for the Anglo-Saxon Church institutions and structures throughout his reign. He even went on pilgrimage to Rome.

For many in England – and later Scotland, when its king, Malcolm II submitted to Cnut in 1031 – his reign marked a return to more settled, predictable times. The threat of Viking attacks evaporated when Cnut became King of Denmark in 1018 and later of Norway, too. Yet, unlike previous kings, Cnut was possessed of no real ambition to engage with or impose his stamp on the Church. He was content to allow it to carry on as was. New Benedictine monasteries were handsomely endowed – notably at Abbotsbury in Dorset – but the King did not interfere in how they were run or dictate what standards were expected of their monks.

After his death in 1035, he was succeeded by his first son, Harold Harefoot, and then from 1040 by another of his sons, Harthacnut. The latter's demise two years later heralded the return of the Wessex line, though there was now an overlap between it and Cnut's family. The new King, Edward, crowned in Winchester Cathedral, was the forty-year-old seventh son of Ethelred, but the first by his second wife, Emma of Normandy. She had married Cnut after Ethelred's death, making Edward and Harthacnut half-brothers.

Edward had spent so many of his early years in exile at court in his mother's country that his English was poor. His pious demeanour is said to have earned him the title 'the Confessor', but the popular image of him as a saintly 'crowned monk' is the result of a later medieval cult that, for political and dynastic reasons, sought to reimagine his life in terms suitable to place him among the patron saints of England.

Whatever the actual state of his soul, Edward had, in his youth, taken to the battlefield in an ill-fated foray to England in 1036 to recover his inheritance (which resulted in another brother being brutally murdered, on Harold's orders, after having his eyes poked out with blazing pokers). As an adult, Edward was known, on occasion, to fly into spectacularly unsaintly rages. His stewardship once king was often unthinking, certainly capricious, with his strongest instinct being to surround himself with a small group of those he knew from having grown up in Normandy, a habit guaranteed to alienate the Anglo-Saxon nobility. They coalesced instead around Godwin, Earl of Wessex, Edward's father-in-law and formerly a powerful figure in Cnut's court.

Church matters inevitably became entangled in such a stand-off. When the see of Canterbury fell vacant, Edward, as was his habit, looked to France and named Robert Champart who, as Abbot of Jumièges in Normandy, had been a prominent supporter of the King's youthful efforts to replace Cnut on the English throne. Already Bishop of London, Champart was Edward's closest advisor. The leadership of Church and State were now to be as one, but his promotion to Canterbury caused controversy with those already feeling excluded from the centre of power. After a clash between the King and Godwin, the Archbishop was forced to flee the country, in fear of his life. In the disputed succession process, he was replaced by Stigand, who combined being Archbishop of Canterbury with continuing as Bishop of Winchester, a situation that caused the Pope to excommunicate him for breaking Church rules. The first non-monk in a century to be leader, Stigand was not widely held in high regard, having shamelessly amassed great personal wealth out of holding high office in both the Church and court.

The stubborn and continuing stench of corruption in the Church that Stigand personified went unchallenged by Edward. He had little of the taste for reform in the Church that had driven his predecessors. A rare exception came with his treatment of the saintly Wulfstan, who managed to win the King's confidence despite being English-born and a confidant of Godwin. In 1062 he was named Bishop of Worcester. More generally, though, profound as Edward's devotion to God appears to have been, he retreated from affairs of Church and State.

The twelfth-century chronicler Orderic Vitalis paints a pitiful picture of the Anglo-Saxon monasteries in this period: 'Monks differed very little from seculars in their way of life. They wore no habit and took no vows; they indulged in feasting and private property and countless foul transgressions'.[7]

Orderic's assessment should be taken with a pinch of salt. Though born in England, his father was French, and he was a great admirer of subsequent Norman reforms of the Church, so he may have sought to portray what had gone on before them in the worst possible light so as to enable the new regime to shine to best effect. And there were certainly achievements to note in

Edward's long reign, not least Westminster Abbey. He had promised to make a pilgrimage to Rome but in the end agreed to found an abbey to spare him the journey. Built in the Romanesque style favoured in Normandy (it may have been modelled on Jumièges), and therefore a reflection of where Edward had grown up rather than of the prevailing Anglo-Saxon vernacular style of England, it was consecrated just after Christmas in 1065. Edward was too ill to attend. He died in the early days of 1066, and his mortal remains were entombed in front of the high altar – a scene depicted in the Bayeux Tapestry.

Edward left no direct heir. He may have taken a private vow of celibacy, in line with the medieval portrait of him as more other-worldly saint than flesh-and-blood king. There may, however, have been more practical reasons. He was long estranged from his wife Edith as part of his long-running dispute with her father, Godwin. Characteristically, Edward had dithered over naming his successor. William, Duke of Normandy, his kinsman, claimed to be his choice, but in the immediate aftermath of Edward's death, it was his brother-in-law Harold, son of the now deceased Godwin, who seized the throne.

William would not be thwarted. With the backing of Pope Alexander II, who sent Saint Peter's banner for him to fight under, he assembled an army in Normandy and crossed the English Channel. Among his stated aims, trumpeted to win support for his invasion, he promised to rescue the Church from the legacy of Edward's neglect and misrule. It seems to have had the desired effect, for when he landed at Pevensey Bay on the south coast, Church leaders were among the first to welcome him. He went forward to defeat Harold at the Battle of Hastings and take the English throne by force.

The Norman Conquest banished any lingering sense that the Church in England, Wales and Scotland was separate from the main tide in Europe of western Christendom. A revived papacy, especially under Alexander's successor, Gregory VII, was taking vigorous steps to make its influence felt by all dukes, princes and kings. William may have signalled his approval for this policy and promised the Pope greater respect, but his actions did not always match his words. The new king was well versed in the theological debates and monastic innovations of the time. Yet he was also acutely conscious of his own authority. To that end, Church appointments, whether of abbots or bishops, were, he insisted, a matter for him and him alone.

At home, the expectations of those English bishops who had hurried to welcome William as their king were largely fulfilled. He quickly restored order to the Church. At a Council in Winchester in 1070, the interloper Stigand was removed from Canterbury. As had Edward the Confessor, William looked to Normandy to bring in not-so-new blood to fill the vacancy. His choice as Archbishop of Canterbury, the elderly Lanfranc, had been born in Italy. William had earlier appointed him as the first head of the Benedictine monastery he had founded at Caen.

The traditional view is that William's nominees as bishops purged the Anglo-Saxon Church of its quirks, as when Lanfranc stripped out of the calendar of saints some of its more parochial figures, or when the newly appointed Abbot of St Albans ordered the removal of the bodies of his Anglo-Saxon predecessors from their places of honour in his church (but not, of course, the shrine of Saint Alban). The reality is more nuanced. There was certainly some spring-cleaning, and more emphasis placed on saints with a wider resonance in the Europe-wide church. Long-delayed reforms and fudged disputes were energetically tackled in partnership by King and Archbishop.

Another Norman, Thomas of Bayeux, was chosen as Archbishop of York. On arrival, he briefly dug in his heels and insisted that York be treated as the equal of Canterbury in ecclesiastical status. It was an argument that had been rumbling on for centuries. William swiftly settled the matter of precedence in Canterbury's favour, and also went further. As his own ambitions grew from enforcing his rule in areas where it had met some resistance, he wanted Canterbury to be seen as the Christian centre of the whole of the British Isles. It never quite happened in his lifetime, or arguably ever, but the claim had been made, and it would resonate with those who came after William, continuing to connect the history of Christianity in Wales, Scotland and Ireland to that of England.

For his part, Lanfranc won many admirers in his almost twenty years as Archbishop, especially for his wisdom and good sense, including among the prelates of Scotland and Ireland who might not have regarded themselves as under his authority, but nonetheless often sought his counsel. His 'constitutions', setting out what was expected of the monks at Canterbury and how their daily life should be structured, were widely adopted in the Benedictine monasteries across the country and further afield. Shaped by a mix of pragmatism married with principle, he upheld the rulings of Rome on such matters as the need for clergy to be celibate, but moved more slowly than the Pope would have wanted, directing that the newly ordained must make vows of celibacy, but allowing those already in the fold to keep their wives.[8]

Most of the time, the priorities of King and Archbishop went hand in hand. There had been considerable initial opposition to William's rule, especially in the north of England and in Wales. In his efforts to quash this and secure his power, William sought to control the major towns and build them up as administrative and military centres. Lanfranc assisted him in this process by switching the centre of the Church's dioceses to reflect this new geography of political power that had come in the wake of the Conquest. Thus Sherborne gave way to Salisbury, and Elmham in Norfolk to first Thetford and then Norwich. Church and civil courts, hitherto one and the same, with bishop and earl sitting side by side in judgement, were separated as part of William's legal reforms, made with Lanfranc's blessing. The move, uncontroversial at the time, was later to come back to distort the relationship between Church and State in the time of Henry II and Thomas Becket.

Lanfranc held no particular candle for the English language, or for Anglo-Saxon traditions in art and architecture. In a letter to Pope Alexander II, written soon after he arrived in Kent, he described himself as 'a novice Englishman, virtually ignorant as yet of English affairs'.[9] And so he led a return to Latin from English as the language of Church affairs, and in his dealings with the court to Norman French.

The most enduring expression of his close cooperation with William, however, was the vast programme of ecclesiastical building works that the new ruler set in train. Saxon cathedrals in Winchester, Worcester, Gloucester, Ely, St Albans and Durham were demolished and, with the expertise of imported Norman masons, replaced by grand, austere, dignified buildings, based on what already existed in northern France. Rugged strength in design and execution projected the presence and permanence of God *and* King. At Durham, the new cathedral stood side by side with the Norman castle.

In Canterbury, there was no need for the Normans to demolish what had re-emerged as the Saxon cathedral after the fire of 1011. In 1067, another blaze had spread quickly through the city and, once again being at its very heart, the cathedral went up in flames. When Lanfranc was installed as Archbishop of Canterbury three years later, the ceremony took place in an improvised shelter amid the ruins. One of his first tasks was therefore to apply the knowledge he had gained during the building of Caen Abbey to the undertaking of providing himself, the King who had appointed him and British Christianity (in William's vision) with a new and fitting central point of focus. Seven years later, a Romanesque building arose, of which the presence can still, just about, be detected in today's cathedral. It had a central tower, plus two more crowning its west front, and a restored priory for its monks.

Work was still in progress when Lanfranc's successor, another Italian, Anselm, arrived and commissioned more building at the east end of the choir. Underneath it, there was to be what was then the biggest crypt in the country. It is preserved largely and wondrously intact today, complete with its mighty columns that hold up everything above them yet are simultaneously objects of beauty with delicately carved capitals. Above the crypt, though, Anselm's new version of the choir survived for less than half a century after its consecration, before it fell victim in 1174 to the third destructive major fire to blight the cathedral in little more than 150 years. Those prone to see God's hand in such catastrophes may have wondered what he was trying to tell the English.

The building project, however, was not the main focus of the new Archbishop. The final decade of the eleventh century saw Anselm locked in battle with William II, who had succeeded to the throne on the death of his father in 1087. With Lanfranc's passing two years later, William Rufus, as he is commonly known, had deliberately delayed naming the next Archbishop of Canterbury so he could seize the archdiocese's revenues for his own projects, which included both resisting the claims of his older brother, Robert Duke of Normandy, to the English throne and imposing his will on the still disgruntled Welsh. Every attempt to compel him to fill the vacancy came to nothing, until 1093 when illness had the effect of turning William Rufus' thoughts to his own mortality. In a moment of wanting to make his peace with his maker and with the Church, lest it be his last opportunity, he finally agreed to appoint Anselm. A noted theologian who had served under Lanfranc in France, Anselm was a significant figure on the European stage.

William Rufus' long prevarication caused the elderly Anselm initially to doubt the wisdom of accepting the King's offer. 'What good,' he is said to have remarked, 'would come of yoking together an untamable bull and an old and feeble sheep?'[10] Yet he did eventually take up the appointment, his decision probably influenced by his loyalty to the ongoing project of reviving the influence of the papacy. He styled himself 'Prime of Great Britain and Ireland' and gave his wholehearted support to Rome's increasingly loud claims that the Pope had precedence over any temporal ruler, not just in choosing bishops, archbishops and abbots, but every other significant matter as well. Once he had recovered his health, William Rufus was in no mood to entertain such notions, and quickly returned to his old ways of keeping vacancies pending for as long as possible in order to line his own pockets with the revenues of leaderless dioceses and abbeys. He even went so far as publicly to lament having chosen the doughty Anselm.

As a foretaste of the problems that lay ahead, there was a battle over the new Archbishop's investiture ceremony. Anselm wanted to travel to Rome to receive directly from the Pope his pallium, the ecclesiastical stole that symbolised every prelate's spiritual authority. William Rufus, however, refused him permission to go, and instead was determined to be the one to give him the pallium – signifying the Church's subservience to the monarchy. The King even managed to get some of the English bishops to side with him against Anselm. Finally, a compromise was agreed – the pallium was laid on an altar in Canterbury Cathedral, from where Anselm took it.

This clash was part of a larger Europe-wide fight over ultimate authority. In England, any spirit of compromise quickly evaporated after the investiture. In 1097, King and Archbishop fell out again when Anselm headed to Rome without clearing it first with William Rufus. The recrimination was such that the Archbishop did not return until the death of the King in 1100.

With William's younger brother now on the throne as Henry I, matters began more promisingly, so much so that he was able to persuade Anselm to come back to Canterbury. Church councils – which had been blocked by William Rufus – were allowed by Henry, and so Anselm got on with introducing into his Church the papal programme of reform over such matters as married clergy and suitable dress for men of the cloth. These were the same changes that were being implemented elsewhere in Europe.

The question of authority – specifically as it affected investiture – had not gone away. After refusing to accept the King's demands that he agree to consecrate bishops whom Henry had already invested with their symbols of episcopal office, Anselm once again went into exile. It took until 1107, two years before Anselm's death, for Henry formally to renounce his rights over investiture and thus pave the way for the Archbishop to come back to Kent.

Anselm's victory was anything but complete. Subsequent kings reversed Henry's concession. The competing claims to power of the monarch and the head of the Church dominated the twelfth century, and led to tragedy in December 1170 in Canterbury. No visit to its cathedral is complete without standing in the place of Thomas Becket's martyrdom, and so – making another exception for the city – we must briefly skip ahead of our timeline.

A simple altar, with a pale stone base and a dark marble top, stands down a flight of steps at the end of the north aisle of the cathedral. It marks the spot known as 'The Martyrdom'. It is curiously visually restrained, next to the grandeur and tombs of the great and good that fill this national church. What reveals its purpose is the modern sculpture that hangs above it, combining four swords dipped in blood, two in metal and two in the shadows they cast on the wall behind. These represent the weapons used by the knights on 29 December 1170, who came to carry out what they took to be the orders of Henry II to 'rid himself' of Thomas Becket, Archbishop of Canterbury. He was, in the King's incendiary words, 'a troublesome priest'.[11] Opposite the altar in this small sunken lobby area stands the pillar of the original Norman door though which Becket's assailants came to commit murder in the cathedral. The fatal blow was struck with so much force that it severed the top of his skull.

Becket was the son of a merchant, but he surpassed higher-born Norman knights at Henry II's court to win royal favour and friendship. He was both a trusted adviser to his king when appointed as Chancellor in 1154 and an able general alongside him on the battlefield in France. When in 1161 the see of Canterbury fell vacant, it seemed a natural enough step to Henry to name Becket as the next incumbent, keen as the King was to impose his will on the Church in the ongoing struggle with the papacy over who was ultimately in charge. It wasn't, after all, as if his Chancellor lacked religious credentials. As a young man, when studying in Paris, Becket had taken a vow of chastity that at least suggests he may have thought about a career in the Church. Subsequently he had worked for Archbishop Theobald of Canterbury as an archdeacon (though he had never been ordained as a priest). Indeed, it was Theobald who had introduced him to Henry, so the King assumed the man who had become his confidant and friend, and who as Chancellor had enjoyed the trappings of office, dressed fashionably and entertained lavishly, would be happy to hold both posts simultaneously.

When he first raised the idea, Becket tried to dissuade Henry but, to the King it seemed a heaven-made opportunity too good to let go. What he discovered, to his cost, when he insisted, was that his new Archbishop was a much more complex character that he had hitherto realised. As soon as he had the pallium – having become a priest the previous day – Becket underwent a dramatic change, in dress, in lifestyle (becoming an ascetic) and in personality. He resigned the Chancellorship and threw his lot in unequivocally with the Pope. Quite why there was this about-turn has been debated ever after, with hypocrisy, pride, overnight conversion and a chameleon aspect to his make-up among the most regularly aired causes.

The mystery of it all and the drama of that early December evening still somehow pervade The Martyrdom. Its very blankness compared to the rest of the ornate cathedral gives the visitor a canvas on which to paint. Henry's shock at how Becket, from the royal perspective, had changed sides turned to anger when the Archbishop, having first consented, decided to oppose the King's eminently sensible efforts to bring an end to the legal nonsense of any offender who could claim to be a clerk in holy orders (all that was required was that their hair was tonsured) be tried by ecclesiastical courts. These had a reputation for delay and passing lighter sentences than the civil courts.

For the reforming Henry, it was a practical question of improving the delivery of justice. And many of the English bishops agreed. For Becket, though, conscious of the Pope's insistence that the Church was separate from the State, and superior to it, the proposed change was a step too far. It handed over to the King the fate of those of even the lowest ecclesiastical rank. Tempers flared and Becket fled to France in 1164. In his six years in exile, his conviction about – as Jesus put it in the Gospels – rendering unto Caesar what is Caesar's and unto God what is God's[12] only intensified. Nevertheless, in the summer of 1170, he allowed himself to be persuaded to return to Canterbury, where the crowds that gathered to greet him served to reinforce his inflexibility.

If Henry believed he now had the upper hand, Becket quickly disabused him by serving excommunication notices, obtained from the Pope, on three of the bishops (York, London and Salisbury), who had sided with the King in their dispute. When he heard the news, Henry flew into a mighty rage and uttered the words in front of his knights that haunted him to his grave.

They headed for Canterbury and confronted the Archbishop, who refused to back down. They formulated a plan to seize him and take him back to face the King, but it unravelled on the spot where I am now standing. Concerned monks had escorted Becket round the cloisters and into the cathedral via the door that stands behind me, but the knights were following. When monks went to bolt the door, Becket forbade it. God's house must be open to all, he said.

When his assailants entered, all but one of his companions, Edward Grim, abandoned Becket to his fate. The Archbishop fought off the knights' attempts to kidnap him and, as they grew more and more frenzied, he was knocked to the floor. One of the four, Richard le Breton, then aimed his sword at Becket's head, ending his life. His killers fled in horror at what they had done, leaving behind the broken point of the murder weapon on the floor.

What stood here for 400 years after the killing was the 'Altar of the Sword's Point', before it was purged in 1538 as part of the Reformation cleansing. Becket's body, meanwhile, was originally placed in a tomb in the crypt, to which Henry II came to perform an elaborate public penance. In 1220, Becket's remains – already a hugely popular draw with pilgrims – were moved back 'upstairs' to the Trinity Chapel, the highest point behind the main altar. They were subsequently to be swept away by royal whim when Henry VIII ordered that the shrine be removed and the bones it contained burnt. Whether they were remains another mystery – though the search for them has thus far proved fruitless.

Nowadays a candle stands and burns where the shrine once was. Behind it, fittingly, for a cathedral whose reach is not just national but international, as the centre of the worldwide Anglican Communion, there is a chapel that is dedicated to the saints and martyrs of our time. Like Becket, these people of faith died because they spoke a higher truth to earthly power.

ALSO WITH A STORY TO TELL . . .

The foundation stone of DURHAM CATHEDRAL was laid in 1093 by William de St-Calais, whom William the Conqueror had named as Prince-Bishop of Durham. The new building replaced the earlier Saxon 'White Church', which had housed the relics of Saint Cuthbert and Bede. Though there have been later additions, the greater part of this majestic, awe-inspiring building remains Norman.

LEWES PRIORY in East Sussex was founded in 1081 by William de Warenne, who had fought alongside William at the Battle of Hastings. It was the first Cluniac house in England, ruled from the mother house at Cluny in France, and was part of a number of new monastic movements that arrived in England from the continent on the coat-tails of the Conquest. Only its ruins remain.

BRECHIN CATHEDRAL IN ANGUS has an eleventh-century conical tower, one of only two in Scotland, but a more familiar sight in early Irish Christianity. With a carved, raised doorway, it is almost as tall as the spire of the more typical Norman Gothic cathedral that stands next to it. The tower is said to have been endowed by the Scottish King Kenneth II who, according to legend, had an Irish wife.

CHAPTER 12
The Twelfth Century

St Melangell, Pennant Melangell: Welsh Fusion

Cwm Pennant galant gweli; cwm uchel
I ochel caledi,
Cwm iachus; nid oes i chwi
Ond cam i Ne'o'n cwm ni.

You see Cwm Pennant shining; a high valley
To ward off hardship,
A healing valley; for you there is not
More than one step between our valley and heaven.

Late eighteenth century *englyn*
(short traditional Welsh poem)[1]

A T THE SMALL village of Llangynog on the southern flank of
Berwyn Mountains in north-east Wales, a turning off the
main road to Bala winds a mile or two up through the flat bottom
of the sparsely populated valley of the River Tanat to St
Melangell's Church. Long a place of pilgrimage and healing, this
low, plain, stone Norman building from the twelfth century is at
one with it remote and magical setting.

Inside is the oldest Romanesque shrine in the whole of northern Europe. The story of its survival is extraordinary. At the
Reformation, the order came from far away in London to smash
it to pieces, but those who worshipped in this isolated valley were
too attached to it to agree to such vandalism. Instead, they took it
apart stone by stone and then concealed its various parts in the
church's thick north wall – and even stashed a few for which there
was no space in the structure of the lychgate. Only in the nineteenth century were they rediscovered, and by the late twentieth
the shrine had been reassembled indoors and placed in the chancel behind the altar.

Just as striking is the unchanging nature of the setting of
this little-known monument to the history of Christianity in
Britain and Ireland. St Melangell's stands in a bowl at the head
of the valley, with mountains and a waterfall rising up behind
it as if linking heaven and earth. The circular graveyard around
it points to its origins as an early Christian place of worship,
while, beyond the stones, a ring of yews believed to be more
than 2,000 years old recall when this was a Bronze Age site

(burial pits have been unearthed nearby dating back to 1500 BC). This is history in the raw.

Melangell, the saint to whom the church is dedicated (pronounced Mel-ann-guh-elle), is said to have been the seventh-century daughter of an Irish king, who escaped betrothal to a prince by choosing to live apart from the world as an anchorite, dedicating herself to God in prayer. Her only friends, the legend goes, were animals until Brochfael Ysgithrog, a local noble from the royal house of Powys, was hunting nearby. He was chasing a hare (sacred creatures for the pagan Celts and in early Christianity) that, in terror, had buried itself for protection beneath Melangell's skirts as she was sitting in contemplation in a thicket. So struck was the hunter by both her demeanour and her oneness with nature that he spared the hare and made a gift to Melangell of the land around her anchorite cell in perpetuity. The tale is recounted in carvings on the church's fifteenth-century oak rood screen.

Other women were attracted to join her, possibly also high-born. They shared her ascetic ways as they lived in community, just as men were doing elsewhere in Wales at the same time in their beehive cells in monasteries. Excavations outside the north wall of the church have uncovered six female skeletons, all once wrapped in linen shrouds. They have been carbon dated to pre-ninth century. Each was found with small white stones laid on her shroud at the time of her burial, believed to denote the number of decades she had lived in the community.

The women's reputation for holiness and healing, and that of the place itself, lived on after their deaths, drawing a continuing flow of pilgrims up this otherwise hidden valley. So much so that, at the start of the twelfth century, construction began of the church that stands to this day, with its shrine to Melangell. In some accounts, it is the work of a local nobleman, Rhirid Flaidd. Through birth he was descended from the Welsh-speaking princes to the west, but what he built owes more to the expanding influence of 'Marcher' barons of the English borderlands to the east (Shrewsbury is thirty-five miles away). The church's font, believed to be original, is Norman, as are the doorway and narrow lancet window in the north wall, while the tall, ornately carved shrine, again from the twelfth century, is of a design seen elsewhere in English and European Christianity in that era, though there are also distinctive Celtic markings among its details.

It was only in the 1950s, during essential building work – at one stage the church had fallen into such a poor state of disrepair that demolition was considered – that the floor was lifted in a small side room, formerly used as the local school before depopulation had emptied the valley. The footprint of the schoolroom had once been a semicircular apse, attached to the church, but was entered separately from outside. Buried underneath the floor was a lead box containing human bones. These, too, were carbon dated to pre-ninth century and are believed to be those of Melangell, again having been secreted away in post-Reformation panic for fear they would be regarded as too 'Catholic'. They were placed back in the body of the shrine during a major restoration in the late 1980s undertaken by the then vicar, Paul Davies, and his wife, Evelyn, later also ordained as an Anglican priest. The apse, where the bones were found, has been rebuilt, and stands beyond the shrine, its floor containing Melangell's small grave, covered with prayer cards, flowers and rosary beads left by visitors drawn to her legend.

William the Conqueror's ambitions stretched beyond seizing power and great swathes of land in England. Wales, too, was among his targets. In 1081, when it had been largely pacified along with much of the rest of his realm, the King paid a visit to St David's. *The Anglo-Saxon Chronicle* has it down as part of a military campaign to enforce English claims of overlordship, and hence Norman rule, in Wales. More local sources record it as a pilgrimage to the monastery founded by Dewi in the sixth century, now the seat of a bishop whose diocese covered almost half of all Welsh lands. Given William's personal piety, it may well have been both. Church and State in his grand plans moved as one.

Back in the colonial age of Britannia, the Romans had only ever operated as an occupying force in Wales, holding strategic locations to keep the population quiet. They made one attempt to colonise, in the south eastern corner closest to England. With their departure in the fifth century, the various medieval kingdoms – principal among them being Gwynedd in the north and west, Powys in the east, Ceredigion on the west coast, Deheubarth in the south west and Gwent in the south east – developed and co-existed in an ever-shifting pattern of alliances and hostilities. Their cultural, spiritual and trading ties with Ireland, especially for those on the west coast, and also with Scotland for those in the north, were as important as those with the Anglo-Saxon kingdoms overland to the east.

For Powys in particular, cheek by jowl with the expansionist Mercian kings of the English Midlands and border country, that proximity was a constant source of worry. And vice versa. The Mercians wanted to extend their influence by forcing Powys to recognise their overlordship. For periods they did just that. At others, though, the Welsh launched raids into Mercia, and later joined forces with princes from further south to resist the incursions of combined Mercia–Wessex forces. Offa's Dyke, the defensive earthworks along the English–Welsh border that stretches from the Dee Estuary and Chester in the north to the Severn valley in the south, dates back to these troubled times.

What stopped the Welsh princes posing any greater threat to the often-fragile Anglo-Saxon kingdoms was their own disharmony. Rare were the moments when they managed to come together, voluntarily or by force of arms, to resist the English, as when Gruffydd ap Llywelyn, ruler of Gwynedd, managed (brutally) to unite the whole country behind him so that he could, between 1057 and 1063, claim to be truly King of Wales. The threat he posed caused tensions with the English and ultimately his defeat, during the reign of Edward the Confessor, by Harold Godwin (who married Gruffydd's widow). Welsh cohesion once again crumbled, leaving its princes vulnerable to the arrival of new and determined rulers of England after 1066.

William entrusted the task of keeping the Welsh in check to three members of his inner circle, Hugh d'Avranches, Roger de Montgomery and William FitzOsbern, who were respectively Earls of Chester, Shrewsbury and Hereford. Collectively, they and their successors are known as the Marcher Barons, the Marches being those areas of England that bordered the Welsh kingdoms. Over the next century, encouraged by being given quasi-independent status by the King, excluding them from the centralising, feudal structures imposed on others in his imported ruling class, they went far beyond subduing Wales. By 1086, the Earl of Shrewsbury had built a castle inside Powys at a place he called Montgomery after his Normandy home, while the Earl of Hereford had taken over the 700-year-old kingdom of Gwent. Under William Rufus they grew bolder still, with Shrewsbury pushing down through Powys and Ceredigion to establish a base – and a castle – at Pembroke on the south west coast.

The Norman grip remained tenuous, however, so Henry I (1100–35) presided over a concerted and sometimes aggressive effort to encourage Norman, Breton, Flemish and English settlers into Wales. It proved particularly successful in the south, across Glamorgan, Carmarthenshire and Pembrokeshire. Later it extended over the Irish Sea into Ireland under Henry II. He led a military force there in 1171, reinforcing Norman claims that had been made by mercenaries sent earlier with his blessing to Dublin and Waterford on the east and south east coasts of Ireland, closest to Pembrokeshire.

While in Ireland, Henry convened a synod of its bishops at Cashel in an attempt to bend them to his will in endorsing his claims to authority over the country. Since the gathering took place less than a year after the death of Thomas Becket, they may not have been entirely convinced by his expression of pious concern for their Church. Indeed, when attending Mass, Henry is reported to have been given to doodling and chatting to those around him.

The dominance of the Anglo-Normans in Wales in the twelfth century waxed and waned, especially following the death of Henry I in 1135. With rival factions in England supporting the claims to the throne of his nephew, Stephen, and his daughter, Matilda, civil war ensued. It only ended when agreement was reached that Matilda's son, Henry II, should inherit the English crown after Stephen's death in 1154. For the Welsh princes, this English drama represented a twenty-year respite, but the new King's advent saw them in the sights of Henry II and the sons who came after him (collectively the Angevin kings, with lands in France and England). Ultimately, only the north western kingdom of Gwynedd held on firmly to its independence, and became the focus for Welsh resistance to English overlordship. So much so that in 1267, at the Treaty of Montgomery, Henry III was forced to recognise its leader, Llywelyn ap Gruffudd, as Prince of Wales, and by association Wales as a principality in its own right.

His death in 1282, followed by the execution by the English of his brother Dafydd in the following year as part of their military campaign, brought Wales firmly back under Edward I and the English crown. Henceforth, 'Prince of Wales' was to be a title given to the heir to the English throne. In May 1285, as King of England and Wales, the victorious Edward was accompanied on a procession through London by the Archbishop of Canterbury and fourteen other bishops. On display was the most precious religious relic in Gwynedd, the fragment of the True Cross known as the Cross of Neith, which had been seized by the English as the spoils of victory from Llwelyn's palace in Aberconwy.

It symbolised the incorporation of the Welsh Church into English Christianity. Its four bishops and their dioceses had long been claimed as under the authority of the Archbishop of Canterbury, but distance and politics meant that, in reality, that influence was not strongly felt. The Welsh bishops did pay heed to what Rome was saying, but had always done so with a sense of their own distinct identity and their isolation from Canterbury. This independence proved hard to maintain, with the English monarchs upholding the Archbishop of Canterbury's claims, while the scarcity of large towns in Wales meant that the local abbey could often feel more relevant to Welsh Christians than a bishop many miles away.

The Normans, as we have seen, regarded the Church and its structures as an important buttress to their claims and authority. They therefore frowned on the lack of oversight of the successors to the traditional *clasau*, or monasteries, in Wales, founded in the sixth century by travelling monks. To rein them in, many were suppressed or forced to redesignate themselves as tributaries of abbeys and priories in England and Normandy, especially those run by reformed Benedictine branches that had been growing in France. The Normans encouraged in particular the rapid expansion of the Cistercians in both England and Wales in the twelfth century. Strata Florida Abbey, established in 1164 near Tregaron in Ceredigion, was one of several established by them on Welsh soil.

This incorporating of the Welsh Church into English structures did not go wholly without challenge. There were even those at Henry II's court who argued that St David's should be elevated to the status of an archdiocese in its own right and its Archbishop given authority over the Church in Wales to match that of Canterbury and York in England. In 1176, when a vacancy occurred, the name of monk, theologian, chronicler and royal favourite, Gerald of Wales, was unanimously put forward by the St David's monks as their preferred candidate. On paper his claim was strong: a scion of the Anglo-Norman de Barri family of Manorbier Castle in Pembrokeshire, his uncle had been a previous bishop there, and his grandmother, Nest, a mistress of Henry I. But the King blocked Gerald's appointment. Even though he held him in high esteem – so much so that he was happy to entrust his youngest son, John, to Gerald's care on a trip to Ireland a few years later – Henry II knew of his ambition to elevate St David's to an archbishopric and feared that it – along with his descent through his mother from the princes of Dyfed – would rekindle Welsh resistance to English rule.

The same plan resurfaced in 1198 when the see was once more vacant. This time Gerald gained the backing of Pope Innocent III and the English King John. For four years he acted as de facto bishop, awaiting final confirmation, but it never came. Ultimately, both Pope and King were persuaded to block him by the powerful Archbishop of Canterbury, Hubert Walter, in whose province Wales continued to stand. Gerald's failure came because he was ultimately too Welsh for the Normans and too Norman for the Welsh.

He may have got off lightly. One of Archbishop Walter's predecessors, Theobald of Bec, had warned the Pope in 1159, 'the Welsh are Christians only in name'.[2]

While a church was being built in those early decades of the twelfth century in the Berwyn Mountains to honour the name of Melangell and the pioneering community of women she attracted in the seventh century, over on the far side of England a similar experiment was taking place that led to the establishment of the only completely English religious order of the medieval period. Gilbert of Sempringham, the son of an Anglo-Norman lord of the manor near Bourne in Lincolnshire, ended up as both land-owner and parish priest when he inherited the family estate in 1130. As a young man he had studied theology at the University of Paris, then the greatest seat of learning in Europe, and had gone on to serve the Bishop of Lincoln. Once back in his home parish, he encouraged and backed a group of local women who wanted to take vows and live as a community of nuns under the Cistercian system, using the Rule of Saint Benedict. He gave them buildings and a cloister attached to his church.

There were, by this stage of the introduction of new religious orders into Britain, other female houses established with the support of landowners. However, Gilbert's nuns had other local women who would pass them food and essentials into the enclosure of their convent, while some local men would work for them on the land that had been given to support the new foundation. The suggestion naturally arose that these helpers would become part of the nuns' religious community as lay brothers and sisters. The idea – in some respects a revival of the sort of double monastery Hilda of Whitby had overseen in the seventh century – went down badly with the Cistercian authorities. Gilbert even travelled to the mother house in Cîteaux in eastern France in 1148 to plead the case, but the idea of men and women in one place was judged too radical. Undeterred, Gilbert established the Gilbertines as a stand-alone order with papal blessing, a small departure at a time when the influence of French monasticism was overwhelming Britain and Ireland.

The Gilbertines' lay brothers and sisters, supporting the nuns, were subject to detailed rules to keep the two sexes apart. The arrangement proved so successful that it eventually spread to twenty-seven convents around the country.

It was to the Gilbertines' mother house at Sempringham that the last native Princess of Wales, Gwenllian, daughter of Llywelyn ap Gruffudd and just an infant at the time of his death in 1282, was sent following Edward I's victory in Wales. The King did not want her to become a focus for Welsh hopes of regaining their independence. She lived there quietly for the remaining fifty-four years of her life.

To each Gilbertine convent was attached a group of Canons Regular, priests who lived as part of the community and would say Mass for the nuns as well as oversee their welfare. Until the twelfth century, there had been a clear distinction between monks who lived in communities and priests who lived in parishes – though it was blurred at those cathedrals that did not have an attached monastery. Now, however, different groups of Canons Regular became another new form of religious life to arrive in Britain. Most prominent among them were the Augustinians, bound by a rule shaped by the teachings of the influential fourth-century north-African theologian, Saint Augustine of Hippo. They were active in the spiritual support of their local communities and eventually had 200 houses, typically smaller than monasteries, including several in Ireland, plus a much smaller number of women's establishments.

Another new arrival at this time were the Norbertines – or Premonstratensians – founded by Saint Norbert in Prémontré in northern France. Their first house was at Newhouse in Lincolnshire in 1143 and they grew to have thirty-one foundations, including some for women.

However, it was the Cistercians who made the greatest impact. Having begun at the start of the twelfth century in France, they based their life as a community of monks on Benedict's Rule, but updated it (or, they would say, returned it to its origins) by insisting on utter simplicity in all things, including the life of their abbeys. A Sherborne-born monk and abbot, Stephen Harding, was among their founders at Cîteaux. Their best-known figure, though, was Bernard of Clairvaux, advisor to popes, supporter of the Crusades and the first of their number to be declared a saint.

The Cistercians arrived in England at Waverley in Surrey in 1128. Four years later, a group of monks from Clairvaux founded Rievaulx in the North York Moors. They preferred remote spots, places where they could shut out the demands of this world and tune in to nature and its God-given rhythms from sunrise to sunset. Rievaulx was to become one of the most renowned monasteries in Europe, not least for the presence there of its abbot, Aelred, whose writings celebrated its prayerful atmosphere: 'Everywhere peace, everywhere serenity and a marvellous freedom from the tumult of the world'.[3]

By 1200 there were some sixty-two Cistercian abbeys in England, Wales and Scotland. In Ireland, where Anglo-Norman influence was growing, they were introduced into the country by Malachy, reforming abbot at Bangor in the north-east, later Bishop of Connor and from 1132 to 1137 Archbishop of Armagh, the principal see in the country, associated by legend with Saint Patrick. Malachy befriended Bernard of Clairvaux and persuaded him to send five Cistercian monks to found Ireland's first Cistercian house at Mellifont in County Louth.

Numerically much smaller than the Cistercians, but influential nonetheless for its distinctive way of life, was the Carthusian order, founded by Saint Bruno in 1086 near Grenoble in the Chartreuse Mountains of France. The order arrived in England in 1181 when Witham in Somerset was endowed by Henry II as part of his penance for the death of Thomas Becket. Its statutes (or rules) harked back to the practices of earlier monasticism in Ireland and Wales. Monks lived separately as hermits in their cells for much of the time, coming together only for services. Unlike their Welsh and Irish forerunners, though, they were enclosed and stayed within the walls of the monastery, serving local communities through their prayer, not their practical involvement. Hugh, the Frenchman who was Witham's first abbot, did, however, emerge from the enclosure to become Bishop of Lincoln in 1186, where his efforts in education and, notably, in rebuilding the cathedral after it had been damaged by an earthquake, won him many admirers.

Buildings, court intrigue and military campaigns with a religious dimension are one substantial part of the history of Christianity in the Middle Ages in these islands. The election in the middle of the twelfth century of the only Englishman ever to sit on Saint Peter's throne is another piece in assembling the picture. Nicholas Breakspear, born and raised in St Albans, had been turned down by the monastery there (even though his father had been admitted and is buried there). Nicholas pursued his vocation in Europe, rising to be Abbot of St Rufus in Avignon, Bishop of Albano in Italy (giving rise to puns about him making it in Albano after being rejected in St Albans) and, after a successful mission as papal legate to Scandinavia, was voted in as Pope Adrian IV from 1154. Over the next five years, he was an implacable defender of papal authority over kings and princes.

What, though, of the lives of the faithful, those who filled the churches and cathedrals; looked up to bishops, abbots and popes; and placed their lives in God's hands? There were occasions when their trust in what their Church taught could lead to mass hysteria, as at Easter 1144 when the death of a young boy, William, last seen in the Jewry area of Norwich, was popularly blamed on the Jewish inhabitants of that quarter. Christian antagonism towards Jews had first developed soon after Jesus' death, as the emerging Church sought to differentiate itself from the faith into which God's Son had been born and lived. Among the false accusations and slurs regularly thrown at Jews by Christians in medieval times in cities across Europe was that they sacrificed Christian children to use their blood in the baking of Passover bread. In Norwich, this 'blood libel' caused local Christians to target the Jewish community that had only been introduced to the city thanks to greater toleration by the Norman kings eleven years prior. Soon miracles were being attributed to William, and he was declared a saint by popular acclaim as communal violence took hold.

It wasn't an isolated incident. Similar charges were heard in 1168 in Gloucester, in 1181 in Bury St Edmunds and in 1255 in Lincoln, each time involving a murdered child. Some monarchs refused to tolerate such prejudice in God's name. Richard I took a stance by inviting Jews to his coronation in 1189, but eventually the crowd turned on them. Other kings chose to go along with the mob, with Edward I in 1290 expelling the Jews from England.

Such outbreaks of hatred were rare. For the most part, the everyday story of Christians' lives in this period was about the continuing expansion of the parish network, largely controlled by lords of the manor, where the practice of religious faith in the local church was tangled up with the ecclesiastical structures of bishops and dioceses, and with the economic and social system known as feudalism. Land was held by peasant farmers in return for services rendered to the local landowner, whose authority over their lives was in most practical matters absolute.

In larger towns, where the stranglehold of feudalism was not so much in evidence, there was more freedom around the structures of parish life. In Norwich and York, by 1300 there were as many as fifty parish churches. In London, now by far the largest city with around 40,000 inhabitants, there were more than a hundred. Yet there was little ambition that they should all follow similar practices. Churches in towns and the countryside would, for example, have their own liturgical rites, often tied with the area in which they were located: the Norwich rite, the Hereford rite, the Sarum (or Salisbury) rite.

What Pennant Melangell and, on a much larger scale, the shrine of Thomas Becket in Canterbury Cathedral both reveal is how much of belief in these centuries was lived out beyond the local parish, and – especially in the towns – beyond the trade and artisan guilds and confraternities that were associated with individual churches. On slender resources, medieval pilgrims would regularly (sometimes annually) set off from their home parish to walk long distances along sometimes dangerous routes that were targeted by thieves, in order to go to shrines such as that to Saint Melangell.

By so doing, they were on one level being fleeced. In his *Canterbury Tales*, accounts written at the end of the fourteenth century by Geoffrey Chaucer about a group of pilgrims en route to Becket's shrine, the Pardoner trades in fake bits of bone that he claims as relics, charging travellers as much as two months' wages to own them. It wasn't, though, just individuals who turned belief into trade. Many monasteries and abbeys relied on the donations to be generated by their collection of relics and associated legends to see them through financially.

Yet, as the same *Canterbury Tales* also tell, the atmosphere on such journeys was often far from solemn. Chaucer mocks the Wife of Bath, a cloth-maker and businesswoman, for her worldliness, making it clear she has taken to the road looking for company and an escape from the restrictions of medieval parish life. For others, these treks were sometimes made as a penance to atone for the pilgrim's sinful state, but important and too easily overlooked was the faith that underpinned these routes as they criss-crossed the countryside of Britain and Ireland. These pathways represented a chance, independent of the control of a parish priest and the lord of the manor, for the walkers to access by their own physical efforts some sort of cure from life's ills – social, emotional or spiritual – and to reach out for a tangible promise of salvation. In that context, the relics on display in the abbeys and monasteries that lined the pilgrim paths were genuinely believed by visitors to possess some power at the very least to close the distance between the believer and his or her God.

In an age of illiteracy, where religious faith for most was fed by listening to a sermon in church or by looking at pictures, carvings and stained glass, a pilgrimage was an opportunity for individuals to take the initiative and put themselves and God to the test. This, after all, was an age when plague and illness could wipe out whole families and populations, when the change from one monarch to another could precipitate civil war, when local lords could give and take away land at will, and when the crops in the fields, upon which so many relied, could be wiped out by a storm or a flood as easily as Lincoln Cathedral in 1185 was brought down by an earthquake – on Palm Sunday of all days. There was a sense that life was fragile and death always close. Anything that could offer some chance, however remote, of exercising control over fate was therefore attractive.

In the late medieval period, this essential appeal was further exploited by the Church-sponsored sale for a modest fee of indulgences to those at pilgrimage spots – essentially a free pass into heaven in the form of a piece of parchment signed by a bishop or an abbot. But those days, when such commerce played a part in precipitating a Reformation, were yet to come. Instead, the story of Christianity in the British Isles is next to be one about education.

ALSO WITH A STORY TO TELL . . .

ST ANDREW'S CHURCH, SEMPRINGHAM, in the Lincolnshire Fens, is the last reminder of the original priory that Gilbert of Sempringham established for his Gilbertine nuns. It was demolished during the Reformation but its church, now St Andrew's, remains. At one time larger, until its chancel and transept were removed in the eighteenth century, it features an elaborately carved twelfth-century doorway and a holy well.

ST WINEFRIDE'S WELL AT HOLYWELL in north Wales was visited by Richard I, son of Henry II, in 1189. Like the pilgrims who had been coming here since the seventh century, he was seeking God's blessing on his forthcoming Crusade at the spot where, it was told, Winefride's rebuttal of the advances of a local prince had caused him to behead her. Where her head fell to the earth, a spring began to pour forth. Winefride's saintly uncle, Beuno, replaced her head on her body and brought her back to life.

MELLIFONT ABBEY, close to DROGHEDA in County Louth, was founded in 1142 by Saint Malachy as Ireland's first Cistercian house, with monks sent from France by Bernard of Clairvaux. It played host to synods of the Irish Church before becoming a private house after the Reformation. Its ruins inspired the opening of a new abbey close by, in the 1930s.

CHAPTER 13
The Thirteenth Century

Blackfriars, Oxford: A New Order

Many, but especially nobles and their wives, sought out Dominican confessors, spurning their own priests and senior clergy.
Matthew Paris, *Chronicon*[1]

Dominic Guzmán, the Spaniard who in 1216 founded the Order of Preachers, placed poverty at the centre of the lives of his friars. They were mendicants, a revolution in religious life across Europe that meant (like their contemporaries the Franciscans) they begged for what they needed rather than relied on the plump royal or noble endowments existing orders received.

Right up there, too, in Saint Dominic's scheme for his new order, was scholarship. So the first-ever Dominican house, in Toulouse in France, had cells where the friars slept *and* cells where they studied.[2] From the start, Dominicans based themselves close to what were then Europe's two great universities in Paris and Bologna, all of which goes to explain the presence today on the wide, tree-lined St Giles, the main route from the north into the very centre of Oxford, of the discreetly elegant, blink-and-you-miss-it façade of Blackfriars, the Dominican priory that is a Permanent Private Hall at the city's university. For on the list of the founding of great European universities, Oxford comes next after Paris and Bologna, and the Dominicans were at the heart of it.

From modest beginnings in the late eleventh century, Oxford had been boosted by Henry II's demand in 1167 that all English students at the University of Paris return home, as part of his dispute with Thomas Becket, who had taken refuge across the Channel. On a visit to Oxford in 1185, Gerald of Wales recorded approvingly that several subject-specific faculties were already in existence. As a university, it was just coming into bloom in 1221 when the Order of Preachers arrived. They quickly made their presence felt. Just seventeen years later, one of their number, Simon de Bovill, was Chancellor of the University.

As I stand outside's today's incarnation of Blackfriars, there are bigger beasts competing for my attention: the grand columned portico of the Ashmolean, Britain's first public museum, just round the corner; the over-the-top Victorian Gothic of the Randolph Hotel, where generations of well-heeled parents have lunched when 'up' to visit their undergraduate children; and the imposing towered entrance to the mighty St John's College opposite (on the site of a pre-Reformation Cistercian foundation). By contrast, the 1929 façade of the home of the Black Friars – as Dominic's followers were popularly known on account of the black *cappa* or cowl they wore over their shoulders as part of their habit – makes a more subtle claim for recognition. The name is spelt out in metal letters above a black, wrought-iron gate that is the entrance. No castellated porter's lodge here, as at other Oxford institutions, to intimidate visitors. Blackfriars' door, as is the Dominican way, is always open.

Inside, as well as the offer of assistance to those in need, there is a simple display case that tells the story of this building and links it with what was established in the 1220s a few hundred metres further south on St Aldgates as the earliest Dominican presence not only in Oxford but in the whole of the British Isles. Among other memorabilia, it contains a silver 'short-cross' penny, first issued during the reign of Henry III, who succeeded his father John to the English throne in 1216. That was the same year Dominic Guzmán founded the Dominicans, and Henry was from the start a great supporter of this new and radical order, intent on renewing Christianity across the whole of Europe.

The actual coin has been dated to between 1230 and 1250, covering the period when the friars expanded so swiftly that they outgrew that first base on land rented from the canons of St

Frideswide's Priory. It was a makeshift affair that initially housed a party of thirteen friars, led by Gilbert de Fresnoy, but now they were in the process of moving further south in the city, this time to water meadows next to the Thames. Their new home was bigger and made much more of a statement about their success and significance. For the next 300 years it was one of the most important centres in the university. So grand, indeed, that in 1258 it played host to the gathering sometimes referred to as the 'First English Parliament', where nobles under Simon de Montfort gathered to challenge the King's authority. (The procedures of the first English parliaments in this century owed much to the Dominican order's own internal system of representation and decision-making.)

This second Blackfriars was destroyed by the Reformation. The short-cross silver penny was among the very few traces found in recent excavations of its site, a slender physical link to bridge the 400 years that passed from when the Dominicans were exiled from the Oxford they had helped to create until they returned to the university in the 1920s and to this current building. Its modern mission may, in scale and number of residents, be much smaller than it was in the thirteenth century, but its essence remains the same. Its friars live austere lives – a daily round of communal prayer, meditation and meals inside the cloister, and a commitment to education. They engage with the teaching work of the university, and beyond that undertake a varied preaching mission that carries them far and wide into parishes.

Oxford University is almost unrecognisable today from when the first Dominicans pitched up. Back then, the curriculum revolved around the *trivium* – grammar, rhetoric and dialectic – and the *quadrivium* (arithmetic, astrology, music and geometry), together known as the Seven Liberal Arts. Most of those studying were in minor orders – clerks on the lower rungs of the Church's hierarchical ladder who had not been ordained as priests. The teaching of theology – generally for those who were what we might now call postgraduates – quickly became dominated by the Dominicans.

Their presence in the city was also about drawing new vocations from the brightest and best studying at the whole university – a strategy in which they were immediately successful, hence their need for bigger premises. Through their parish work – where they addressed themselves both to raising standards in what was still largely an ill-educated clergy by preaching to them in Latin and to inspiring the congregation by preaching to them in the vernacular – they injected new energy and vigour at every level into the Church. As a result, the thirteenth century is referred to as the age of 'friar fever', with the existing orders coming to resent the rise of both the Dominicans and the Franciscans, who shared a similar ethos and approach. By 1272, the heights had been scaled in a remarkably short time. Robert Kilwardby, who had studied and taught at the University of Paris before joining the Dominicans in Oxford, was named Archbishop of Canterbury.

At the time of the death of Edward I in 1307, the Dominicans had in the space of just eighty-six years established no fewer than eighty-three priories. There were five in Wales, all in or near towns that were bases for English rule in the principality. Likewise, the twenty-four new Dominican houses in Ireland, starting in Dublin in 1224, were largely found in that part of the country dominated by the Anglo-Normans. Over the course of the thirteenth century, the order came to epitomise the link between the Church and the Plantagenet kings.

The stability that Henry II had achieved in government during a reign that ended in 1189 was subsequently squandered under his sons. First, Richard I spent less than six months of his ten years on the throne actually in England, preferring instead to play a prominent part in the Crusades that aimed to defeat the Muslim rulers of the Holy Land and establish in their place a Christian kingdom. His brother John, who succeeded him in 1199, stayed at home, but was hampered by both his temperament and his poor choice of counsellors.

With the death in 1205 of the Archbishop of Canterbury, Hubert Walter, John determined to install his personal friend, John de Grey, already the Bishop of Norwich, as his successor. De Grey may not have been as ill suited to ecclesiastical office as Geoffrey Plantagenet, soldier and illegitimate son of Henry II, who had been appointed as Archbishop of York in 1189 at the age of thirty-seven by his half-brother, Richard (probably to eliminate him as a rival claimant to the throne). Yet Innocent III refused to confirm John's choice for leader of the English Church because De Grey was someone to whom the King owed money. It was as if he were buying the role. Moreover, as a young man, Innocent had visited the shrine of Thomas Becket in Canterbury, so was acutely aware how royal appointments of a favourite adviser as archbishop could unravel.

In a further twist in the already long-running dispute between kings and popes over senior ecclesiastical appointments, the determined Innocent, himself elected at the age of just thirty-seven to the papacy, sought instead to impose his own candidate, Stephen Langton, an English priest based in Rome and a graduate of the University of Paris (where he had been a student friend of the future Pope). Neither King nor Pope would back down on their insistence on having 'their' man in post. John refused even to allow Langton into England, despite Innocent having already consecrated him as Archbishop. He therefore became the third Archbishop of Canterbury, after Anselm and Becket, to be forced into exile by a king.

Innocent combined the same exalted theory of papal supremacy over secular kings promoted by his predecessors with a steely disposition when he felt his authority was being challenged. He responded to John's intransigence in March 1208 by placing the whole of England under a papal interdict. It may not have greatly disturbed John's daily life. Indeed, it gave him an opportunity to seize church revenues where priests, abbots and bishops felt obliged to join Langton in exile. For believers, though, the interdict was a calamity. Churches were closed, Masses went unsaid, funerals were cancelled and access to the sacraments curtailed.

In 1209, Innocent upped the ante one more notch when he excommunicated the unrepentant King. Even that sanction had no effect in encouraging John to compromise, so the Pope began openly to plan with Philip of France a war to depose him. Being ejected from his throne by force finally proved sufficient threat to persuade John to back down. In 1213, he surrendered his kingdom and his crown to the Pope, receiving them back as Innocent's vassal once he had agreed to pay an annual tribute of a thousand marks and to accept – as all his predecessors since William the Conqueror had refused – the presence of a papal legate in England.

Innocent's triumph seemed complete when Langton arrived in Canterbury, where he correctly read the mood of the times and gave his blessing to the rebel nobles who in 1215 forced John to grant the Magna Carta, a charter of rights. The Pope, however, instinctively opposed a document that declared in its first clause, 'the English Church shall be free' to elect its own officers. While those words had been included to temper the role of the monarch, they also potentially dispensed with that of the papacy. King and Pope, hitherto sworn enemies, suddenly found themselves on the same side of an argument. Langton, though, was on the other. As a result, he ended up once again in exile.

John's death the following year, and the ascent to the throne of his nine-year-old son, Henry III, brought about the high point of papal influence in England. Successive papal legates played significant roles at the royal court during Henry's minority. When he reached adulthood, there could be no doubting his personal piety.

A daily Mass-goer, he regularly relied on his Dominican confessors for guidance. An unhappy measure of his loyalty to the Church and its teaching was that he enacted more punitive measures towards Jews in his kingdom than any of his recent predecessors. Antisemitism was now part and parcel of medieval Christian teaching and culture.

Henry was also responsible for the development of the cult of Edward the Confessor as a patron saint of England, rebuilding Westminster Abbey where his shrine was located. He made regular pilgrimages, including to the Marian shrine at Walsingham in Norfolk. It had been established after a local noblewoman, Richeldis de Faverches, reported in 1061 seeing a vision there of Jesus' mother. In the centuries that followed it became a particular royal favourite, and was visited by every king up to and including Henry VIII.

Religion was in many ways Henry's escape from political and dynastic entanglements at home and on the continent. He showed little real inclination to push back against papal encroachments in his domains, whether by nature, by calculation or in gratitude for the support provided by papal legates in the early years of his reign. And Innocent's thirst for papal dominance of Europe in temporal as well as spiritual matters required money. He needed to pay the central bureaucracy he was gathering around him in Rome to enforce his will. One method he hit upon for raising funds was to hand vacant posts of canons at great cathedrals and significant churches in England to his own nominees, some of them just boys. In return, the new office-holders redirected straight to Rome the tens of thousands of marks in revenue attached to their new roles. Moreover, as papal appointees, they saw no need to go to England to do the job.

To cover day-to-day needs, ill-educated jobbing priests were hired for a pittance. A new and despised class of absentee placemen was distorting Church life. 'Wretched men, without manners, full of cunning, proctors and "farmers" of the Romans,' complained the celebrated Benedictine monk, Matthew Paris of St Alban's Abbey, of Henry III's reign in his *Chronica Majora*, 'seizing whatsoever in the country is precious and serviceable and sending it away to their lords living delicately out of the patrimony of the Crucified.'[3]

His was not a lone voice. Robert Grosseteste, Chancellor of Oxford University (in some accounts), and from 1235 Bishop of Lincoln, represents with Matthew Paris the best of thirteenth-century churchmen. He stood up to both King and Pope in equal measure. He rebuked Henry III on more than one occasion, and in 1253 refused a demand that he appoint a nephew of Innocent IV, Frederick de Lavagna, as a canon at Lincoln (and thereby permit revenues to be sent to Rome). 'With all filial respect and obedience,' he replied to Rome, 'I will not obey, I resist, I rebel.'[4]

That same fear that the papacy now had too much influence in national life, and was using it corruptly, was felt in political as well as ecclesiastical circles. A proposed 1240 levy to fund the latest chapter of Innocent's feud with the Holy Roman Emperor, Frederick II, was widely resisted throughout the English Church, as was a subsequent tithe to support the Crusades. Simon de Montfort – a close friend of Grosseteste – led efforts by barons to force Henry III to change course in his slavishness to papal demands.

The Oxford Parliament in the Dominicans' second priory took place against this backdrop, but ultimately it, too, failed to achieve its goal of change. Instead, civil war followed in 1264, with first the King defeated and taken captive at the Battle of Lewes, and then the following year de Montfort beaten and killed at the Battle of Evesham by Henry's son, Edward. Though released, the King never fully recovered his powers, and was succeeded by Edward in 1272.

While he shared his father's dutiful attitude to faith, Edward I was more willing to resist faraway Church leaders whose demands would bring him trouble at home. His first two Archbishops of Canterbury, the Dominican Robert Kilwardby until 1278, and then the Franciscan John Peckham through to 1292, had been chosen by Rome, but in practice offered him no real challenge. His third, Robert Winchelsey (1294–1313), a graduate of Paris, Chancellor of Oxford and a disciple of Thomas Aquinas, the greatest theologian of the medieval period, proved much more troublesome. He vigorously upheld ecclesiastical liberty against what he regarded as royal encroachment, notably following Boniface VIII's 1296 ruling that clergy should never pay taxes to lay rulers. Indeed, Winchelsey was so diligent that the Pope had to sideline him and agree his own compromise that allowed Edward to fund his wars. King and Archbishop again fell out over Walter Langton, who combined being Bishop of Lichfield with serving as Edward's treasurer. It came to a head in 1305, when Winchelsey went into exile, the fourth archbishop to do so in just over two centuries, but this time it was as agreed by Pope and King. He was largely unmourned by his fellow bishops. When Edward II took the throne in 1307, he returned, but once more fell out with the monarch when he sided with those barons who demanded the banishment of the King's favourite, Piers Gaveston.

In less than a century, both Dominicans and Franciscans had quickly established themselves as forces to be reckoned with in the delicate and flammable relationship between kings, popes and barons. Soon after Edward II's coronation, an eighty-fourth Dominican priory was established at Kings Langley in Hertfordshire, next door to the royal palace. It was to be the last resting place of Piers Gaveston, after he was murdered in 1313 by those nobles who opposed his influence. His body was taken first to Blackfriars in Oxford and then buried at Kings Langley with great ceremony.

Involvement in such court tussles had not been the friars' main purpose in coming to Britain. Their mission from the start was practical, and their enduring contribution in this century came in education and in the parishes. As scholars of international renown in the first decades after the Norman Conquest, Anselm and Lanfranc had striven to improve the levels of education found in both monks and clergy. In the decades after their deaths, their efforts bore fruit, as the stranglehold exerted by monasteries on learning was broken, initially by the 'secular' cathedrals (those run not by monastic communities, but by clergy). They created the role of cathedral chancellor to organise lectures to drive up standards of learning among local priests and, increasingly, to develop schools attached to the cathedrals where local boys, often from well-to-do families, could be educated.

Following that lead, larger churches in towns and cities next stepped up to open schools. By the thirteenth century, most places of any size would have a school teaching Latin grammar and arithmetic. And, at a parish level, humble village schools attached to the local churches were increasingly in evidence. Such developments were not happening in isolation. The Fourth Lateran Council of 1215 had passed a raft of reforms around the education and conduct in the clergy and the laity, promoting the sacraments in the lives of Christians (including the rule that all must attend confession and communion at least once a year) and urging bishops to focus their attention on preaching to their people and teaching them, using their own language, to help them understand God better. The arrival of the Dominicans in England just six years after the Council can also be seen, therefore, as part of Europe-wide efforts to embed the Council's decrees in the lives of national churches.

Another aspect of this trend in the thirteenth century was the beginning of the tradition of medieval mystery, morality and miracle plays, dramatisations that brought Bible stories to life for the large crowds who gathered in churches and on the streets of cities and towns. As a means of instilling the faith in largely illiterate congregations it proved highly effective, sometimes by accident. At Beverley Minster, at the start of the century, a resurrection play, performed outdoors one summer's day, drew such a crowd that a young boy climbed high on the Minster to get a better view. When he fell to the ground, it was assumed he was dead, but he revived and got to his feet. To most of those who witnessed it, his survival proved that, with God's grace, the miracle of resurrection was possible.

ALSO WITH A STORY TO TELL . . .

SALISBURY CATHEDRAL, built between 1220 and 1258, is one of the glories of the softer early English Gothic architecture that replaced the bulkier Romanesque of previous centuries. Its octagonal Chapter House contains the best-preserved of the four surviving original copies of the Magna Carta.

ST ASAPH'S CATHEDRAL IN NORTH WALES claims to be the smallest Anglican cathedral in the British Isles. The current building contains some features that survived the great fire, started by English soldiers in 1282, during Edward I's campaigns to conquer Wales. The King wanted to move the diocese, but a new cathedral was rebuilt on the same site.

ST ETHELDREDA'S CHURCH, IN ELY PLACE, LONDON, next to Smithfield Meat Market, was built in 1290 as a chapel attached to the Bishop of Ely's Palace in London. It is one of only two buildings from Edward I's reign that are still standing in London.

CHAPTER 14

The Fourteenth Century

*St Andrew's, Fillingham: Wycliffe
and the Age of Dissent*

Englishmen learn Christ's law best in English. Moses heard God's law in his own tongue; so did Christ's apostles.

John Wycliffe (c.1330–84)

CHALLENGES TO CHRISTIANITY since its earliest days in Britain and Ireland had come from above or outside: from greedy, overbearing kings and barons, anxious to control or to fleece the Church; or from heavily armed invaders intent on plunder, disruption and conquest. In the late fourteenth century, for the first time, dissent arose from within and below.

At the start of the century, heresy, as the Church would label it, was something that happened in continental Europe, notably with the Cathars in southern France, around the city of Albi, from the twelfth to the fourteenth centuries. These devout ascetics were in good faith attempting to cleanse corruption and impurity from Catholicism by leading purer, simpler lives, but their efforts were brutally crushed by a Crusade dispatched by the Pope, fearful for his authority if they were allowed to succeed. There had even been a short-lived attempt to import the Cathar ideals into England in the early 1160s by a group of around thirty missionaries. It ended in tragedy when they were handed over by the English bishops to Henry II, who had them scourged and branded on the forehead. Released into the midst of an exceptionally cold winter and denied any sustenance, by royal order, they died of exposure or hunger.

The popular revolts that sprang up in the late fourteenth century proved more robust and popular, and ultimately harder to freeze out. The name most readily associated with this wave of dissent is that of the theologian, priest and polemicist, John Wycliffe. The connection, though, is a complicated one. It was not so much that Wycliffe chose to be a rebel leader, rather that his writings inspired protestors. The link is more tenuous in the Peasants' Revolt, an uprising in 1381 against an unpopular poll tax imposed by Richard II, which briefly saw rebels seize control of London. There was at least one, John Ball, who publicly declared himself a follower of Wycliffe, and religious grievances were certainly bound up in the dissatisfaction that led to the uprising. It was eventually put down, first in London by Richard II, and then in one of its strongholds, Norwich, by the city's bishop, Henry le Despenser, who led an army into battle with the rebels at North Walsham.

Lollardy, the other bottom-up radical campaign to cause alarm at the end of this century was, however, more explicitly religious in its aims, and more direct in claiming Wycliffe as the champion of the reforms it wanted to see in Church life. No one is quite sure of the origins of Lollardy. The word itself comes from the Dutch meaning to murmur or mumble, and was initially used to denigrate the oratory of Lollardy's roving preachers. In 1395, the movement presented its Twelve Conclusions to Parliament, a list of demands also posted on the doors of both Westminster Abbey and St Paul's Cathedral in London. Much of what was being attacked as objectionable in Church practices had already featured in Wycliffe's public utterances.

Both Lollards and Wycliffe, for instance, stood against the insistence that the bread and wine used in the Eucharist was symbolically *and* physically the body and blood of Christ (the doctrine of transubstantiation had been endorsed at the Fourth Lateran Council of 1215). It was, they argued, simply a commemoration of the Last Supper. Rejected, too, was the new emphasis on confession with a priest as the principal route to access God's forgiveness for sin. It put the cleric between each believer and the Lord, the Lollards objected. And they decried as unjust the practice of clergy making the poor pay to have prayers said for their dead relatives. Other shared concerns included the obsession, as they saw it, with ever-greater ostentation in Church buildings, and the ruinous burden that fell disproportionately on ordinary people of Church taxes.

Such attacks on how the Church operated conjure up a picture of John Wycliffe as the ultimate anti-establishment figure. Yet, in many ways, the life of this contradictory man suggests the opposite, as what is referred to as 'Wycliffe's church' in Lincolnshire makes all too plain. For seven years from 1361, when he had only just entered his thirties, Wycliffe was the rector of St Andrew's Church, Fillingham, which shelters on the west-facing slopes of rich farmland a few miles from the cathedral city of Lincoln. Yorkshire-born Wycliffe – some accounts have him raised on a sheep farm, so he may have enjoyed the rural setting of Fillingham – had distinguished himself at Oxford as an academic, rising quickly to become Master of Balliol College. The college system at the university had been developing since the late thirteenth century, in part to counterbalance the dominant presence of friars.

As Master, Wycliffe had the pick of any of the 'benefices' that had been donated by benefactors to support the college. Under ecclesiastical law, the right of advowson – which had grown up with the expansion of the parish system after the Norman Conquest – allowed a patron, in this case Balliol, to name the rector of certain churches or benefices. That rector then enjoyed financial benefits from the 'living' – in terms of the taxes and tithes paid to the church, and even in some cases the use of a vicarage, the first of which were starting to be built to provide homes commensurate with their status for clergy. Until then, many had lived either in the same basic housing as those to whom they ministered, in a room over the church porch, or in the tower.

While it as yet boasted no vicarage – the handsome stone one that today sits opposite St Andrew's only came later – the parish of Fillingham was by repute the most lucrative of all the livings in Balliol's portfolio. The Domesday Book, the survey of much of England and parts of Wales that William the Conqueror had ordered in 1086, records that it was home to both a church and seven manors. Whatever his later criticisms of a Church system where clerics had little real connection with their congregations, Wycliffe appears in 1361 to have had few qualms about taking on the living at St Andrew's. His reasons may have been practical – that as an ambitious young academic without a wealthy family behind him, he needed money. There is debate about whether Wycliffe, in addition to holding the living of Fillingham, continued to teach in Oxford (at that time part of Lincoln diocese) or took on several more Church posts. What all agree on is that he had no intention of living in his 'living'.

His visits to Fillingham were at best irregular. During his long absences, services were led, as was standard in such benefices, by a stand-in cleric, probably local and ill-educated, who would have received a tiny portion of what Wycliffe was paid as rector. And the understudy's role, it is clear from the century's most celebrated Middle English narrative poem, William Langland's *Piers Plowman*, could be arduous (as Langland may have known from personal experience, his text seeming in places to suggest that he may have been just such a substitute cleric). Sundays, he writes, were especially busy:

> *Upon Sonedayes to cease. godes servyce to hear*
> *Bothe matyns and messe. and after mete, in churches*
> *To hear their evesong. Every man ouhte.*[1]

The church that Wycliffe took on was not the original building listed in the Domesday Book, but rather a late-twelfth-century replacement that remains at the core of today's St Andrew's. Approached via a path lined by tall trees from the high street of a

Fillingham much shrunken in size from its medieval heyday, it was built in newly fashionable Early English Gothic. The main doorway, protected by a porch that supports a much later tower, is its oldest surviving feature. Indoors, at either end of the nave, two main arches are delicately pointed, as was the Gothic style, rather than solidly rounded as had been the Norman way. Fragments of thirteenth-century glass remain in three irregularly shaped windows in the north wall of the nave, and there may once have been arcades running off to either side, but these are long gone, as at All Saints, Brixworth. The one extant fixture that would have caught Wycliffe's eye on his pastoral visits is an outsized fourteenth-century wooden chest that sits in the chancel, its panels decorated with rosette whirls.

Heavily restored in Victorian times, and now used only occasionally, St Andrew's struggles to conjure up much of the spirit of Wycliffe, the popular radical theologian, though on the basis of his later writings he would, I feel, have warmed to its essential modesty and absence of fussy, expensive ornamentation. The orator in him might bemoan its lack of a pulpit, which from the 1340s, under Dominican influence, was increasingly a standard feature of even modest parish churches, and a symbol of the Church's stated focus on its mission to educate the faithful in the teachings of Jesus.

Otherwise, there are only posthumous reminders dotted around of the church's association with the most controversial churchman of late-fourteenth-century England. A copy of the standard portrait of him, bearded and wise, made long after his death, sits in a modern frame on the organ. An entry in the list of rectors on display next to the main door places him tenth in chronological order of service, followed by a procession of Balliol nominees. His predecessors, though, are not described as such, suggesting the young Wycliffe may have been the first to profit from this cushy benefice.

If he subsequently felt any pangs at his absentee role here, he never admitted them in writing. Quite the opposite. In *On the Truth of Sacred Scripture*, written a decade after he had swapped this living in Lincolnshire for another one closer to Oxford, at Ludgershall in Buckinghamshire, Wycliffe argued that his long absences actually benefited the local congregation:

> It is lawful for a rector, for a time, to gather the seeds of faith in theological schools away from his parish with a view to sowing it at an opportune time. Spiritual food is more effective and permanent than bodily food, so it is appropriate that the pastor feeds his charges at appropriate times during the year provided that he trains a suitable substitute.[2]

For him, it was a case of rare feasts followed by long famines. Such seems to have been the orthodox view of parish management of the day, unquestioned by many, however inadequately the substitute had been trained. In that sense, Wycliffe was absolutely a man of his time. Yet it was certainly not the orthodoxy of self-confessed Wycliffite John Ball. Once a priest in York, he had turned his back on the parish system to become a travelling preacher, his sermons on social and Church reform attracting such large crowds that the Archbishop of Canterbury had him excommunicated in 1366.

Likewise, absentee parish priests were anathema to the Lollards, many of whom had taken up a similar itinerant ministry to Ball in an effort to make good the damage caused by poor pastoral stewardship of parishes by stand-in clergy. How, then, did Wycliffe end up in the rebel camp, ultimately shunned by almost all of his former associates? Part of the answer lies in the particular circumstances of what was a blighted century.

Discontent with Church practices was just one element in a wide-ranging malaise that afflicted the second half of the 1300s.

Discontent had been steadily building since the papacy had moved from Rome to the fortified city of Avignon in southern France in 1309. Intended as a temporary measure by Clement V to assuage the incessant demands of King Philip IV of France, the exile lasted for seventy years and ended in a schism that divided Europe between two and at times three rival claimants as pope.

The fall-out of these squabbles left the papacy diminished and degraded in many eyes, and regarded as little more than a French plaything. That belief was especially strongly felt among the English, as since 1337 they had been engaged in a conflict with the French known as the Hundred Years' War. The result was resentment at all levels of society, high and low, that at least a proportion of their Church taxes were going to the Avignon papacy to sustain their mortal enemy, France. This outflow of money was even more begrudged when further demands fell on already empty purses to support the English war effort.

On one level, this was a practical and social dilemma, with the poor apparently paying for both sides in a rich man's war. Yet, politically, theologically and ecclesiastically, it gave renewed impetus to those questions that had arisen in previous centuries about the extent of the authority of the papacy over national churches. If it could be so wholly subsumed to the ends of just one of the players on the European stage, how could it claim as it did a role that transcended mere kings and princes? Wycliffe's contribution, with his sharp brain and even sharper tongue, was to coin a theological formula that effortlessly put the papacy – in his words, 'a poisonous weed' – in the wrong.

In the years after he left Fillingham, he developed arguments around authority in the Church that he referred to as the theological principle of 'dominion'. It sought to distinguish between, on the one hand, the invisible Church of the saved who the Bible promised would enjoy eternal life with God in heaven, and on the other the visible, corrupt institutional Church on earth. Since 'dominion' comes from God, Wycliffe argued, those in the visible Church who were in a state of mortal sin were excluded from exercising authority, or benefiting from the exercise of it. And that could include both individuals and institutions. At the top of his list of the excluded was the papacy.

Theological arguments don't usually set off popular rebellions. Something more is required to impel people to rise up. In this case, that was the devastation caused by the Black Death, a plague that had a traumatic effect on the century and magnified all other ills. Believed to be the most costly pandemic in terms of human life in human history, the Black Death struck Europe, Asia and parts of Africa in the middle decades of the century, with recurring outbreaks thereafter. It is estimated to have killed between one-fifth and one-third of the population of the British Isles, with the figure rising in overcrowded cities to nearer 60 per cent. For all the protests about the corruption of the Church and lazy clerics that animated the late 1300s, it is perhaps worth pointing out that there were those among the clergy who during the pandemic proved themselves worthy of their calling. John Moorman, in his definitive *A History of the Church in England*, notes:

> The mortality was certainly heaviest among the clergy ... Parish clergy, by the exercise of their normal duties, were inevitably brought into close contact with the dying and the dead; the friars were mostly living in the more congested districts of towns where infection was likely to be most severe; and the monks lived in close and sometimes unhealthy quarters.[3]

Death on such a scale, however, precipitated social change. With a decimated workforce, the resulting shortages of labour saw the rise of the yeomanry – commoners who freed themselves of feudal obligations and worked their way up to middle-ranking offices in the court, in the service of noble families, in the army or to farm small plots of their own land. That was from most perspectives a positive development, but the Statute of Labourers, introduced in 1351 as the first peak of the plague passed, sought to stop those who had survived charging more for their work. The cap it placed on the maximum wage that could be paid became one of the main grievances of those who marched on London in the Peasants' Revolt (sometimes called Wat Tyler's Revolt, after the leader of the Kent faction).

Economic disruption strained the relationships between the lords of the manor and their feudal tenants all across the countryside as both struggled to keep their heads above water. And it prompted questions, heard at all times of trial in human history, about why God could have allowed such a tragedy to befall his people. Some of the reflection on such matters was profound and long lasting. If the Black Death was a form of hell on earth, some sought as their response the opportunity to contemplate heaven with determination and detachment as hermits, anchorites and anchoresses. They left behind texts that continue to inspire: the Augustinian Walter Hilton's *Ladder of Perfection*, the anonymous author of *The Cloud of Unknowing*, and especially Mother Julian of Norwich's *The Revelations of Divine Love*. This 1393 account of sixteen mystical visions of Jesus, which she had experienced while recovering from an illness that may have been the Black Death, was written while in a cell attached to, but walled off from, St Julian's Church in Norwich. At the end of a century that had witnessed unimaginable loss of life, she was trying to discern her own answer about God's role in suffering in the world.

Others, more caught up in the daily business of feeding themselves, were quicker to find an explanation and a scapegoat. The finger of blame was widely pointed at a bloated, corrupt and worldly Church, highlighting how far it had strayed, and allowed others to stray, from the gospel ideals. It is there loud and clear in William Langland's *Piers Plowman*, written around 1377. He personifies the deadly sin of sloth as a parson who has been thirty years in his parish yet could scarcely read a line to share the Scriptures with his congregation. He was, though, someone to count on to 'fynde in a felde or in a fourlong an hare'.[4]

Langland was highly critical of the mendicant friars – Dominicans and Franciscans – who took vows of poverty yet lived off a diet of 'sondry metes [and] egges yfryed with grece'[5] while ordinary folk were dying of hunger. He wrote more approvingly of the longer-established monastic orders.

Wycliffe took the opposite view. Labelling monks as representing 'the religion of fat cows', he said their monasteries and abbeys no longer had a purpose and should be dissolved.[6]

Such invective in debates within the Church were nothing new, but in these later decades of the fourteenth century the accusations hit home more than before because anti-papal feeling and anger at the corrupt practices of the Church had given rise to a more general anticlericalism. In such an atmosphere, Wycliffe's utterances found a wider audience than the lecture halls of Oxford or his fellow theologians. They were music to the ears especially of ruthless, ambitious individuals at court who were looking for a plausible reason to retain taxation and revenue that should be sent to the Pope. In 1374, therefore, Edward III named Wycliffe as his representative at a meeting in Bruges with papal delegates on these vexed money questions. Wycliffe played his part to perfection, as far as the King was concerned. His refusal to give ground to those sent by his spiritual leader endeared him more than ever to those at court, especially to John of Gaunt, Duke of Lancaster, the King's younger brother. After Edward's death in 1377, the Duke became the power behind the throne of his ten-year-old nephew, Richard II.

His interest in religion was purely practical. John of Gaunt's influence over his nephew earned him many opponents, including senior Church figures who aspired to hold high political office in addition to their ecclesiastical role and felt that the King's uncle was blocking their way. His response was to pack the bench of bishops with his own placemen, including in 1398 his twenty-four-year-old son, Henry Beaufort, as Bishop of Lincoln. For John of Gaunt, Wycliffe presented another means of sidelining his Church critics. So, rail against Wycliffe as did Pope Gregory XI in Avignon, issuing five condemnations ('bulls') of 'the master of errors', such efforts came to naught because John of Gaunt effectively blocked attempts to carry out disciplinary action in 1377 against his new ally.

With the papacy deeply unpopular, Wycliffe may have judged that he was free to act on his beliefs with no fear of the consequences. When next he was deployed by John of Gaunt against Westminster Abbey, however, he managed to isolate himself from the mainstream of opinion in the Church. He agreed in 1378 to defend the actions of royal forces in breaking the long-standing tradition of sanctuary offered by the Abbey to fugitives from justice. There was, he believed, an academic argument to make, and the Abbey could easily have been conflated in his mind with the bloated Church he saw as an offence to God. However, many clerics, even those sympathetic to some parts of Wycliffe's argument for reform, felt he had gone too far in siding with the Crown against the Church.

It was to be his last public appearance. He retreated to his books and writings, but controversy once unleashed is slow to be forgotten. Though Wycliffe could not in any way be held directly responsible for what happened when the Peasants' Revolt landed on the streets of London in 1381, many suspected him, on the basis of his writings and past pronouncements, of being in sympathy with the rioters. That meant guilt by association when the mob that besieged the Tower of London seized the Archbishop of Canterbury, Simon Sudbury, and executed him.

Wycliffe's list of enemies was now much longer than that of those who lionised him. Among the former was Sudbury's

successor as Archbishop, William Courtenay, who was determined to get his man. And, because the rioters had destroyed
John of Gaunt's Savoy Palace on the Thames, this time there was
no royal intervention to halt the synod held at Blackfriars in
London in May 1382 to pass judgement on Wycliffe's alleged
heresies. Known as the Earthquake Synod because the building
was shaken during proceedings by tremors, it voted to condemn
and ban his writings.

The accused did not attend to defend himself, and instead
stayed put in his latest parish in Lutterworth in Leicestershire,
where, undeterred, he spent the last two years of his life pursuing
an argument he had raised over Church teaching around whether
Christ was in some way present in the bread and wine at communion. For many, this was the final straw. Even for lowly clergy who
continued to admire him, Wycliffe was now attempting to take
away the one thing that they alone could do: change the bread and
wine into Jesus' body and blood.

Abandoned, too, by his university, Wycliffe was unbowed. He
began work on what is both his best-remembered project and
something of a literary mystery. In some accounts, he set about
translating the Bible for the first time into English, something the
Church had always fiercely resisted, wanting to stick to its own
universal language of Latin (which made it accessible only to the
well-educated). In other versions, Wycliffe worked not alone but
with a team, including Nicholas of Hereford and John Purvey, to
accomplish the task. Or he may just have given his blessing to the
idea, attached his name to it and encouraged others to do the
hard work.[7] No consensus has ever been reached, but the text that
emerged has long been referred to as Wycliffe's Bible, of which
around three hundred copies, mostly incomplete, remain.

Whatever the way he participated in the production of a
vernacular Bible, it was a key moment in the history of Christianity
in Britain and Ireland. For this was a text that would make the

Scriptures accessible, if not to the largely illiterate masses, certainly to those in the growing artisan class with sufficient learning to read. They would be able to use the texts, Wycliffe believed, to hold up a mirror to the activities of the Church and the failings of its clerical leadership.

Among the most enthusiastic backers of an English Bible were the Lollards. It was central to their ongoing quest through travelling preachers to bring the Scriptures to a wider audience outside the confines (as they saw them) of parish churches. As had been the case with Wycliffe, some in the ruling class, especially in Parliament, had initially made a show of embracing Lollard arguments so as to advance their own attempts to rein in the power of the Church. But the range of challenges Lollardy presented – in addition to the English Bible, they questioned the Eucharist, baptism, the value of pilgrimages and the cult of saints – pushed them beyond the pale in the early years of the fifteenth century.

In 1401, at the behest of the new King, Henry IV, son of John of Gaunt and the first of the Lancastrians on the throne, a statute was passed to punish those who expressed 'wicked, heretical and erroneous opinions' with burning at the stake. Lollards were the target, and the first to suffer was one of their number, Sir John Oldcastle, soldier and scholar, arrested and convicted in 1414. He briefly escaped from the Tower of London to mount a revolt, but was recaptured. Despite his friendship with the new King, Henry V, who had succeeded his father in 1413, he was consigned to the flames.

Lollard arguments based on Wycliffe's ideas did, however, go on to influence European reformers, especially Jan Hus of Bohemia, who was condemned to be burnt at the stake for heresy by Church leaders from across Europe meeting at the Council of Constance in 1414 (They had promised him safe conduct to get him to attend.) Hus's example, in turn, inspired an obscure German monk, Martin Luther. In 1517, his publication of the

Ninety-five Theses – nailed, legend has it, like the Lollard Twelve Conclusions, to the door of his local church – was to tear apart Catholic Europe.

There is an unmissable echo between Luther's arguments about the primacy of Scripture, the need for a vernacular Bible and the corruption of the institutional Church, its practices, structures and sacraments, and those advanced by Wycliffe 130 years earlier. Over the centuries it has caused some to trace the origins of the almighty upheaval Luther brought to western Christendom back to England and to Wycliffe, and therefore to refer to him as 'the morning star of the Reformation'. He has been variously hailed as the first communist and the original Protestant. All such judgements involve a stretch, but if it was fame – or infamy – that Wycliffe sought, then he has certainly achieved it. He would, I suspect, protest that he was simply an academic telling the truth as he saw it.

Wycliffe's alleged crimes were on the agenda of the Council of Constance, alongside the charges against Jan Hus. He was excommunicated, though the verdict came almost thirty years after he had gone to his grave. In his lifetime in fourteenth-century England, Wycliffe had escaped physical injury despite his outspokenness. In death, he was not so fortunate. Orders were issued that his body should be removed from its final resting place in Lutterworth, burnt and thrown in the local river.

Because of the continuing tensions between Rome and the English crown, this curious, gruesome and ultimately pointless act of revenge couldn't actually be carried out until 1428. 'Thus,' wrote the seventeenth-century historian Thomas Fuller, 'the brook hath conveyed [Wycliffe's] ashes into Avon, Avon into Severn, Severn into the narrow seas, and they into the main ocean. And thus the ashes of Wycliffe are the emblem of his doctrine which now is dispersed the world over.'[8]

The point is well made, but it leaves Wycliffe without a shrine. The key-holder of St Andrew's highlights that absence as I am bidding my farewell to Fillingham. He points to a large monument in the churchyard, its original inscription long ago completely worn away by the weather. It has, he tells me, been unofficially adopted as Wycliffe's final resting place by some of those overseas visitors who turn up, often by the coachload, with guides, and even floral tributes, to see the church that, ironically, Wycliffe so seldom visited himself.

ALSO WITH A STORY TO TELL . . .

Before the Black Death, rising prosperity saw the building in market towns of aspirationally grand churches, such as ST PATRICK'S IN PATRINGTON, EAST YORKSHIRE. The local lord of the manor was the Archbishop of York, and work started at the dawn of the 1300s in the Decorated Gothic style, which favoured more ornamentation than previously (200 carvings of human faces and animals throughout the church), as well as tracery in windows and vaulting in ceilings. Its fifty-five-metre spire caused locals to refer to it as 'the Queen of Holderness'.

The thirteenth-century tower of ST PETER'S AT WALPOLE ST PETER in Norfolk was all that survived floods in the 1330s. Rebuilding came later that century, once the Black Death had abated, again in Decorated Gothic, with an abundance of intricately carved bosses (junctions between ribs in the ceilings). Its size is striking. Fenland soil, even before the area was drained, brought prosperity and an appetite to use that wealth to the greater glory of God. But it is the subtlety of its many details and quirks (including a tunnel under the chancel, to accommodate processions round the tight churchyard) that captivates.

ALFRISTON CLERGY HOUSE IN EAST SUSSEX, now owned by the National Trust, is one of the oldest vicarages in the British Isles. A timber-framed, thatched building dating back to the fourteenth century, it stands next to St Andrew's Church.

CHAPTER 15

The Fifteenth Century

Henry VII's Chapel, Westminster Abbey: Calm Before the Storm

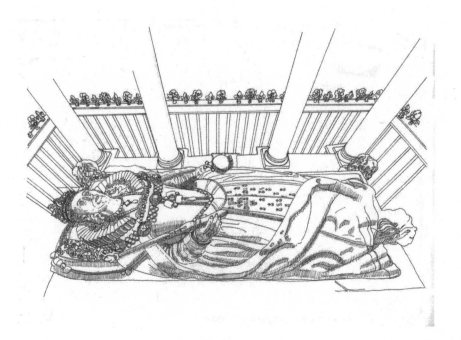

There is not a parish church in the kingdom without crucifixes, candlesticks, censors, patens and silver cups worthy of a cathedral.

An Italian visitor to England in 1497[1]

AFTER THE UNPREDICTABILITY of the fourteenth century, the fifteenth was, for the most part, an extended and welcome period of calm in the life of the Church in Britain and Ireland, even if it co-existed alongside continuing turbulence in the realm of kings, princes and popes. With prosperity and population once again rising as the shadow of the Black Death receded, wealthy wool merchants, burgeoning trades' guilds and a growing and assertive class of educated citizenry in the towns combined to enlarge, embellish and, where necessary, endow new churches that reflected the vibrancy of their communities. The results, outside and in, were elaborate, elegant and enduring in equal measure. Their spires and towers continue to define the skyline of the British countryside to an extent unrivalled anywhere else in Western Europe. Collectively, they speak of late medieval optimism and faith in God. Though the winds of change from Italy blowing in the Christian humanist ideas of the Renaissance were slow to reach the shores of Britain and Ireland, when they did, they brought a contagious and empowering belief in the potential of individuals, through God's grace, to shape their own destinies in this world as well as the next.

Beyond the walls of these new churches, with their vast expanses of clear and coloured glass as favoured by the period's dominant Perpendicular style of Gothic, affairs of court and state singularly failed to find any parallel equilibrium. Just one year before the century had begun, Henry IV, with the support of yet another exiled Archbishop of Canterbury, Thomas Arundel, had brutally usurped his cousin, Richard II, leaving him, according to some accounts, to starve to death in prison.[2]

In the first decade of the fifteenth century, Owain Glyndŵr's failed rising in Wales showed that it was by no means settled in its status as part of the English crown. Meanwhile the Hundred Years' War with France dragged on, at intervals, until 1453, draining the treasury and distracting kings and nobles. Even the high point of the English victory at Agincourt in 1415 – thanks to the intervention of winged, heavenly bowmen, it was reported, setting off a trend for decorating church roofs with angels[3] – did not prevent the final ignominy of defeat, with Henry VI's claim to the throne of France sunk as his army was driven into the English Channel. Only the foothold of Calais remained to him.

Such a crushing disappointment should have exhausted the appetite for conflict. Instead, it fuelled the War of the Roses, a struggle between Henry's Lancastrian branch of the ruling house of Plantagenet and its Yorkist cousins. The large numbers of soldiers returning from France with nothing to employ them were fuel to the fire of dynastic rivalry. Settlement only came in 1485 with the death of the Yorkist Richard III at Bosworth Field. The accession, in his place, as Henry VII, of Henry Tudor from the Lancastrian branch saw him take Elizabeth of York as his queen. He was by instinct a unifier, and his successful reign ultimately saw an extension of the control exerted by the Crown at the expense of the nobility. Finally, if unspectacularly, Henry delivered the feeling of security and good order that his subjects had long been enjoying in their churches, and for which so many had long been craving in those who ruled them.

Haggling with the papacy over senior appointments in the Church rumbled on throughout the century, but the flourishing of the local church and the parish network took some of the sting of resentment out of this. The Pope may have named as absentee bishops his own Italian favourites – such as Silvestro de' Gigli to

Worcester from 1497 to 1521 – in preference to better-qualified, native-born men, but the lack of oversight the bench of bishops as a whole exercised in their dioceses (subcontracted to vicar-generals and assistant bishops, who in some cases also held Irish appointments) only empowered local priests and congregations. Often led by newly assertive Churchwardens, they made their own decisions.

In the same way, the great abbeys and friaries, which had previously sent their monks to run the many parishes they controlled, were in decline and their hold was weakening. The high point of monastic institutions had passed, with vocations falling and their formerly close connection with their orders' (often French) mother houses on the continent forcefully severed during the Hundred Years' War. In the most practical terms, they lacked the manpower to run their own parishes and were grateful that the local community was able to step in, just as long as no one imagined they were equally willing to surrender their ownership of vast swathes of land around the country.

A fog of decay and decline descended on many of these religious houses. Some of the smaller ones closed – including the twelfth-century Augustinian Creake Priory (later Abbey) in North Norfolk, where first fire in 1483 and then an outbreak of sweating sickness in 1506 wiped it out altogether. Those who might in the past have directed a portion of their wealth to endow monasteries or convents, in the hope that their gift would help ease their own passage to heaven, were in the fifteenth century increasingly endowing institutions that were both religious and educational. Margaret Beaufort, heiress and mother of Henry VII, into whose hands the lands of Creake Abbey passed when it closed, founded both Christ's College and St John's College in Cambridge in the years immediately before her death in 1509.

The Black Death itself may no longer have been posing such an immediate threat as it had in the previous century, but the widespread fear that death might strike at any moment remained visceral, especially among those at the bottom of the pile. Such anxiety fostered an approach to faith throughout the medieval period that emphasised the real and ever-present danger of eternal punishment in hell, or at the very least before getting into heaven, a long stretch in the antechamber of purgatory (which had become part of doctrine in the twelfth century).

For those with means, there were options other than making gifts to monasteries and colleges. The fifteenth century saw the proliferation of chantries – chapels that were either built on private land or housed in separated-off areas of churches large and small. They had their own altars and were served by their own designated priest or priests, employed out of the endowment and tasked daily with offering prayers and saying Mass for the souls of the dead donor and his or her relatives. The money could fund a 'perpetual' chantry, with, as the name suggests, the prayers going on for as long as it took, or – if the donors' pockets were not quite so deep – a designated chantry for a set period, typically between one and ten years.

These proved popular arrangements. Funds flooded in on an unprecedented scale to the English parish churches that incorporated chantries into their floor plans. The money stoked a fifteenth-century building boom. Some of the grandest chantries were found within cathedrals, where competition arose among those who could pay for the most lavish decorations, ornate carvings and splendid vestments to be worn by their attached priests. By 1500, York Minster is said to have housed fifty-six perpetual chantries, while St Paul's in London had as many as eighty. In the larger towns, churches would have rows of these chantry chapels lined up along the aisles and close to their main altars.

Many of the clergy who served in them received a decent wage for relatively light duties, plus accommodation in the chantry house nearby that sometimes came with the post. They were exempt from the authority of the parish priest or the local bishop, and could, if they wished, make the minimum of effort. Yet many did more than their required tasks by offering a helping hand in supporting the wider parish too. This was especially true of those who served in more meagerly endowed chantries, who would routinely supplement their wages by taking on teaching roles.

At the time, some questioned these chantry arrangements as favouring the few over the many and distracting the Church and its clergy from the principal role of serving everyone in the parish. Dissent, though, was muted, thanks to draconian heresy laws that came into being at the start of the century to silence the Lollards. And there is a positive case to be made for chantries as the century went forward. First, they increased the availability of education. When the chantries were later outlawed in 1545 by Henry VIII, having initially survived his earlier raid on monasteries, some of them opted to continue their teaching mission by reopening as grammar schools. Several examples are still around today, named after the new King from 1547, Edward VI.

Second, chantries encouraged active involvement in a parish church by a wider range than hitherto of the well-to-do and the educated laity. The living relatives of those who had endowed a chantry had an obvious stake in seeing that the church where it was located was properly run. These busy, bustling, local churches could, with some justification, be held up as truly in touch with everyday life, rooting the Church as a solid presence in every corner of the land, spiritually and physically. In the following century, Thomas More, distinguished lawyer, Christian humanist and statesman, was to write admiringly that, in learning and honesty, English parish churches were 'well able to match, number for number, the spirituality of any nation Christian'.[4]

Against this backdrop, work began in 1503 in Westminster Abbey on the Henry VII Lady Chapel. The cult of the Virgin Mary, which had grown powerful in the medieval Church all across Europe despite her meagre appearances in the Gospels, had prompted Henry III in the thirteenth century to add a Lady Chapel at the eastern end of the Abbey as part of a more general rebuilding. It was now to be replaced with a new, more magnificent structure, money no object, that Henry VII intended should give legitimacy to his own kingship, which had started out in such contested circumstances. When he died six years later, the chapel that now bears his name had not yet been completed, but it is impossible to believe he wouldn't have been pleased by the result. When it was unveiled in 1516, the contemporary historian, poet and court favourite John Leland hailed it as '*orbis miraculum*', or 'a wonder of the world'.

As a statement of the power of faith to elevate the fifteen kings and queens who rest in it, including Henry, his wife and his mother, Margaret Beaufort (who had given birth to him as the thirteen-year-old widow of Edmund Tudor, half-brother of Henry VI), it simply cannot be bettered. The Abbey as a whole has so many other eye-catching architectural features and connections to British history: Nicholas Hawksmoor's unmistakeable great West Towers at the entrance; the Tomb of the Unknown Warrior; Poets' Corner; and the Edward the Confessor Chapel.

For all this, the chapel that awaits me at the furthest point of my walk through the Abbey is the spot that takes my breath away. Its tall windows are filled with jewel-like stained glass. Elsewhere, Tudor emblems of rose and portcullis in stone are liberally scattered around. The mighty tombs and monuments resonate permanence and majesty. But the chapel's undoubted glory is its spectacular fan-vaulted ceiling, with elaborately carved hanging pendants, apparently staying up miraculously in defiance of earthly gravity as they reach down as if from the clouds of heaven.

This last great masterpiece of Perpendicular Gothic is a testament to the genius of the late medieval period, just as it was being overtaken by the arrival in England of the classical symmetry and order that characterised the Renaissance approach to church (and other) building. As if to capture perfectly the changes afoot, when it came to commissioning a tomb for his father and mother, their son and heir, Henry VIII, chose the Renaissance Florentine sculptor, Pietro Torrigiano, a contemporary, friend and sometime rival of Michelangelo. The result, in black marble, with the two recumbent figures in gilt bronze, both with hands joined and raised in prayer, their robes falling in natural folds around them, has pride of place in the chapel.

The combination of Perpendicular architecture and Renaissance sculpture illustrates a point in history when so much was in flux: the transition from one reign to another, from one century to another, from the late medieval to the early modern, and from the calm development of the Church in England over the fifteenth century to the traumas and tragedies that were to overwhelm it in the sixteenth. There are here, too, down both sides of the chapel the tombs of Henry and Elizabeth's grandchildren, the children of Henry VIII: Edward VI, Mary and Elizabeth. The last two, half-sisters, share a final resting place in the north aisle, where the effigy of Elizabeth with a great ruff, her hand clutching the orb and sceptre of majesty, manages to eclipse Mary in death as she did in life. And then, by what surely can be no accident, in the opposite corner of the chapel, that sense of drama continuing to play out in death is heightened by the huge, lavish canopy tomb of Mary, Queen of Scots, great-granddaughter of Henry VII. The lion of Scotland is at her feet in a monument erected by her son, James VI of Scotland, who became James I of England on Elizabeth's death in 1603. The son who hardly saw his mother in life wanted to celebrate her in death and reclaim her place in this Tudor pantheon.

In bridging the fifteenth, sixteenth and even seventeenth centuries, the Henry VII Chapel provides a perspective not available as the actual events they describe unfurled. Mary, Queen of Scots' first resting place, after her execution on Elizabeth's orders in 1587, was in Peterborough Cathedral, while in life she and her cousin never once shared the same room.[5]

And so, at this crucial moment in the history of Christianity in Britain and Ireland, our strict matching of Church events to a century-by-century structure must be extended by a few decades into the 1500s to accommodate the smooth flow of the story.

On becoming King of England in April 1509 at the age of seventeen, Henry VIII was in many ways a conventional Catholic. What he did over the course of a reign of almost forty years, however, was to unpick the settled nature of the relationship between the Crown, national Church and papacy that had been in place since the Synod of Whitby in the seventh century. What came in the later decades is all the more surprising since, in his early days of power, he was more publicly faithful to the papacy than many of his predecessors had ever been. In 1521, he weighed in with a polished piece of Catholic polemic in defence of the Church's traditional list of seven sacraments and of the Pope's authority, both under ever-more-vicious and ever-more-popular attack by the German reformer, Martin Luther, and his supporters. Leo X was so pleased that he rewarded Henry with the title *Fidei Defensor*, Defender of the Faith, still used by English monarchs to this day.

It is rumoured that Henry's text had been written, at least in part, by his great friend, the scholarly Thomas More, but this was a king who prided himself on his own theological learning. And the profound loathing he had of Luther's arguments as a result is to be found running through in its pages. Yet Henry's own inherited concept of kingship as divinely instituted – so powerfully expressed in the Henry VII Chapel by his father – simultaneously caused him to regard the Church and its domestic leaders as in practice under his command rather than the Pope's.

The young, good-looking, energetic, breath-of-fresh-air King was an egotist to the core. In his early years he achieved his ends by persuasion and charm. Later, when those qualities had paled and he had grown impatient, he got results by tyranny and blood-letting. In whatever sphere of life he was operating, he expected to have his own way. His dealings with the Church were no exception. He alone would choose those who was to be appointed to high office – often simultaneously spiritual and political – and he would tell them what to do.

As his Archbishop of Canterbury and Lord Chancellor, Henry had inherited from his father William Warham, the son of a tenant farmer. Loyal to the Crown, having first entered royal service under Henry VI as a diplomat, Warham gave up his politi-cal office in 1515 to make room for Thomas Wolsey, who was Henry's own man. Wolsey was quickly loaded with preferment and power, acting as de facto head of the Church as Archbishop of York, his senior status confirmed when he was named a cardi-nal. In post, Wolsey enthusiastically carried out Henry's wishes to neuter the bench of bishops, and to make the institution they led subservient to the Crown.

Though he continued for two decades as Archbishop of Canterbury, Warham accepted without much protest playing second fiddle to Wolsey. When summoned into the spotlight in 1527 because Henry wanted to discard his first wife, Catherine of Aragon, as she could not give him a son, Warham did as the King wished and wrote to Pope Clement VII to urge the annulment of the marriage he himself had carried out in 1509.

After that request was refused – the Pope was virtually a prisoner in Rome of Catherine's favourite nephew, Charles V of Spain, the Holy Roman Emperor – Henry set about severing links with Rome via a series of bills that passed through a compliant Parliament between 1532 and 1534. The final one, the Succession Act, brought in an oath of loyalty to the King and new arrangements for the Church in England. To refuse would be to commit high treason, punishable by death, as Thomas More, the King's old friend, and Bishop John Fisher of Rochester found to their cost.

Warham took no such stand in defence of principle when, in 1531, by now an old man, he gave way once again, this time to Henry's insistence that the King be acknowledged by all clerics as Supreme Head of the Church in England. There was, however, a caveat added, with the words, 'as far as the law of Christ allows'. Warham did not live to see how little they meant in practice. The following year he was dead.

His replacement, Thomas Cranmer, needed no get-out clauses in his commitment to Henry's Reformation. His challenge was not to restrain the King, but – as a Protestant, often in league with Thomas Cromwell, his chief minister from 1534, and charged with dealing in Church matters – to push him on to take the Reformation further. It proved a struggle. Having begun a Reformation, Henry had only intermittent appetite thereafter to see a constitutional and political change develop into something close to the new Protestantism on the continent which he still distrusted.

The Ten Articles, agreed in 1536, had gone a good deal of the way to just such an outcome, to the dismay of many conservatives, but by 1539 Henry had changed his mind on them. They were replaced by the Six Articles, which endorsed the continuing validity of Catholic doctrines that Protestants rejected – including clerical celibacy. Cranmer had hastily to spirit away his wife, Margarete, the niece of a prominent German Reformer he had married in 1532 while on a visit to Nuremberg. Soon afterwards he lost his closest ally, Cromwell, who paid with his life in 1540 after Henry blamed him for his fourth disastrous marriage to the German princess, Anne of Cleves.

For all his instinct to stop the Reformation in its tracks once he had disposed of his first marriage and become Supreme Head of the Church in England, Henry nevertheless continued to benefit from the practical rewards of the upheavals he had set in motion. The Dissolution of the Monasteries, led by Cromwell between 1536 and 1540, saw their great wealth and landholdings transferred over to fill the coffers of the Crown. In many cases, now-redundant buildings were handed out to royal favourites to make homes and fortunes. Some became parish churches. Others were left to crumble, overnight deemed symbols of a bygone age.

What is most remarkable about Henry in the years between 1530 and his death in 1547 is how he managed to transform the life of the Church with so little opposition. The only halfway serious challenge came with the Pilgrimage of Grace in October of 1536. Taking its cue from a small uprising earlier that year in Lincolnshire, it started in Yorkshire and then spread to Lancashire and Cumbria. Protestors included local gentry, their tenants and the new class of townsfolk. All were united in opposition to what was happening to the Church. When they entered York, they showed their colours by allowing nuns and monks who had been evicted from their convents and abbeys to return to them. Yet their essential demand for a return to the established order in ecclesiastical matters was shot through, too, with economic anxieties (the previous harvest had been poor and hunger was widespread) and personal animosity to Henry's lieutenants, notably Cromwell and Cranmer. In the popular mind, these two were extreme Protestants leading the King astray. The rebellion was put down, and its leaders arrested and executed.

If the autocratic older Henry had little tolerance for those who valued more than he did the link with Rome, neither did he take kindly to those citizens who were too energetic in wanting to journey in the opposite direction towards embracing the tenets of Lutheranism (Protestantism was not a word Luther ever used or liked). He feared that what he regarded as an extreme version of Christianity would seed all too easily in a land already prepared for such dissent by the Lollards and Wycliffe a century before.

The English scholar William Tyndale, who, inspired by Wycliffe and Luther, had worked to produce his own translation of the Bible into English in the 1520s, was one target. When he wrote that Henry's annulment of his first marriage violated Scripture, the King struck. Tyndale had to flee for his life to Brussels. By a cruel irony, he fell foul of the Catholic authorities there, was arrested and executed in 1536 on the order of the Holy Roman Emperor, an ally of the Pope. Yet for all Henry's distaste for Tyndale, in 1539, just months after the Six Articles Act, he allowed the publication of an English translation of the Bible based heavily on Tyndale's work. By 1541, a version was mandatory for all churches.

What, though, did those in the towns and parishes far from the court in London make of Henry and what he had set in motion in the Church? The wars of the previous century had created an appetite for forceful leadership, which meant they were predisposed to tolerate a lot from a king they regarded as capable of taking charge. Henry was particularly astute at playing on that. Security and order depended on having a male heir, he and his courtiers insisted, as he manoeuvred to have his marriage to Catherine annulled after she had failed to produce one. And anyway, they pointed out, playing on their listeners' faith, Henry had confessed his sin in agreeing to marry Catherine in the first place, she being the widow of his older brother and therefore in theory forbidden to him as a wife. Though the Pope at the time, Julius II, had given a special dispensation from this rule, the lack of a surviving son was presented as punishment for a union that offended God.

Relying on a residual anti-papal feeling at large in the population, Henry's lieutenants could also reliably present a corrupt, overbearing papacy as the real problem getting in the way of the King taking a new bride. And, in the same vein, existing anticlerical sentiments ensured a good reception for official suggestions that the vast wealth and land holdings of some 2,000 monasteries, the legacy of an earlier age, had made them bloated obstacles to progress and prosperity.

The fact that some of these claims cut across the realities of everyday life did not in the end seem to count for much. Catherine of Aragon had been popular, certainly in death in 1536, when she was widely mourned. And almost half of the monasteries and convents that were closed to benefit the King had operated in some form or measure as hospitals, so their loss would be keenly felt by those who relied on them.

Despite all this, the changes were accepted in the parishes, though the upheaval was mitigated for practical reasons. A proportion of the redundant monks simply moved over and served as parish clergy. In those cathedrals that were in the care of monastic orders, there were instances of the prior simply taking on a new title as dean when the establishment had to become a secular (rather than monastic) chapter. And those other monks, friars and nuns? They seem to have been silently absorbed, leaving behind little sign of any fuss for subsequent generations to pick over.

The shrines they once watched over were suddenly gone. The greatest medieval shrine of all in the country, Walsingham in Norfolk, was left in ruins – the 'lonely arch' all that remains today of its abbey, now found in the garden of the local stately home. Relics that once had drawn crowds because of claims that they had miraculous powers now commanded an audience when they were exposed as frauds. The Holy Rood of Boxley Abbey in Kent was a crucifix where the eyes and lips of Jesus appeared to move. It had once attracted even the young Henry VIII. In 1538, it was revealed by the local Bishop of Rochester, Henry's chosen successor to the martyred John Fisher, to be a mechanism with invisible strings. It was taken to London where a crowd gathered to witness its burning.

Yet for many faithful believers in their village, town or city church, even with its chantries now unmanned, the pattern of their religious life and their essential beliefs about God's grace and mercy remained as they had always been: the example of the saints; the consolation of the liturgy; and the sense of how very easy it was to fall into sinful ways, or be tempted to sup with the Devil. These essentials would take much more than a king's whim to disrupt. Quite how the Reformation made that happen belongs to the larger remaining portion of the sixteenth century, and the next chapter.

ALSO WITH A STORY TO TELL . . .

KING'S COLLEGE CHAPEL, CAMBRIDGE, is one of the finest examples of the Perpendicular in church architecture in the country, with its huge windows, abundance of light, and the grace and delicacy of its stonework. Started by Henry VI in 1446 and completed by Henry VII on either side of the Wars of the Roses, its founding vision included boy choristers from poor families.

ST PETER AND ST PAUL, LAVENHAM, was built – or rebuilt – in the fifteenth-century heyday of this Suffolk town, when it was one of the richest in Britain on account of the cloth trade. Among the principal donors was local landowner John de Vere, Earl of Oxford, commander of Henry VII's army. He wanted the church to celebrate Henry's victory at Bosworth Field. It is one of the last churches finished before the Reformation.

ST GILES, HOLME, north of Newark, is typical of the fashion in the fifteenth century to renovate and embellish existing churches to reflect the status of a town's wealthy merchants. In this case, John Barton, who had made his money in wool and died in 1491, lies beside his wife Isabella next to the chancel that is lit by the large Perpendicular windows installed as part of his bequest, amid an array of carved treasures, including the screen and bench ends of angels, dogs and birds.

CHAPTER 16

The Sixteenth Century

St Giles Cathedral, Edinburgh: The Reformation Spreads

Remember that the theatre of the world is wider than the realm of England.

Mary, Queen of Scots (before her judges, 1586)

I CAN'T HELP WONDERING what John Knox would make of his life-size statue standing against the north wall of the nave of St Giles Cathedral in Edinburgh's Old Town, sometimes referred to as 'the mother church of world Presbyterianism'. The details certainly do justice to what we know of the firebrand preacher and leading light of the Scottish Reformation. In his left hand he grips the Bible – the *Sola Scriptura* that, according to him and his fellow Protestant reformers across Europe from Luther onwards, was the only basis for discerning how to live a truly Christian life. Knox's forefinger is leafing through the pages, as if to find a pithy quote to use from the pulpit to damn the ungodly, unscriptural corruption he saw in the behaviour of the papacy, the bishops of his national Church or his Catholic monarch, Mary, Queen of Scots, to whom he refused to bend even an inch in their repeated clashes.

Most arresting, though, is how the sculptor has reproduced Knox's famously direct gaze. It almost beams out from the statue's deeply drilled irises, as compelling as it is (almost) alarming. But that is not what is most troubling about the statue. It is something more fundamental. Knox is on the record time after time as decrying the presence of any statues in churches, regarding them as akin to the graven images condemned in Scripture, in the Ten Commandments. When he became Minister of St Giles in 1559, it took a full nine days to clear all signs that this had once been a Catholic church, or a 'puddle of papistry' as he referred to the Church of Rome.[1] Statues, stained glass and silver were removed.

Some fifty stone subsidiary altars, each with its own sets of vestments and silverware, were destroyed, pillars were painted green and walls were whitewashed before the texts of the Lord's Prayer and the Ten Commandments were inscribed onto them.

Knox's arrival in the church that stands today on the Royal Mile was accompanied by a mob of his supporters. His seizure of it for the Protestant cause did not go uncontested. Soldiers loyal to the Crown and Catholicism took it back briefly in November of that year and it was even reconsecrated. The Reform movement in which Knox was influential was, however, ultimately to triumph the following year, when in August the Scottish Parliament formally voted to end the authority of the Pope and ban the Catholic Mass. Thereafter, the new pulpit Knox had installed in the south east end of St Giles – no longer part of the building today – was his and his alone as a Reformation gathered pace that was separate from, but inextricably linked to, the English one.

Such a legacy gave rise to confused feelings about any statue of Knox. For more than three hundred years following his death in 1572, there was no memorial at all in St Giles to the man who had been its minister for twelve years. Only in the second half of the nineteenth century was any serious proposal made for one. Today's statue was installed in 1906, close to where it stands now, but it was originally placed in a Gothic niche with a canopy over it, to blend in with the architecture of the rest of the building, much of which dates back to 1390 and an extensive renovation following an attempt by the English under Richard II during a raid into Scotland to burn it to the ground.

In the 1950s, Knox's statue was moved to make way for a war memorial, and in 1965 it ended up outdoors in the square in front of St Giles. When the inclement weather started to damage it, it was allowed back indoors in 1983, but there is a slightly begrudging undercurrent to its presence.

Though it is today at the very heart of the Protestant Church of Scotland, St Giles does not exactly trumpet the details of the Scottish Reformation. A nineteenth-century makeover stripped the walls back to their reddish stone and restored stained glass to its windows. There may be the occasional memorial to those who brought about the Reformation – the Earl of Moray, a staunch friend of Knox among the Scottish nobility, is recalled in the Holy Blood Aisle – yet a walk around its precincts does not, perhaps by design, bring back to life the drama and the intrigue of those decades in the middle of the sixteenth century when a popular rebellion overthrew the established Church. Even one of the names by which it is popularly known today – St Giles Cathedral (others call it the High Kirk of Edinburgh) – is curiously misleading, as another thing for which Knox campaigned fiercely and (posthumously) successfully was that the Church of Scotland should go forward without bishops, governed instead on the Calvinist model by assemblies, church sessions and elders, or 'presbyters' (hence Presbyterianism). No bishops should in theory mean no cathedrals, but not here.

Though English kings claimed overlordship and repeatedly invaded, Scotland largely charted its own course in the centuries following the landmark Synod of Whitby, slower than others further south to accept the rulings of the Pope in Rome, but eventually to assert its independent relationship with the papacy. Regular conflicts on either side of the border, sometimes flaring up into more substantial wars and periods of occupation, revealed that the destinies of Scotland and England, politically and spirituality, were inseparable.

Following the Norman Conquest, as we have seen, William the Conqueror had ambitions to extend his kingdom into Scotland. To that end, he claimed for the Archbishop of Canterbury authority over the bishops and Church there, too. And, indeed, his first archbishop, Lanfranc, was greatly respected by Scottish prelates. In 1070 he sent monks to establish a new Benedictine abbey at Dunfermline. But the diocesan structure that developed in Scotland was proudly independent of Canterbury. Throughout the twelfth century, the Archbishops of York tried to assert their rights over the Scottish bishops (including the right to consecrate them after they were chosen by the Pope). There was a flimsy historical pretext for this power grab, York having been the ecclesiastical centre of the early Northumbrian kingdom that spread into southern Scotland, as well as that of Anglo-Saxon Bernicia that stretched from the River Tees to the River Forth in central Scotland. It was left to Pope Celestine III in 1192 to resolve the dispute, declaring in his papal bull *Cum universi* that the dioceses of St Andrews, Glasgow, Dunkeld, Dunblane, Brechin, Moray, Ross and Caithness had a separate relationship with him as 'a special daughter'.

Such parental care did not extend to allowing for a leader among these bishops, meaning that the Scottish Crown could adopt divide-and-rule tactics in its relationship with the various Church prelates in its lands. St Andrews and Glasgow had to wait until the fifteenth century to get their own archbishops, with St Andrews finally taking up the primacy. Yet even this was compromised, since the Bishop of Galloway, in the south west, based in Ninian's Whithorn, remained under the authority of York.

The relationship between the Scottish monarchs and the Church was as close and complicated as in England. In both realms, it was the Crown that encouraged and facilitated the arrival of newer religious orders. At the start of the twelfth century, Alexander I, known as The Fierce, sponsored the first Augustinian priory at Scone in Perthshire. It housed the Stone of Scone, sometimes called the Stone of Destiny, an oblong block of pale-yellow sandstone used in the coronation of Scottish kings until it was seized as spoils of war in 1296 by the English King, Edward I, and placed in Westminster Abbey.

With papal authority weakened in the fourteenth century during the exile of the popes in Avignon, the balance of power in Church appointments in Scotland came thereafter to rest firmly with the Crown. For the Church, there was compensation in that it accumulated as gifts and endowments, often from the King, great tracts of land throughout Scotland. In 1556, a report sent to Pope Paul IV suggested that almost half the revenue of the whole Scottish kingdom came to the Church.[2] Such riches were accompanied by the same sort of corruption that beset the English Church of the same period. In 1504, James IV named his illegitimate eleven-year-old son, Alexander, as Archbishop of St Andrews, though it ultimately benefited neither of them since Alexander died alongside his father at the hands of the English in 1513 at the Battle of Flodden in Northumbria.

The wealth of the Scottish Church was grist to the mill of the Reform movement that emerged in the early decades of the sixteenth century. It also decried the Church's liturgical practices, its attachment to the papacy, its enthusiasm for Latin and the seven sacraments, and – explaining in some measure its popularity – the failure of clerics properly to care for the poor. The landed estates of the Church were deeply resented by some Scottish barons. For them, a break with Rome would be an opportunity to extend their own holdings. And for many young priests, such as Andrew Johnston, one of the chaplains at St Giles in the 1530s who was condemned as a heretic and forced to go into exile, there was frustration that they were left with few clerical opportunities because as many as 80 per cent of parishes in Scotland were in the gift of monastic houses. At the end of the fourteenth century that had even been the status of St Giles, under the control of Scone Abbey. While the young priests struggled to find posts, what John Knox referred to as 'a greedy pack'[3] of lazy, corrupt clerical placemen, loose in their morals, monopolised what openings there were, despite living with scant regard for the requirements of Scripture.

These accusations filled the anticlerical and anti-papal pamphlets circulated by the Reformers. They had learnt from Martin Luther's Reform movement in Germany how developments in mass printing in the previous century could be harnessed to the rapid spread of dissenting views. If the words in such cheap, often single-sheet publications were carefully chosen to be simple to read (aloud by the only just literate when they were sharing them with the illiterate), they were accompanied by crude illustrations to get their point over. In such a fashion, popular resentment built and gave momentum to the drive for change.

Few were better at inciting public discontent than John Knox. Details of his upbringing are vague. In the late 1530s he is said to have trained as a priest in St Andrews, Scotland's premier ecclesiastical centre, home at the time to Cardinal David Beaton, a staunch defender of the status quo. The city's Catholic leaders had already seen off the efforts of an earlier wave of reformers, inspired in the 1520s by Luther, and increasingly in the 1530s by the changes being made under Henry VIII in England. One of the leading voices for the new Protestantism had been Patrick Hamilton, Abbot of Fearn in Ross-shire in the north, who had travelled to Luther's Wittenberg. On his return home, he spoke out for Lutheran principles and in defence of his new wife, but in 1528 was found guilty of heresy by a Church council in St Andrews and burnt at the stake.

In his early days in St Andrews, Knox appears to have been conventionally Catholic in his views. The King, James V, was as unconvinced by Luther's theses as Henry VIII, his uncle, and blocked any progress. His death in 1542, though, enabled the Protestant tide to rise again. His heir was his six-day-old daughter, Mary, now Queen of Scots. The regent, the Earl of Arran, was pro-English and – like others of the noble class – taken by the arguments of Protestantism of Europe.

The following year, a translation of the Bible in the vernacular was allowed, despite opposition from Cardinal Beaton. To seal the bond with the English, it was agreed in that same year, in the Treaty of Greenwich, to betroth the infant Scottish queen to Henry VIII's six-year-old son and heir, the future Edward VI. Their eventual marriage promised a shared Reformed future with the unity of the two Crowns. Appalled, the pro-Catholic forces in Scotland rallied, with the support of Mary's widowed mother, Mary of Guise, whose family had considerable influence at the royal court of Catholic France. They favoured instead a Catholic union, with the Scottish queen set to marry the Dauphin, the future Francis II.

The two camps fought it out over the next six years, a period known as the 'rough wooing' because English forces harried the Scots so as to strong-arm them into sticking to their promise about Mary's betrothal to Prince Edward. In 1544, English forces reached Edinburgh, and once again set fire to its buildings. In defence, the regent stationed gunners in the tower of St Giles.

By 1549, the English had been driven off, with the help of French troops. Mary Queen of Scots was now promised in marriage to the Dauphin Francis, fourteen months her junior. She was to be educated in France, while her mother would stay behind in Scotland, eventually as regent, to protect both the alliance and the Catholic Church.

It was during this troubled period over the future of Scotland's queen and its Church that Cardinal Beaton in 1546 condemned to death another prominent Reformer, George Wishart — by all accounts a gentle man of deep Protestant faith who criss-crossed the country as a travelling preacher. He was to be hanged and burnt at the stake for heresy. Beaton was already not a popular man with many Scottish nobles, some of whom were favourable to the Protestant cause, others disliking his vanity and resenting his influence. They feared he wanted to make their country a province of France and to keep the riches of the Church under his control. Wishart's death galvanised them into an act of savagery.

They broke into the castle in St Andrews, murdered the Cardinal and put his mutilated body on public display.

It proved to be a rallying cry. A large group of Protestants took control of the city and held on to it for fourteen months against royal forces, hoping all the time that Henry VIII in England, whom they saw as their natural ally, would send troops to relieve them. But he was to die the following year, and instead it was a French fleet that crushed their revolt.

During those months of siege, John Knox came into his own as a chaplain to the rebels. His sermons made his name celebrated among those who shared his beliefs. When the French rounded up the vanquished, they took Knox off along with the other leaders to stand trial. He was condemned to serve as a galley slave for life, but help was at hand. After eighteen months' hard labour, thanks to an intervention by Edward VI, who in 1547 had become King of England, Knox was released into the custody of the English.

The Protestant advisors around Edward, keen to destabilise the situation on the border with Scotland to their advantage, sent Knox off on a provocative tour of the far north of England, distributing Protestant texts. In 1551, after spending time in Berwick and Newcastle, he was recalled to court. Turning down an offer to become Bishop of Rochester – such episcopal titles would be redundant in the new Church he envisaged – he chose instead to serve as royal chaplain. His rise came to an abrupt halt in 1553 when Edward died and was succeeded by his half-sister, Mary Tudor, a Catholic determined to turn back the clock on the Reformation. Knox, who had described her as a 'wicked English Jezebel', headed for safety in Europe.

His next six years were spent in Geneva, centre of the new Protestantism in Europe. There he mixed with Ulrich Zwingli and John Calvin, heirs to Luther's Reformation, both keen to go beyond those parts of Catholic tradition that Luther had retained (including bishops). Knox admired their innovations and planned for a time when the laity in Scotland would, like their continental cousins, have much more power than in the hierarchical, clerical structures of Catholicism.

He returned home for a few months in 1555, to test the temperature, and could see events were once more on the move. As regent, Mary of Guise had allowed a degree of toleration of Protestantism, in the hope of drawing its fire. It had had the opposite effect, however, emboldening its advocates. Opposition to French rule coupled with the practices and privileges of the Catholic Church increased the more people were exposed to Protestant ideas. In December 1557, a group of nobles, known as the Lords of the Congregation and including the Earls of Argyll, Glencairn and Morton, joined forces on a covenant that demanded reform. It in turn encouraged local groups of like-minded Protestants meeting in 'privy kirks', secret churches, to promote the new ideas, all the time maintaining the appearance of conformity to Catholicism on Sundays.

In such a volatile situation, the marriage of Mary, Queen of Scots, to the French Dauphin in 1558 further deepened divisions. So much so that, in the spring of 1559, John Knox felt the time had come to return home permanently. One of his earliest sermons after arriving back, that May in Perth, had as its theme Jesus driving the corrupt moneylenders out of the Temple.[4] His hearers took the Gospel story literally and set off round the city, stripping out statues and artworks from the latter-day temples that were churches. When royal troops, sent by Mary of Guise, failed to quell the riots, the rebellion spread to Edinburgh and elsewhere. Knox was able to take St Giles and begin to return it, in his view, to being a place of God. French assistance was needed to regain control from the rebels that autumn and winter, but a series of deaths left a vacuum. The way suddenly and unexpectedly opened up for a peaceful Scottish Reformation.

In July of 1559, Francis II had become King of France, with Mary, Queen of Scots, as his consort. On their coats of arms, alongside those of Scotland and France, were those of England, now once more separated from Rome following the death of the Catholic Mary Tudor after five years on the throne restoring the link. Those who held that Henry VIII's second marriage to Anne Boleyn had not been sanctioned by the Church regarded the new Queen Elizabeth, the couple's daughter, as illegitimate. The crown rightfully belonged, they argued, to Mary, Queen of Scots, a descendant via a legitimate line of Henry VII. The result of such speculation was that the English suddenly became a lot more interested in the fate of the Scottish Reformers, at precisely the same time as French engagement with troubled Scotland waned following the death of Mary of Guise, the regent, in July of 1560.

As the two interested outside parties, the French and the English in the Treaty of Edinburgh of July 1560 agreed to avoid a conflict and leave the matter to the Scots. Earls, lords, bishops, abbots, and lairds (landowners) gathered in the Scottish Parliament, hitherto a limp, unimportant body, to vote on a Scots' Confession, drafted by John Knox and others. They passed it. They may have been a minority in the land, but their coup meant that Scotland's allegiance with the papacy was decisively broken, and the Catholic Mass outlawed.

By 1562, the General Assembly of the Church of Scotland, set up on Calvinist principles, was able to hold its first meeting, while in the parishes a new system was being introduced, based on another text written by Knox, *The First Book of Discipline*. It covered the reordering of churches, the clearing-out of statues and the positioning of a pulpit in their centre. Bishops were to be replaced by superintendents, priests by ministers (like Knox at St Giles) and a Presbyterian system of local synods, while above them a General Assembly was put in place for the new national Kirk.

Victory, however, was far from assured. In some places bishops simply referred to themselves as superintendents and priests as ministers without changing their views. In others, bishops just remained in post. And in the north, in the Highlands and Islands, least touched by Protestant propaganda and literature, the 'old ways' were remarkably resistant to change. The death in December 1560 of Francis II effectively ended French interest in Scotland, but also meant the return of a Catholic queen to her Protestant nation. As a concession, she was allowed to attend Catholic Mass in private.

There were those around Mary who hoped she might inspire a Catholic fightback. For six years, she played a difficult hand with greater aplomb than many had imagined possible, even trying on occasion to reason with John Knox. It was not her theology but the complications of her second and third marriages, to Lord Darnley and the Earl of Bothwell, with one husband accused of murdering another, that dented her authority and robbed her of popular support. She was forced to abdicate and, in 1567, the new Protestant leadership took her infant son, James VI, from her and had him crowned as King of Scotland.

With no other viable options, Mary went into exile in England, in the care of her cousin Elizabeth. Though many of the details of the Scottish Reformation remained to be resolved, notably over the position of bishops, its direction away from Rome seemed all but secure.

The same could not be said of the English Reformation at the stage where we left it in the previous chapter. When Henry VIII died in 1547, much Catholic practice remained in place, but with the King as Supreme Head of the Church rather than the Pope. His son and successor was a nine-year-old boy, incapable yet of using the powers that Henry had amassed for the Crown in matters of religion. Though himself in many things a Catholic,

Henry had done his best to prepare Edward VI for the challenge. Curiously, given his own views, he had decided that the boy should be schooled by Protestant teachers. He had also carefully assembled a regency council to rule until Edward reached adulthood that was dominated by Reformers, led by the new King's maternal uncle, the Duke of Somerset.

Working hand in hand with Thomas Cranmer as Archbishop of Canterbury, Somerset set about using royal powers to remove conservative bishops, many of whom had been picked by the dead King. Instructions were issued, along Protestant lines, for a first wave of cleansing of churches of anything that might cause 'superstition'. Artworks were taken down and the bells were no longer allowed to ring during Mass. In 1549, a first English Prayer Book, written by Cranmer, was introduced. Its language was every bit as majestic and sombre as the Latin texts it replaced, but it also sought in its content and approach to the major doctrinal disputes to appeal to the broadest audience in what were still divided congregations. That was the carrot. The stick meant that refusal to use it in church services was punishable by imprisonment.

Clergy were now once again allowed to marry, as Luther had advocated. Margarete Cranmer returned to her husband's side in public, while the arrival of a group of distinguished Protestant theologians from Europe at Oxford and Cambridge, including the former Dominican Martin Bucer, who had been among Luther's inner circle, spurred on the pursuit of radical change, even as others found the existing pace too much for them. The 1549 Prayer Book prompted a rising in Devon and Cornwall, which was brutally put down. Meanwhile in Norfolk, in the same year, Kett's Rebellion, mostly a protest at the enclosure of farmland but also acting as a focus for other discontents, revealed a country ill at ease with itself after so much turmoil. That piled pressure on Somerset.

With an empty treasury, he enacted plans Henry had drawn up but not acted upon for the dissolution of the chantries. The justification given was that the proceeds would fund education, but when much of the money raised ended up in royal coffers it only served to anger those who had endowed such chapels to remember their dead relatives. The unpopular Somerset was eased out and replaced by the Earl of Warwick, soon Duke of Northumberland, who continued to develop the reform programme in the young king's name.

A drastically revised Prayer Book emerged in 1552, with the most significant updates around the Communion service, where participants were told no longer to regard the bread and wine as the 'real presence' of Jesus, but rather – as most Protestant Reformers argued (but not Luther) – as part of what was simply a commemoration of his sacrifice. Churches were to be further stripped back of any remaining 'papist' fittings and objects. Stone altars were to be replaced by simple tables, ornate vestments for priests were outlawed, and plates and silver were seized by the government. The following year the 42 Articles, drawn up by Cranmer, defined the Church of England's place as being in the middle ground between Catholicism and the Anabaptists, a new strain of extreme Protestantism coming from the continent.

So much that was so new had had little chance to bed in when Edward died of pneumonia in the winter of 1553, not yet sixteen. Henry VIII and the Church in England had both paid a very high price to have a male Tudor heir, but it all was now in vain as the succession passed to his older daughter by Catherine of Aragon, Mary Tudor. A strong Catholic, she had spent more than half of her thirty-seven years a virtual prisoner. Northumberland tried in vain to exclude her from the throne in favour of the more pliable Lady Jane Grey, a cousin once removed of Edward VI and a great-granddaughter of Henry VII. She was swept aside (and was subsequently tried and executed) as Mary successfully asserted herself as the rightful heir, on grounds of legitimacy and not of religion, which she deliberately played down. Greeted by cheering crowds, she entered London as England's first ever Queen Regnant.

Mary's approach was essentially conservative, but initially not confrontational. The bishops who had been displaced from their dioceses under Edward were brought back, and the reforms enacted in the previous reign were repealed by Acts of Parliament. Clerical celibacy was reimposed, stone altars restored, torn vestments mended. There were even stuttering efforts to revive monasticism, at Westminster Abbey and in a handful of other places, but it was a goal that would have required many years to achieve. All the evidence, however, points to such a tentative return to familiarity going down well at first with her subjects. It might even have carried the day, but for subsequent poor judgements on Mary's part.

By agreeing in haste to marry Philip, the Catholic heir to the Spanish throne, probably because she was anxious to have children, she was obliged to restore formally England's link with the papacy, something she had promised but had carefully avoided actually doing thus far because it would be provocative. Suddenly, all those who had benefited from seized Church lands and closed monasteries had reason to fear that the Queen might be about to deprive them of their ill-gotten gains at the Pope's insistence. Still, there was only one uprising as a result – Wyatt's Rebellion in Kent – which was put down with ease.

Mary tried to navigate round the problems facing her by, in 1554, repealing all laws passed since 1528 *except* the Dissolution of the Monasteries. Guided by Cardinal Reginald Pole, once a favourite of her father and now a keen advocate within Catholicism of the need, as part of a Counter-Reformation, to go some of the way to meeting the demands of Luther, she might yet have survived. Pole replaced Cranmer as Archbishop of Canterbury.

The latter had refused to recant and joined an ever-lengthening line of those, of high and low birth, condemned to burn under new heresy laws. It is estimated that 300 died in this way during Mary's reign.

Many explanations have been offered that try to downplay the personal responsibility in all of this of 'Bloody Mary', as she became known, but that is not how it was seen at the time. She had underestimated the depth of the roots the new Protestantism had already grown. Fear alone was not sufficient to drive some of her subjects back to the old ways. When she then became embroiled in a falling-out between her husband, Philip, and a new anti-Spanish Pope, Paul IV, the transformation in such a short time of Mary's reputation was complete.

Her death in November 1558 (most likely from cancer, though believing that her swollen body was caused by the longed-for pregnancy) was followed within hours by that of Cardinal Pole, a victim of an influenza epidemic. News of their passing saw crowds out again on the streets, this time to cheer her departure from this world.

John Knox would have joined in, had he been in London. In the year of Mary's death he published perhaps his most notorious text, *The First Blast of the Trumpet Against the Monstrous Regiment of Women*. In it he attacked female monarchs, and Mary in particular, arguing with his usual vehemence that rule by women is contrary to the Bible. Had he known how precarious the health of his principal target was, he might have paused to reconsider publication, not out of any embarrassment at such an onslaught against a dying woman, but because her successor on the English throne, on whom the eventual success of the Scottish Reformation rested, was also a woman.

Elizabeth, daughter of Henry VIII and Anne Boleyn, was twenty-five in 1558 and inherited the responsibility for a Reformation that was still delicately poised. During her subsequent forty-three years as Queen, and ever after under the ceaseless scrutiny of historians,

Elizabeth's own private religious inclination on the Catholic-to-Calvin spectrum has remained tricky to pin down. Even in public, in her early years as Queen, she appeared anxious to include as many people as possible in what is called the Elizabethan Settlement that she introduced in 1559.

Left to herself, she is said to have preferred a more Catholic style of worship, but as 'Supreme Governor' of the Church of England – the switch from 'Supreme Head' was significant and enduring – she brought back the Prayer Book of 1552 (more radical than that of 1549, which she could also have chosen). In matters of doctrine, her own instinct was that clerics should be celibate, but her stated policy was to allow them to marry, as long as they weren't based in a cathedral. She made plain that she found long sermons tedious, but during her reign the latest in a long line of reorderings of churches placed renewed emphasis on the pulpit.

What greeted Elizabeth on her accession were three groupings. There were those keen to continue Mary's return to the embrace of Rome. Heavily represented on the bench of bishops, they were also liberally scattered among the nobility in Parliament, and were present, too, across the country, often in deep pockets such as in Lancashire and Norfolk. They were said to include the family of William Shakespeare (and by some accounts the man himself). At the other end of the religious spectrum were those anxious above all to resuscitate the 'progress' towards Protestantism made under Edward VI but forcibly reversed by Mary. They were mostly found among parish clergy as well as exiles returning home from Geneva and Germany, brimming with new ideas. Somewhere in between were the moderates. To judge by her choice of the three Archbishops of Canterbury who served her during her reign, Elizabeth shared this moderation. Two – Matthew Parker and John Whitgift – were firmly in the middle ground.

Yet Elizabeth also had to contend with events she would not have chosen and over which she had no control. At the very start of her reign, as we have seen, she felt obliged as the best in a list of bad options to give shelter to Mary, Queen of Scots, the cousin who had already announced her claim as the (in Catholic terms) legitimate heir to the English throne by including its symbol in her coat of arms while married to the French Dauphin. Despite all efforts to lock her away from outside influence, Mary proved an irresistible draw both to those in England hankering for a Catholic restoration and to powers on the continent intent on teaching the, in their opinion, upstart Elizabeth a lesson. For a quarter of a century, Mary was the subject, knowingly or not, of endless schemes to usurp Elizabeth, including the Northern Rebellion of 1569 that briefly seized Durham Cathedral, and the Throckmorton and Babington Plots of 1586.

Then there was papal pressure, especially after the election in 1566 of the austere and saintly Pius V, who wore the coarse clothing of a friar under his grand robes and was determined to restore papal supremacy over Europe's secular rulers. He excommunicated Elizabeth in 1570, a copy of his judgement smuggled into England and nailed to the door of the Bishop of London's palace.

In the face of such provocation, the English Queen tried to convince herself that her Scottish cousin wasn't complicit in such acts of treason, but finally, reluctantly, allowed herself to be persuaded. This resulted in Mary's execution in February 1587 at Fotheringhay Castle in Northamptonshire. It prompted the despatch of the Spanish Armada the following year. Plans had been laid as early as 1585 to retake England by sea for the Pope and Catholicism, but when the Armada arrived in the English Channel, both the military preparedness of the English and public opinion about Protestantism had been misjudged. It was swiftly defeated by Francis Drake, among others, to national rejoicing.

More severe measures were introduced to constrain remaining Catholics, who now were increasingly regarded as traitors. The compromise that had seen eyes averted to those who continued to seek out the (in theory banned) Catholic Mass on a Sunday no longer held. From 1568, a seminary at Douai in northern France had started to send young priests to replace the dwindling band left over from Mary's reign, who were serving the remaining Catholic community in England, Wales and Scotland, known as 'Recusants'. In grand Catholic houses, such as Oxburgh Hall in Norfolk, then as now home of the Bedingfeld family, they would say Mass in secret chapels and hide in 'priest holes' from those instructed by the Crown to seek them out. It is thought that around eight hundred such priests were smuggled into England by the end of Elizabeth's reign, of whom around 130 were captured and executed, along with sixty lay supporters.

As an outcome, it is hard to reconcile with the approach that Elizabeth took on religion at the start of her reign. The Act of Supremacy of 1559 simply reversed Mary's decision to accept once more papal authority, and required an oath to the monarch as 'Supreme Governor'. It restored matters to where they had been in 1547 when Henry VIII died, though it was accompanied by the Act of Uniformity, which reintroduced the 1552 Book of Common Prayer. If the intention was to return to a Protestant direction of travel without completely alienating Catholics, it was only successful in the short term. And it felt like a betrayal to that second group among Elizabeth's subjects, those who felt that the Reformation had many more miles to go to match the innovations of Calvin and, after 1560, of the Scots, with bishops replaced by synods and a General Assembly. For them, the restored Prayer Book still allowed too many frills and fancies: organ music was not banned, saints were not banished and believers could still make the sign of the cross.

Like the Recusant Catholics, these Protestants made the necessary oaths in public and attended Church of England services through gritted teeth, but in private developed a network of Bible study groups, which gradually included their own simple services. Far from the ambition for uniformity, the key plank of the Elizabethan Settlement, diversity was growing inside as well as outside churches. 'Administration of communion,' lamented Edmund Grindal, Elizabeth's second and least effective Archbishop of Canterbury in 1565, 'is done by some with unleavened bread, some with leavened; some receiving kneeling, others standing, others sitting; some baptise in a font, others in a basin; some sign with the sign of the cross, others sign not.'[5]

Far from being settled by the end of the sixteenth century, the English Reformation remained a work in progress, with many minds feverishly plotting around the succession while the ageing, childless queen gave no indication of her views on the candidates being mentioned. Nothing felt secure.

ALSO WITH A STORY TO TELL...

HOLY TRINITY CHURCH IN ST ANDREWS is said to have stood for 1,000 years, but its oldest surviving parts – its tower and some of its pillars – date back to the early 1400s. John Knox, the father of Presbyterianism in Scotland, preached here and is commemorated in the south porch.

OLD ST LEONARD'S CHURCH AT LANGHO in Lancashire is one of a handful of churches built during the reign of Mary Tudor. Completed in 1557, its stonework, windows, plinths, roof timbers and fragments of medieval glass were all rescued from nearby Whalley Abbey, a Cistercian foundation left to rot after the Dissolution of the Monasteries.

ST FAITH'S, BACTON in Herefordshire, a thirteenth-century building, may have been far removed from court intrigue, but it contains the first known depiction of Elizabeth I as Gloriana, symbol of her nation, part of a monument commissioned for her own eventual burial by locally born Blanche Parry, Chief Gentlewoman of the Privy Chamber to the Queen, and Elizabeth's close confidante for sixty years. Though Parry wasn't eventually buried here, she composed the epitaph, which includes the words, 'with maiden queen a maid did end her life', suggesting that Elizabeth was indeed a 'Virgin Queen', a claim not borne out by the historical record.

CHAPTER 17
The Seventeenth Century

St John's, Little Gidding: Trial and Error

Blessed be God, whose love it was
To double-moat thee with his grace,
And none but thee.

George Herbert, priest and poet, 'The British Church'[1]

To CALL LITTLE Gidding a hamlet would be an exaggeration. It stands in the middle of the flatlands of Cambridgeshire, down long, high-hedged, country roads, which out of the blue take a ninety-degree turn to conform to the logic of the vast fields on either side of them. A collection of trees, ponds and a sprinkling of houses, Little Gidding clusters around the small Church of St John. To any traveller who stumbles upon it in any time or season, it is a place unlikely to stop them in their tracks. Yet it has done precisely that, twice, and with memorable effect.

The first occasion was brief and unhappy. In early May 1646, King Charles I arrived after his defeat by parliamentary forces in the English Civil War at the Battle of Naseby. He was on the run and seeking sanctuary among a small royalist religious community based at the church he knew well. Reluctantly, they told him that they could not guarantee his safety and directed him elsewhere.

The second was more leisurely, but also in May when the hedges were in blossom. In 1936, having read of Charles's visit and grown curious, the Anglo-American poet T. S. Eliot was brought here by friends from nearby Cambridge. He found the spot so inspiring that he immortalised its name as the title of the fourth and final section of his *Four Quartets*.

Part of Little Gidding's appeal for Eliot was that this isolated and – on closer inspection – introverted place had for him the quality of being able to transcend both time and itself to reveal something about the place of religion in the nation's collective memory.

There are other places
Which also are the world's end, some at the sea jaws,
Or over a dark lake, in a desert or a city –
But this is the nearest, in place and time,
Now and in England.
If you came this way,
Taking any route, starting from anywhere,
At any time or at any season,
It would always be the same: you would have to put off
Sense and notion. You are not here to verify,
Instruct yourself, or inform curiosity
Or carry report. You are here to kneel
Where prayer has been valid.[2]

For just how long prayer had been valid at St John's is unclear. There are today three Giddings – Little, Great and Steeple – but only a single mention of *Geddinge* in the Domesday Book. In 1626 the local manor house at Little Gidding had been empty for sixty years, while the adjoining medieval church was being used as a barn after congregations had migrated to the alternatives at Great and Steeple Gidding. Such dereliction, though, did not deter the Ferrar family from buying house and church as a job lot, apparently sight unseen. Composed of a mother, Mary, her two sons, Nicholas and John, and her daughter, Susannah, along with their various children and servants, around forty in total, the new arrivals were – in modern terminology – downsizing. The family fortune had largely been lost in the bankruptcy of the Virginia Company, set up in 1606 to establish coastal settlements in America.

Yet there was also a strong religious imperative to their escape to the country that was simultaneously ancient, contemporary and even prophetic in terms of the Church in England. Monasteries, abbeys and convents had disappeared with Henry VIII's break with Rome, reaffirmed by his daughter Elizabeth. In these early decades of the seventeenth century, the opportunity to live in a self-proclaimed and self-regulating community of faith, so as to search together for spiritual insight, seemed lost forever. The Protestant reformers regarded any efforts to revive the practice with suspicion, but that did not deter the Ferrars. They wanted to revive community living as a distinctive part of the new Church of England, and thereby – after the turmoil of the previous century – define what it stood for as Church in a positive way, rather than by reference to what it wasn't – namely Roman Catholicism or the Protestant, Presbyterian and Puritan approaches.

Nicholas Ferrar in particular was part of a group of linked and influential individuals, sometimes called the Caroline Divines ('Caroline' from the reign of King Charles). They shared a desire to nurture new beginnings in the Church so as to establish its identity as something more than created as a result of Henry VIII's insistence on a divorce. Among the group was William Laud, from 1633 Archbishop of Canterbury, keen above all on finding a modus operandi for a Church that was both reformed and catholic, with a small 'c' and so meaning universal. Others included Lancelot Andrewes, Bishop of Winchester, who played a prominent part in the Authorised 'King James' Version of the Bible in English, published in 1611 and used as standard in the Church of England into the twentieth century. And then there was the Welsh-born George Herbert, a poet celebrated to this day for his gift of conveying the challenges and joys of lived faith. He had been a rising star at Cambridge, appointed the University's Public Orator at a precocious age, but had opted instead to train for the priesthood – alongside Nicholas Ferrar, who was an ordained deacon.[3] Herbert then chose a life of quiet service as a country rector and sub-dean at St Andrew's in Bemerton, west of Salisbury.

The windowless, limestone façade of St John's, topped by an ornate bellcote – Eliot called it dull – stands at the end of a short path that contains the table tomb of Nicholas Ferrar. He died at the age of forty-five in 1637, leaving his brother and sister, John and Susannah, to lead the community. The church was partially rebuilt in 1714 by a subsequent generation of Ferrars, but the red-brick walls around its sides and back, as well as its interior, bear witness to what the original Ferrars did to bring this abandoned house of God back to life.

The oak panelling they used on the walls and ceilings survives in its original form on the south side of the chancel. Elsewhere it has been replaced and renewed to what are believed to be the original designs. The organ they imported remains – anathema to the pared-back Puritan tendency within Protestantism, strong in Europe and growing in England, which believed that only human voices, not instruments, should have a place in worship – along with the cedar Communion table and the brass font and lectern. On tablets on the walls are the Protestant standbys, the words of the Ten Commandments, the Creed and the Lord's Prayer. And then there are the curious seating arrangements, with a single row of pews facing each other on either side of the narrow nave, with the altar beyond them in the even narrower chancel.

The overall effect is that of a hybrid, halfway between the stark simplicity favoured by Calvin in Geneva and taken up by both the Presbyterians in Scotland and the Puritans, and the (to Protestant eyes) distracting, abundant, even idolatrous decoration to be found in Catholic churches. For the Ferrars, more important than the style of the interior was to establish a practical connection between what went on in the church and what went on in their home and community. Liturgy, hearing passages from Scripture and preaching were one component of the daily search for God, but there was also the equally essential challenge of living out their faith.

It sounds remarkably like the ideal of an abbey, friary or convent, but in the Catholic model of religious community, discarded in Britain at the time of the Reformation, family had always been seen as a distraction, and celibacy was among the vows demanded of monks and nuns. The Ferrars, by contrast, regarded family as a strength and so required no formal pledges, no Rule, and no enclosure as they followed together a life of religious devotion. Several times each day they would process in prayer from their manor house to the church. And for the rest of the time they would study and discuss the Bible, or make books, known as harmonies or concordances, where related passages from the four Gospels were cut out and pasted onto new sheets so as to be side by side, with the aim of revealing their parallels and differences. These collections were illustrated, sometimes with pictures, adapted and reused from older Catholic texts that were no longer thought suitable for general consumption.

The harmonies were used in the community, but also – in more intricate versions bound by Mary and Anna Collet, daughters of Susannah – shared with patrons. George Herbert received one, and wrote back in gratitude that 'he had lived now to see women's scissors brought to so rare a use as to serve at God's altar'. Another found its way into the hands of Charles I, which is how he heard about Little Gidding, and made the first of what are believed to have been three visits to commission his own harmony, now kept in the Royal Collection.

Such detailed work carries a ready echo of what went on in monasteries for centuries in making illuminated manuscripts before printing presses came along. And the Ferrars also embraced the outreach work of the Dominican and Franciscan friars, supporting the poor of the area. Part of their home was converted into an alms-house for elderly and infirm local women. Another section was repurposed as a dispensary to provide medicine and broth to those who turned up at their door in distress. And then there was the schoolroom (though there is some debate about whether only family children or all local youngsters were admitted).

Some have gone so far as to suggest that the Little Gidding community, with its combination of 'good works' and Bible study, fused the best of the Catholic and Protestant traditions and became a blueprint in miniature for the 'middle way' that was the Church of England's hallmark in centuries to come. That may be ascribing too much to an experiment on such a modest scale, but the well-connected Ferrars continued long after Nicholas' early death to attract attention from the wider world, despite their remote location. A measure of their perceived influence came in 1641 when they were publicly attacked by Puritan writers for being far too similar to a Catholic nunnery.

In the polarised times that followed in that same decade, when the stand-off between the King and Parliament descended into Civil War after 1642, Little Gidding's royal connections made it vulnerable, especially when the surrounding county of (then) Huntingdonshire, birthplace of Oliver Cromwell, was so strongly in the Parliamentary fold. That is why Charles's visit after defeat at Naseby in 1646 was so short. He came 'at night like a broken king', Eliot writes in 'Little Gidding',[4] but the community feared for his safety if he were to remain with them. Within three years, he was dead, beheaded in front of the Banqueting Hall in Whitehall.

For a short period, the pressure in polarised times was such that the Ferrars felt obliged to leave Little Gidding, but that seemed to them an abandonment of their mission and they soon returned to continue with their work. It survived local hostility and the deaths, in a flu epidemic within a month of each other, of John and Susannah at the end of 1657.

Since Henry VIII's break with Rome, each of his successors had laboured to restore uniformity in matters of religion to the kingdom they inherited. And each had failed because dissenters of different shades refused to conform, resulting in outbreaks of violence. The seventeenth century continued this pattern, as James I, Elizabeth's successor in 1603, soon discovered.

The first of the Stuarts on the English throne, he was the son of Mary, Queen of Scots. As James VI he had been King of Scotland for thirty-five years since his coronation at the age of just one. His claim to hold the English throne simultaneously was disputed on a variety of grounds by others who were, like him, great-great-grandchildren of Henry VII. On her deathbed, having lost the power of speech, Elizabeth – who had always refused to reveal her choice of successor – is said to have responded to those around her reading aloud a list of potential candidates by raising her wasted arms above her head at the mention of James, and then bringing her fingers together in the shape of a crown. She died the next day, and her closest advisor, Sir Robert Cecil, followed her wishes, no doubt also impressed by James' successful record in Scotland, since he had taken over the reins of government in 1583, in resisting the more hardline Presbyterians. They had yearned, most of all, to abolish bishops in the Church of Scotland, as James was told from the pulpit by John Knox's successors in no uncertain terms on several occasions while attending services in St Giles. Yet the young King had refused to concede and outmanoeuvred those who sought to force his hand.

As King from 1603 of both England and Scotland – or of Great Britain, as he styled himself – his ambition was to bring the two Reformed Churches north and south of the old border closer together in their practices, and so to fuse two different Reformations into one. In pursuit of that goal, he made his one and only journey home from London to Scotland in 1617 to appear at the General Assembly and persuade it to agree, reluctantly on the part of its Presbyterian members, to his Five Articles for the Church of Scotland. These sought uniformity with the less Protestant Church of England over such matters as kneeling during Communion, confirmation by a bishop and the observance of holy days.

James's arrival in England had raised hopes among two oppos-ing factions. Catholics unreconciled to the break with the Pope wanted him to act as his mother's son and turn back the clock. Their frustration at his refusal – he blamed the constant plotting against Elizabeth by Recusants for causing his mother's death – led to a failed attempt by Guy Fawkes and a handful of Catholic extremists in November 1605 to blow up the Palace of Westminster with gunpowder, as it hosted both King and Parliament. Their willingness to kill him ended any instinct James may have harboured towards granting greater toleration to Catholics, and was followed by the imposition of a new oath of loyalty designed to root out papists in public service.

And then there were the Puritans. Inspired by the achievements of the Presbyterians in Scotland in bending the national Church to their will, they were anxious to enlist James in England to sweep away the compromises they so disliked in the Book of Common Prayer. He agreed to a gathering with them and his bishops at Hampton Court in 1604, over which he presided. As a result, a series of tweaks to the Prayer Book were granted, but nowhere near sufficient for the Puritans' liking. Unlike the Catholics, these dissidents neither retreated nor were forced into the shadows. Instead, they increasingly established a presence in Parliament as representatives of the rising class of squires, from which many were drawn. Such a platform allowed them both to push for the Reformation to be carried further and to complain bitterly about the burden of taxes levied by the King and his aris-tocratic advisors.

In dealing with such insistent demands, James brought not only his vision of what kingship meant, but also his considerable skills as a theologian. In 1597, he had produced a volume on demonology. More significant, though, was his *Basilikon Doron* (*Royal Gift*) of two years later, in which he argued in favour of the divine right of kings to rule. It was a belief that informed his twenty-two years on the English throne, and those of several of his successors. In his own mind, he was God's appointee, divinely guided as he strove to lead God's Church in settling its differences. His biggest achievement in this regard was the production in 1611 of a new translation of the Bible, to replace the several, competing English versions that had been circulating in the latter part of the previous century. The King James Bible, in which he took a hands-on role, was highly successful in bridging the differences between the factions, and it remains to this day the best-ever-selling English-language book in the world.

There were, inevitably, some in the Protestant ranks who objected to its language as inaccurate or too Catholic and who remained loyal to the pocket-sized Geneva Bible, handy for travelling round the countryside on evangelistic missions. The Puritan scholar Hugh Broughton, for one, pronounced the King James' version to be 'ill done': 'Tell his Majesty I had rather be rent in pieces by wild horses than that any such translation . . . should be urged upon poor churches. It crosseth me and I require it to be burnt.'[5] Such voices, though, were in a minority.

James ended up with much more of a head-on confrontation with the Puritans over their desire to ban all sports and merry-making on the Sabbath, as the Ten Commandments ordered. The King resisted. His Declaration of Sports of 1618 reaffirmed that such traditional pleasures as Morris Dancing were not sinful if undertaken on Sundays. His ruling was ignored in areas where Puritan numbers were strong, and his rejection of their Bible-based Sabbatarianism added to their perception that further reform of the Church of England to conform with their views was a lost cause. Some Puritans, known to history as the Pilgrims, had already left the country for the more conducive Dutch city of Leyden, where religious toleration had been granted in the new republic that emerged following the defeat of the Spanish colonial powers. From Leyden in 1620 they were among those who joined the *Mayflower* on its voyage from England to the United States to establish a Puritan colony.

James's son, who succeeded him as Charles I in 1625, shared his father's belief in the divine right of kings, and in the paramount importance of achieving uniformity in matters of religion. But he was more impetuous, and believed he could use his royal authority to force others to agree with him. As head of the Church in England and in Scotland, he made it plain that he and he alone would decide what was best for it. Given that he was married to a French Catholic princess, Henrietta Maria, for whom special arrangements had to be made so that she could hear Mass in private in London, Charles was inevitably distrusted by the Puritans. Their suspicions only deepened when he treated Parliament with imperiousness, and in 1629 decided he could rule without it. It took eleven years for him to change his mind, and only then because he had blundered into a war that he was losing, and needed Parliament's blessing for new taxes.

James's Five Articles may have been voted in by the General Assembly of the Church of Scotland in 1617, but they remained deeply resented by many. The Church was effectively split between Presbyterians who relied on the authority of the Assembly to uphold their beliefs and practices and a bench of Protestant bishops, with Catholic leanings, who depended on the support of the King. Charles acted clumsily in this delicate situation, declaring in 1633 for the first time that St Giles was now officially a cathedral (at the centre of the new diocese of Edinburgh he had created). If that increased friction, it was nothing compared to the reception in 1637 for the King's Prayer Book for Scotland, designed to replace Knox's Book of Common Order. More 'Catholic' even than the version used in England, in July of that year it provoked a riot in St Giles against the royal imposition. Local market trader Jenny Geddes is said to have set it off by throwing a stool at the dean, in protest against the new Prayer Book.

Opposition quickly gathered pace. A National Covenant was circulated, signed by thousands of Scots, opposing what was characterised as Charles's attack on the Church of Scotland. That in turn led to the two Bishops' Wars of 1639 and 1640. The King tried initially to undertake them with his own resources but, facing defeat by a Scotland that was now under the control of the Covenanters, he was forced to recall Parliament to raise funds for his military campaign.

Charles's instinct, as ever, was to bulldoze his way through, but public opinion in England as well as Scotland was turning against him, emboldening Parliament to resist his demands. On 11 December 1640, it received the Root and Branch Petition, signed by 15,000 Londoners, demanding the abolition of all bishops and their replacement by a Presbyterian system of Church governance. Such was the groundswell of popular dissent that, within a week, William Laud, the Archbishop of Canterbury, had been accused of treason, arrested and impeached on the orders of Parliament.

A year of ever-rising tensions followed, culminating in Parliament presenting Charles with the Grand Remonstrance, a list of 200 grievances. News was arriving of the outbreak of war in Ireland, and Charles was more desperate than ever for funds to sustain his military campaigns. As a condition of providing the means, the Parliamentarians demanded he relinquish sole control of the army, fearing that, left to his own devices, he might use it against them. 'By God, not for an hour,' the King replied, his belief in his divine right undimmed.

Worried that his Catholic wife was about to be impeached like Archbishop Laud, Charles gathered a force of 400 men and attempted to enter the House of Commons to arrest five members. His actions were taken by his opponents as an attempted coup against Parliament. Its failure saw the King leave London for the north, with the Queen heading to Holland, supposedly to pawn the Crown Jewels.

The scene was set for a civil war where religion would dictate the sides. Parliament allied itself with the Scottish Presbyterians against the King, signing up to a covenant to root out 'popery, prelacy, superstition, heresy, schism, profaneness and whatever shall be found to be contrary to sound doctrine and the power of godliness'.

As well as being engaged in conflicts in Scotland and England, Charles was facing a challenge on a third front, this time in Ireland. Together, this trio is known as the Wars of the Three Kingdoms. The Irish Confederate Wars broke out in 1641, an uprising in which Catholic Ulstermen and others were prominent in opposing the Crown. All were angry at the increasing number of English, Welsh and – in particular – Scottish settlers that Charles (like his father and Elizabeth before him) had been encouraging to migrate to Ireland. The northern province of Ulster was a particular focus for new arrivals. They brought with them English Protestantism, Scottish Presbyterianism and an acceptance of the Reformation and its break from Catholic Rome that was not shared by the great majority of the Irish. These 'plantations', as the settlements of migrants were known, raised fears among the existing population over land rights, anti-Catholic discrimination and the whole future of self-government in Ireland under English rule.

Since Henry II's bold incursion into Ireland in the 1170s, with only the kings of the north west able to resist his demand that all rulers in the land bow down before him and accept his supremacy, English power in Ireland had been in slow but steady retreat. It had rested largely on a small group of aristocrats, the 'Old English', who could trace their origins back to the Anglo-Normans but who had increasingly been assimilated. Their loyalty to the English Crown, while crucial, often came third to their loyalty to Ireland and to themselves.

The Irish Church had worked with these arrangements but had carefully maintained its independence from its counterpart in England, though bishops leading dioceses on both sides of the Irish Sea were not uncommon. When Henry VIII broke with Rome and named himself head of the Church of England, the whole system in Ireland was thrown into turmoil. Henry was determined that the country should fall into line with the rest of his domains. A tame Irish Parliament had existed in Dublin since 1297, doing the King's business, though by the first half of the sixteenth century its writ did not run far beyond what was known as the Pale, a semicircle of territory stretching out on all three landward sides of Dublin. It was, therefore, in the Pale that the most immediate impact was felt when the Irish Parliament dutifully voted in royal supremacy in Church matters in 1537, and accepted the dissolution of Ireland's monasteries in 1541.

Displaced abbots, monks and nuns headed to the west of the country, where links were maintained with Rome in open defiance of the King's dictates. State domination of the Church, as achieved in England, proved impossible in Ireland, given the fragile hold the English had on the country and the loyalty of its ruling class. While Henry used some of the revenue he reaped as a result of seizing the monasteries in the Pale to strengthen his administration in Ireland, it was not sufficient to prevent an independent Catholic Church continuing to thrive everywhere that was any distance from Dublin. There were simply not enough subjects loyal to the Tudors on the ground with livelihoods that depended on that royal connection.

To correct that imbalance, first Henry and then Elizabeth encouraged the plantations. They feared Ireland's potential as a launching ground for attempts to disrupt newly Protestant England. And, indeed, the Catholic powers of Europe and the papacy were busily engaged in various such schemes, sending envoys to Ireland with talk of raising armies and plots to unseat Elizabeth, but all ultimately to little effect.

Quite how treacherous were the shifting sands of loyalty in this period in Ireland is shown by the case of two archbishops who died within two years of each other. Richard Creagh was named by the Pope as Archbishop of Armagh in 1564, but he remained publicly staunch in his defence of Elizabeth's rights over Ireland, even in the face of threats to his own life from the Ulster chiefs. Yet he was taken prisoner by the English, in spite of his loyalty to the Crown, because he refused to renounce Catholicism. He ended his days in 1586 in the Tower of London.

Three years previously, Archbishop Dermot O'Hurley of Cashel had been smuggled into Ireland where a rebellion was underway that had initially been prompted by the Pope's excommunication of Elizabeth in 1570. His role, in contrast to that of Richard Creagh, was openly to sustain the covert activities of the Catholic Church in the face of the threat posed by the Queen's priest-hunters, who finally tracked him down at the home of the Lord Treasurer of Ireland, the Earl of Ormond. So fluid was the line between pro-Crown Protestants (like Ormond) and pro-Pope Catholics (like O'Hurley) that the Earl vigorously defended the Archbishop when he was arrested. It was insufficient to save him. When even the torture of having his legs boiled over a fire failed to convince O'Hurley to renounce his loyalty to the Pope, he was condemned to death and hanged in Dublin in 1584.

The final decade of Elizabeth's reign saw continuing unrest and uprisings in an Ireland that was impossible to pacify. On his accession in 1603, James decided on a more nuanced approach. He accelerated the plantation programme, bringing over more lowland Scots and border English, and promoted Protestant translations of the Bible into Irish. At the same time, though, he allowed greater toleration towards the open practice of the in-theory outlawed Catholic faith, especially in the west of Ireland. His son Charles went further in trying to buy off Catholic Ireland, offering 'graces' or concessions to Catholics in return for them sending the money and men-at-arms he required to sustain his rule once he had dispensed with Parliament in 1629.

Such adjustments in official policy did not stop the tide of resentment against the English King continuing to rise, with the growth of the plantations seen as a threat to the Irish language and culture, as old as any in the British Isles. A particularly bad harvest in 1641 further inflamed tensions and tipped the country into the Irish Confederate Wars. They took their name from the confederation of Catholic Ulstermen and descendants of the Old English, which quickly had Charles' forces overstretched and the threadbare English administration in Dublin on the run. The battle, though, turned out to be a drawn-out, ugly and brutal one, with what would now be called ethnic cleansing deployed in disputed Ulster and scorched-earth tactics used elsewhere.

Initially, the governance of Ireland fell into the hands of the rebels, but both sides in the English Civil War – Royalists and Parliamentarians – along with contingents from Scotland came to Ireland in an attempt restore order. As his position weakened further at home, Charles formed an alliance with the Irish Confederates, some of whom then crossed the Irish Sea to join Royalist forces in their fight with Parliamentary army. Their ultimate defeat alongside the King left Ireland open to the wrath of the victors.

Following Charles' execution in 1649 and the declaration of a republic, styled as the Commonwealth, Oliver Cromwell was named as Commander-in-Chief of the forces sent to end the war in Ireland. Charged with defeating the Royalists and the Confederates, he launched a bloody campaign that resulted in as many as 600,000 deaths before peace was declared in 1652. Under its terms, Catholicism was banned, and priests faced execution if arrested.

Before the conflict had broken out in 1641, it is estimated that 60 per cent of the land in Ireland was in Catholic hands. After the peace, that figure fell to 10 per cent – and the poorest 10 per cent at that. To resist confiscation, Catholics had to prove consistent support over a number of years for the Parliamentary cause. Very few could, and were therefore powerless as whole swathes of Ireland were handed over as rewards to the commanders who had fought in Cromwell's armies and those who had funded the war. The inflow of Protestants continued in Ulster, intensified in the 1690s by a famine in Scotland, so much so that by the 1720s they were in the majority there.

The English Civil War saw widespread destruction of churches and church property. Where the Parliamentary forces were in control, bishops were thrown out, the Book of Common Prayer was replaced, and parish clergy were obliged to become ministers rather than priests and to work with the system of synods and assemblies required in the Presbyterian model. Those who refused – according to some estimates as many as one-quarter – were deprived of their living and their home, under rules set by an agency appointed by Parliament and called the Committee for Scandalous Ministries.

Some headed into exile in Europe, but many carried on in conditions not unlike those already being suffered by Recusant Catholics. The redundant bishops largely kept their heads down, but were willing to carry out secret ordinations to maintain some sort of coherence in a Church of England that steadily went underground. In the pre-war Puritan strongholds, notably East Anglia, commissioners were appointed on the authority of Parliament to inspect churches and chapels so that remaining 'idolatry' could be stripped out of them. Over the course of a ten-month period in 1643 and 1644, just one of these commissioners, the devout Puritan William Dowsing, little qualified for the task but well connected in the Parliamentary ranks, was charged with visiting 250 churches in Suffolk and Cambridgeshire (including all the Cambridge college chapels, though not St John's, Little Gidding). He was often accompanied by soldiers to enforce his whims. In a diary entry he describes how, in a single Suffolk church and on the basis of his judgement alone, he was responsible for the smashing of thirty 'superstitious' pictures, the removal of forty carvings of angels and the levelling of the chancel floor to do away with the 'unnecessary' steps that led up to the Communion table. Even inscriptions on brass plaques did not escape his attention. Any 'too Catholic' wording had to be removed.[6]

Yet Dowsing – and by association the Puritan faction that steadily took control of the Long Parliament that sat between 1640 and 1649 – did not always have things his own way. Some of his 'visitations' were greeted by local churchwardens and parishioners who denied him entry, even summoning the local constable to their aid. They refused to let his view of what was acceptable in the worship of God go unchallenged. And for all the churches that suffered in Suffolk and Cambridgeshire, there were others just over the border in Norfolk, though still in Puritan East Anglia, that to this day retain their angel roofs, their chancel screens and their medieval glass windows. Churchgoers were, it seems, as divided and disorganised as the country's leaders.

Just as Charles I had made himself unpopular by too rigid an insistence that his choices in matters of religion should be followed by his subjects, so too was Parliament now facing the same accusation on account of its lack of toleration. Imposed Puritanism and Presbyterianism fared no better than imposed episcopal leadership. 'New Presbyter is but old Priest writ large,' reflected the Puritan poet, John Milton.[7]

At the beginning of the 1640s, Milton had been a strong supporter of the Parliamentary cause, denouncing bishops and the King's claim to a divine right to rule. As the decade progressed, he widened his attack to include all those – including the Presbyterians – who wished to restrict Christian liberty. In this he allied himself with a new strain that was emerging among the Puritans, known as the Independents. While loathing both Catholicism and the Church of England as Charles had led it, they were keen that it should not be replaced by another imposed system, but rather by giving individuals the choice of how and where and when they wanted to worship God. Prominent among these Independents was the conqueror of Ireland, Oliver Cromwell, who, after a profound religious experience in the 1630s, had come to believe that God was guiding him in each step along the way.

Born into a wealthy family in Huntingdon, he had sat as the town's MP from 1628, and then for Cambridge in the Short Parliament of 1640 and its successor the Long Parliament. He had distinguished himself on the battlefield in the Parliamentarians' victory over the Royalists at Marston Moor in July 1644 that gave them control of northern England, and was a leading figure in the New Model Army established by Parliament in 1645.

With victory over the King in 1647, a Presbyterian system was introduced into England. When Charles indicated that he might make an accommodation with this, many Parliamentarians were inclined to accept such an arrangement, wanting to bring the conflict with the King to an end. Cromwell, however, was not. There could not be peace and security in matters of religion or state, he insisted, while Charles was still alive. And so he was among the initially small band that pushed for, and finally orchestrated, Charles I's trial and execution in front of the Banqueting House in London's Whitehall on 30 January 1649.

Milton was enamoured and hailed Cromwell as 'our chief of men':

who through a cloud
Not of war only, but detractions rude,
Guided by faith and matchless fortitude,
To peace and truth thy glorious way hast plough'd . . .[8]

The new Commonwealth sent Cromwell and his army first to Ireland, then in 1650 to Scotland to see off an alliance between Presbyterians there and Charles II, son of the dead King. On the back of his victories, and with strong backing from his troops and the Independents in the Rump Parliament, he was declared Lord Protector in 1653.

The old goal of uniformity in religion was now discarded and replaced by the pursuit of individual liberty. The 1653 Instrument of Government declared that all were free to go wherever they chose to worship and were 'protected in the profession of the faith and exercise of their religion'. Liberty excluded, however, those whose choice would be 'popery or prelacy', but even here there was a degree of leniency. Catholics who went to the embassy chapels of Spain, Portugal and Venice in London to attend Mass were left undisturbed, but the same toleration was not seen in Ireland, where even Cromwell's placemen were now struggling to force their tenants to break their ties with Rome. The toughest measures, though, were reserved for those who remained attached to the Church of England, its Book of Common Prayer, its calendar of feast days and its sacraments. Christmas Day services were banned under Cromwell, likewise readings from the Prayer Book, even at a graveside. All marriages had to be civil unions, notions of a sacramental dimension to such ceremonies having no place in Puritanism.

That, at least, was the theory promoted by the new ruler. Enforcement was another matter. In his diary, the layman John Evelyn records many examples of Prayer Book services in churches and of the marking of holy days, but equally of being confronted, while at a Christmas Day service in London in 1657, by armed soldiers: '[They] examined me, why contrarie to an Ordinance made that none should any longer observe the superstitious time of the Nativity, I durst offend & particularly be at Common prayers, which they told me was but the Masse in English.'[9]

If the Church of England was persecuted, Cromwell gave free rein to others, in line with his public promises of toleration. In 1656, he allowed the settlement of Jews in England for the first time since they had been expelled by Edward I in 1290. Within Christianity, the years of the Commonwealth and Protectorate saw a great increase in the number of independent sects, to the horror of the more ordered Presbyterians.

What united these new groups was a dislike of all forms of organised religion, and a conviction that they, and they alone, were the true Church. Chief among them were the Congregationalists – closely linked to Cromwell's own Independents – who followed the Presbyterian/Puritan mainstream but believed that each congregation should make its own decisions, without reference to any other group or governing body. In theory they shared an attachment with others who followed the teachings of Robert Browne, an English cleric who in the early years of the century had developed the concept that each congregation should answer only to itself. Yet, in practice it was a recipe for fragmentation and dispute. Sometimes called 'Brownists', his followers were well represented in the ranks of Cromwell's army, and had also been included among the Pilgrim Fathers who set sail for America on the *Mayflower* in 1620. Yet in later life, Browne himself (who died in 1633) was reconciled with the Church of England.

Then there were the Baptists, who established churches in England and Wales to live out the insights of another former Church of England cleric, John Smyth. He had decamped for the freedom of the Dutch Republic in the early years of the century and taught that liturgy got in the way of spontaneity in worship. Like the earlier Anabaptists, his followers held that true baptism was not for infants but for adults, so each one could make a mature commitment to God.

George Fox, who was born in 1624 to a family of Leicestershire weavers, was another who thrived under the Protectorate, and met Cromwell on a number of occasions. A charismatic preacher and prolific pamphleteer, he spoke and wrote for many of similar artisan origins in lamenting the social upheaval caused by the religious wars of the middle years of the century. He appealed to that 'Independent' spirit in Cromwell – and is said to have brought tears to Cromwell's eyes – with his message that all believers had to put aside rituals and even church buildings and instead find God in life, in the Bible and most of all as an 'inner light' inside each individual.

If Fox appealed to Cromwell, he appalled others in authority in the Protectorate who found him and his message particularly subversive, especially as his followers began to expand from rural areas in the north to reach London. They were often called Quakers – allegedly because Fox had once told magistrates, during one of his many appearances before them, that they should quake because God was watching them.

There were many other smaller sects – such as the Ranters, Muggletonians, Levellers and Diggers, whose religious convictions, once given free rein by the government, led them to take equally radical positions on how society should be arranged. This time the results did manage to dent Cromwell's stated belief in tolerance. The Levellers, who advocated the removal of all class distinctions, were again found in numbers in the Parliamentary and later the Commonwealth army. When a group of around three hundred and fifty of them rebelled in 1649 and sacked their officers, they were rounded up by loyal troops and herded into St John's Church in Burford, Oxfordshire, to hear a sermon from Cromwell himself. Afterwards, three of the ringleaders were taken out and executed by firing squad in an effort to restore order in the ranks. It led other Levellers to declaim Cromwell as more despotic than the king he had replaced.

On Cromwell's death in 1658, possibly from blood poisoning linked to an infection, his son Richard succeeded him as Protector, but he was a pale shadow of his father and did little to inspire his followers. A new Parliament was elected at the instigation of the army leaders, and it agreed to invite Charles II to return, which he did, amid universal acclamation – and sighs of relief – at the end of May 1660. Before setting out from his court in exile at Breda in the Netherlands, Charles had issued a general pardon for all in the overthrow of the monarchy, making an exception only for a handful involved in the death of his father. He declared 'liberty to tender consciences', adding 'that no man shall be disquieted or called in question for differences of opinion in matters of religion which do not disturb the peace of the kingdom'.

His pledge followed a familiar pattern when put into practice. Some tender consciences were not eligible, among them the Quakers and other more radical sections of Protestantism, collectively known as Nonconformists on account of their refusal to conform to anyone's demands but God's. The conformity that Charles demanded was to be a communicant in the Church of England. Those who weren't were excluded from all civic and military roles, suffering the same fate that Recusant Catholics had long been enduring.

In making this distinction, Charles was in practice dividing society along class lines. The wealthier aristocracy and gentry generally passed the test and dutifully took Communion in their local church whatever their private convictions. They were joined by many of the poorest in their areas, where the habit of following the example of their overlords was well established and hard to break. The urban tradesfolk and artisans, however, stuck to their principles in religion, and refused to relinquish the 'Nonconformity' they had embraced in the middle years of the century. They were, therefore, pushed into the category of dissenters.

Charles's private religious sympathies remain a cause of much debate, with rumours of a deathbed conversion to Catholicism (his mother's faith). In public, in his twenty-five years on the throne, he oversaw the return of the Church of England bishops who set about restoring a shattered ecclesiastical structure across the country. The success of this endeavour owed much to the moderation and general good sense of the majority of the priests, who came back after more than a decade of being excluded from parishes. The Republican interlude appeared to have exhausted any appetite for further change in such clerical ranks. So back, too, was the Book of Common Prayer in England, albeit in an amended version that appeared in 1662, alongside another Act of Uniformity. The changes were, of course, too little to satisfy a minority of Puritans among the clergy, who refused to make the legally required public declaration in its favour. The result was that an estimated seven hundred were ejected from their livings, the latest in a long line of purges. 'I hear most of the Presbyters took their leaves today,' noted Samuel Pepys in his diary on 17 August 1662.[10]

Some headed to Scotland, where the more Protestant Presbyterian Kirk was restored, albeit still with bishops. The presence of such prelates caused renewed discontent, with dissident Presbyterian ministers leading open-air services known as conventicles. These were then targeted by new legal prohibitions and increasingly brutal suppression.

In the later years of Charles's reign, however, it was his own suspected leanings towards Rome, and the open embrace of Catholicism by his brother and heir, James, Duke of York, that caused most alarm. James's accession in February 1685 after the death of Charles, who had no legitimate children, brought the first Catholic to the throne since Mary Tudor, and threatened to reopen the Reformation wounds once more.

The new King, though, was, initially at least, a popular figure with many. His earlier role in leading the fight against the Great Fire of London in 1666 had won him considerable and enduring popular acclaim. Actions, it seems, counted for more than doctrinal attachments. And James tried his best in his early months to quell any fears of religious extremism on his part and pledged to protect the existing settlement, which won approval in England, Scotland and Ireland.

Yet rumours were soon rife of his plotting with the Pope, which James chose to do little to dispel. Instead, he grew steadily bolder in revealing his hand, offering concessions to Recusant Catholics. The King banned the popular spectacle of lighting bonfires on 5 November to celebrate the failure of Guy Fawkes' Gunpowder Plot, and he agreed to readmit Catholics to public office. Such a relaxation wasn't only for Catholics, though, and in his Declaration of Indulgence of 1687 James signalled his wish to remove the 'conformity' tests that his brother had put in place, to allow a more general freedom of religion. This so alarmed the Archbishop of Canterbury, William Sancroft, and six other bishops that they publicly questioned whether the King could act in good faith as the Supreme Governor of the Church of England. James's response to such questioning was to commit them to the Tower for seditious libel. But the King had misjudged the mood in the country, which was now running against him to such an extent that the seven bishops were regarded as popular heroes. At their trial they were acquitted. Crowds took to the streets of London in celebration.

Rioting spread across the country and into Scotland. Another civil war over religion loomed when the birth of a son to James's second wife, Italian princess Mary of Modena, took place in the same month. This infant would precede in the line of succession James's two Protestant-raised daughters, Mary and Anne, from his first marriage to Anne Hyde, who had died in 1671. The new heir could mean a return for years to come to the Catholic fold.

With the whole nation, according to John Evelyn on 29 June 1688, 'disaffected and in apprehension',[11] overtures were made by

Parliamentary leaders to Mary, now married to the Dutch Protestant William of Orange. On 5 November, of all days, a Dutch army landed in Torbay. By 18 December they had entered London and James had fled to France. Parliament declared the throne vacant and offered it jointly to William and Mary. Some of the bishops, including Archbishop Sancroft who had played such a major role in precipitating the crisis, were wary of so lightly once more overturning the principle of the divine right of kings, and so refused to take an oath of allegiance to William and Mary while James was still alive. They were punished by being deprived of their office. Yet a century and a half of what had felt like continual upheaval, based on religious disagreement, had caused a profound weariness in the country. Parliament courted this by introducing new rules of tolerance for Nonconformists.

In March 1689, the 'Glorious Revolution' was secured at the Battle of the Boyne. James's attempt to reclaim his throne with the support of French troops was defeated in Catholic Ireland, the only part of his realm that had refused to accept either the Reformation or its new protectors, William and Mary.

ALSO WITH A STORY TO TELL . . .

THE QUEEN'S CHAPEL, alongside St James's Palace in central London, is the work of Inigo Jones, built in 1625 in the Classical style. No new Catholic churches were allowed, but here Charles I's French Catholic wife, Henrietta Maria, could attend Mass, which was also banned. It was used as a stable during the English Civil War, and later refurbished by Christopher Wren, architect of St Paul's Cathedral.

THE CONGREGATIONAL CHAPEL AT WALPOLE in Suffolk was originally two farm cottages, but following the 1689 Act of Toleration it was leased by local Congregationalists and converted into a chapel. It continued in use until 1970. The plain, unadorned, white-walled interior, with clear glass windows, is dominated by its hexagonal pulpit, with seating in tiered galleries on the side walls.

ST ILLTYD'S CHURCH IN ILSTON on the Gower Peninsula is believed to have housed one of the first Baptist congregations. In 1649, the Royalist rector was replaced by a Parliamentarian, John Miles, who held both Church of England services and Baptist meetings in the medieval building throughout the Commonwealth years. With the restoration of Charles II, he was thrown out, so he used the local disused pre-Reformation Trinity Well Chapel as his Baptist meeting house.

CHAPTER 18

The Eighteenth Century

Heptonstall Methodist Chapel: Ancient and Modern

Give me one hundred preachers who fear nothing but sin, and desire nothing but God, and I care not a straw whether they be clergymen or laymen; such alone will shake the gates of hell and set up the kingdom of heaven on Earth.

John Wesley (1703–91)[1]

THE TWO MARGARETS – Margaret Coupe and Margaret
Morgan – who show me round have between them clocked
up 130 years of attendance at Heptonstall's handsome octagonal Methodist chapel. Its stonework blackened but resolute, it
sits in the middle of a multi-tiered graveyard on a steeply sloping hillside above the Upper Calder Valley. One Margaret
is Senior Steward, the other Margaret Treasurer. 'In the Church
of England,' they explain together, 'they'd call us Churchwardens.'

But they are not Church of England. Despite the founder
John Wesley's insistence right up to his death in 1791 that
Methodism was and must always remain a reform movement
within the Church of England, soon after it went its own way.
'When I say I'm going to chapel,' explains Margaret Coupe,
'from our point of view as Methodists that separates us off
from the Church of England. If you are Church of England,
you are going to church.'

The combined long service of these two unflappable women in
what is the world's oldest Methodist chapel in continuous use is
remarkable. It still leaves them, though, a good few years short of
the 250-plus years that have gone by since it first opened its doors
in 1764. Wesley had visited Heptonstall seventeen years earlier as
part of his near-constant travelling missions, typically giving
three or four sermons a day and covering (according to calcula-
tions made from the journals he kept) almost 250,000 miles over
his lifetime.

Itinerant Nonconformist preachers had already been drawing crowds to their open-air meetings at this spot halfway between Manchester and Leeds before Wesley came. Perhaps their success is what attracted him – to the place and to the style of evangelisation they favoured, so very different from his training as a Church of England priest where he had followed in the footsteps of his father. Their rousing oratory, their energy, their immediate connection with the lives of their listeners and their absolute conviction that God was giving them the words that sprang from their lips were winning over many working people who had been alienated by what was on offer in their more subdued, ordered, dutiful but detached local parish churches.

If Wesley was – unlike the Nonconformist preachers – part of the established national Church, he also became a one-man movement for change within it. He could see all too readily that it was too often too comfortable, too complacent and too distant from the poorer members of its congregations that it was supposed to serve. Of course, the century also contained some remarkable individual clerics who dedicated themselves unsparingly to parish work.

One such was Wesley's friend, John Fletcher, who served in a parish at Madeley in Shropshire, turning down wealthier, more prestigious livings to remain there for three decades, long enough to witness in 1781 the opening on the parish boundary of the Iron Bridge over the River Severn that was the first of its kind and remains a symbol of the Industrial Revolution. Though he shared many of Wesley's beliefs about how the Church of England needed to respond more vigorously and imaginatively to rapidly changing times, Fletcher chose to do so in one place, not on the road. He earned such a reputation for saintliness that even the great French *philosophe* Voltaire, forerunner of the French Revolution and not one over-enamoured with clerics, is reputed to have named him as the person who, in his experience, was closest in life to the perfection of Christ.[2]

More generally, though, after 200 years of ceaseless upheaval, the eighteenth-century Church of England was most anxious to stand still, and so adopted a stance in most things of studied moderation. On the positive side, that meant it succeeded, as it hadn't in the previous century, in holding together what was in the European context a unique coalition of both a 'High' Catholic wing, hankering after some of what had been lost with the break with Rome, and a 'Low' or Evangelical side that was much more drawn to the simplicity and emphasis on Scripture of Protestants, Presbyterians and Puritans. Yet the 1700s also saw the Church and those in authority within it grow too focused on stability and retrenchment, and on not rocking the boat. Climbing the ecclesiastical ladder of preferment became a goal in itself, leaving the Church often bereft of a clear, strong and engaging sense of mission when operating in a society that was witnessing huge upheavals in the second half of the century.

Mission and immediacy, by contrast, ran through everything John Wesley did. As an earnest young man studying at Oxford in the 1720s, he and his brother Charles had joined a group of like-minded fellow students who wanted to distil the wisdom and radical edge of the early Church into a way of living more actively as Christians. They would gather regularly to read the Scriptures and pray together, to fast and practise a strict rejection of life's luxuries, to receive the Eucharist weekly (at a time when quarterly or annual Communion services were not uncommon in parishes), and to engage in charitable and educational projects in the city. Martin Luther had decried the Catholic claim that 'good works' could play a part in earning a place in heaven, but these young idealists parted ways with him on this point. Their carefully calibrated methods of living out their faith earned them the nickname 'Methodists' from their detractors. Wesley turned the insult on its head and made it the name by which his new movement was known.

After university, in 1736, he had set sail for the British colony of Georgia in America with the Society for the Propagation of the Gospel, bursting with zeal to bring God to the indigenous population and to inject some spiritual discipline into the settlers. His enthusiasm and inflexibility, however, put backs up (he also suffered an unhappy love affair), and within eighteen months he was back home. In May 1738, at a service in Aldersgate, London, he underwent what he later described as a physical experience of God's presence. Akin in modern Evangelical terms to being 'born again' – though they were not words he would have used – he wrote of feeling 'my heart strangely warmed . . . that He had taken away my sins and saved me from the law of sin and death'.

It brought about a profound change in him. Thereafter, he eschewed the traditional path of church pulpits and preferment to embark instead on preaching tours of a bigger version of parish, where he spoke to groups around the country at open-air meetings. Initially, he concentrated on London and Bristol, later the Midlands, Yorkshire and the North East, but ultimately covered Scotland, Wales and Ireland, too. Wherever he went, he would, if possible, leave behind Methodist 'societies', run by local people enthused by his message and approach. These would meet regularly to discuss the Scriptures, as well as Wesley's own writings on them, which eventually stretched to thirty-two volumes. Lay preachers would come to speak to the gatherings, and Wesley was ahead of his time in allowing women to take on this role. Such assemblies, quite separate from weekly attend-ance at church – and absolutely not a substitute for it, Wesley made plain – were his chosen method of shaping and binding his followers into what he described as, 'a company of men . . . united in order to pray together, to receive the word of exhorta-tion, and to watch over one another in love, that they may help each other to work out their salvation'. He also urged that there should be a 'community of goods', where those with more shared their good fortune with those with less.[3]

It was a radical spiritual, political and social gospel that chimed with those who heard it, especially when coupled with Wesley's charisma, his way with words, the dynamism he exuded and the simple but rousing lyrics of the hymns that his brother Charles set to music. The focus on personal morality – preaching temperance and the virtues of hard work, of bettering yourself and of keeping the Sabbath – provided his listeners with a blueprint for a righteous, God-fearing way that would guide them through life's many and increasing challenges and towards life everlasting.

On his estimated twenty visits to Heptonstall, Wesley drew large crowds, many walking miles to hear him. 'The people,' he recorded in his journal, 'stood row above row on the side of the mountain. They were rough enough in outward appearance; but their hearts were as melting wax.'[4] On one occasion, he is said to have preached out of a first-floor window of the house where was staying in Heptonstall. So popular did he prove in a community whose livelihoods were rooted in agriculture, or as artisans and craftsmen, that it was decided to put up what was to be called a 'meeting house' in Heptonstall (referring to it as a chapel only came later, after the split with the Church of England that followed Wesley's death). The octagonal shape was favoured, it was said, to make plain this wasn't a church (although in their youth, the Margarets tell me, it was ascribed to not wanting to allow any corners for the devil to hide in, Wesley being as keen as any Evangelical preacher on putting a spotlight on the traps that Satan had laid for those who strayed).

As the building was going up, Wesley returned to urge on the construction by preaching in its unfinished shell. 'Ye hills and ye dales,' he enthused, 'continue the sound, break forth into singing ye trees of wood, for Jesus is bringing lost sinners to God'.[5]

Two years after the completion of the meeting house, he was there again. This time there was, his journal reports, some shifting of allegiances between members of the Methodist societies and those who went to other Nonconformist churches in the area that had made a clean break with the Church of England. 'At Heptonstall,' he writes, 'the renegade Methodists, first turning Calvinist, then Anabaptist, made much confusion here for a season, but they have now taken themselves away again, and the poor people are in peace.'[6]

By the end of the century, the Heptonstall meeting house had 337 members and 1,000 children attending its adjoining Sunday school, still standing today but now closed up and disused. In 1748, the first Methodist school had opened at Kingswood in Bristol. Education was from early days a central part of the mission, extending in the nineteenth century from Sundays to cover every day of the week, and in the twentieth to running state-funded primary and secondary schools. So popular did Heptonstall Chapel become that an extension had to be added, elongating and distorting the original octagon, with the old front door today filled in by a stained-glass window of workers in a vineyard.

No sooner had more space been made than the community it served started to relocate. A series of Enclosure Acts from the seventeenth century onwards had seen rights to use common land and open fields eroded. The latest of these, in 1773, set off a wave of displaced agricultural workers heading into towns in search of employment. The Industrial Revolution hugely accelerated that process, with those from the local hillsides and moors around Heptonstall migrating to the valley floors to earn their living in the mills and factories of Hebden Bridge alongside the new Rochdale Canal, opened in 1804 and linking Yorkshire with the booming manufacturing centre of Manchester. New meeting houses and Nonconformist chapels opened there to serve and sustain those who worked in harsh, unforgiving conditions.

The restoration of the monarchy in 1660 had seen the previous goal for kings and queens of uniformity in religion abandoned in everything but name. The drive ever since Henry VIII had broken with Rome to define a single national Church and then force everyone into it had, after all, brought only bloodshed and turmoil. A new beginning after the free-for-nearly-all of the Commonwealth years allowed Charles II to adopt a more nuanced approach. The Church in every part of his kingdom was henceforth to be broad enough to accommodate both those whose instincts were towards the Catholic end of the spectrum and those drawn to the more moderate forms of Protestantism that had travelled from Europe in the wake of Luther's Reformation.

There were, however, limits. Roman Catholicism – as it became called (though it was never a term used by Catholics) – remained outlawed. Any instinct Charles might have had towards relaxing measures was quashed by dubious but regular reports of continuing scheming by Recusant Catholics that culminated in 1678 with Titus Oates's (fabricated) revelation of a 'Popish Plot'.

It caused fifteen innocent men to be hanged. Its final victim – and indeed the last Catholic martyr to die in England – was Oliver Plunkett, the Archbishop of Armagh. Given the immoveable Catholic sympathies of the majority in Ireland, greater toleration was practised there under Charles II than in England, but the hysteria of the Popish Plot saw Plunkett accused of planning a French invasion of Ireland, brought to trial at Westminster Hall (on the basis that no Irish jury would convict him) and, at the second attempt, found guilty of high treason. He was hanged, drawn and quartered at Tyburn in July 1681.

For their part, while Nonconformists might freely go to their chapels under Charles II, they could not also hold public office.

Toleration went so far, but no further. Unless they were seen to be within the Church – principally by attending its Communion services – they were effectively outcasts. After Charles, first the Catholic James II and then the Calvinist William III both tried to shift the definition of toleration towards their own sympathies at either end of the religious spectrum, but both failed. As a result, the eighteenth-century Church in England, Wales and Ireland continued with its bishops, its hierarchical structure, its sacraments, its rituals and its formal link with the State, but also with the challenge that went with being a national Church of extending its boundaries beyond its moderate centre, somewhere between Protestantism and Catholicism. Only in Scotland, joined legally with England in 1707 by the Acts of Union, was a greater degree of divergence permitted, with bishop-free Presbyterianism as its national Church and a separate Episcopalian (with bishops, as the name suggests) denomination formally incorporated in 1712 and particularly strong in the north and east of the country.

Yet even this low-key degree of divergence proved challenging to navigate. There remained right up to the 1750s some Anglican bishops wedded to old notions of the divine right of monarchs and who had therefore refused to accept the accession of William and Mary as the legitimate King and Queen while James II was still alive. These 'non-jurors' had continued to raise the same objections when Mary's Protestant sister, Anne, came to the throne in 1702, and remained a distracting thorn in the side of the Church of England during the failure of two major 'Jacobite' uprisings by first James II's son in 1715 and then his grandson, 'Bonnie' Prince Charlie, in 1745.

Queen Anne, her instincts High Church but not so much as to risk any religious strife, had no surviving children. After her death in 1714, under the terms of the Act of Settlement of 1701, the Crown could not pass to anyone on the Catholic side of her family. She was therefore the last Stuart monarch and was

302

succeeded by her second cousin, a grandson of James I, George, the suitably Protestant Elector of Hanover, who ruled as George I. He, too, stayed as clear as he could of religious disputes and worked alongside Parliament. It was on its benches that religious differences continued to count for something, so much so that they shaped the identities of its two main parties.

The Tories were associated with High Church sympathies that on occasion saw them toy with the Stuart pretenders to the Crown. They were conscious of a more Catholic approach to tradition, structure and ritual, whereas the radical Whigs unequivocally backed the Hanoverian line, and were inclined towards a Low Church approach, close to the ever-growing number of Nonconformists. The question of how far to extend or restrict religious toleration of such Nonconformists in matters of access to public office was one of the great issues of the age. The Tories, for their part, were keen to root out those of stronger Protestant tendencies, who only made a show of occasional attendance at Church in order to be eligible. Yet, with the Whigs in power from 1714 through to 1760, the direction of travel was the opposite way, towards a further watering-down of existing barriers and tests of conformity.

Some, however, remained beyond the pale. The Quakers, whose refusal to bear arms made them pariahs, were still subject to restrictions. The passing in 1753 of laws that removed the requirement for immigrants to receive Church of England Communion before they could be naturalised prompted so much antisemitic protest on the streets that it was swiftly repealed. Old prejudices, such as Christian antisemitism, were slow to shift. And in 1778, a mild measure to tone down the penal constraints on Catholics in the name of toleration led to riots in Scotland and in London, incited by the Scottish MP Lord George Gordon (labelled by the Whig politician, Horace Walpole, as 'the lunatic apostle'[7]). In the capital, so potent did the cry 'No Popery' remain that 1,000 people were left dead. Even 10 Downing Street, the official residence of the prime ministers whose role became central under the Hanoverian kings, was attacked in the middle of the night by a torch-carrying mob.

With the centre of political power moving from sovereign to Parliament, bishops of the Church of England fixated increasingly on making their influence felt via their seats in the House of Lords. Some would spend as many as eight months each year in London embroiled in its sessions and disputes. There were those who were inspired by the highest motives, but it was undoubtedly a distraction from their wider pastoral role. For those with weaker moral fibre there were temptations aplenty.

Under the four generations of Georges who ruled Britain and Ireland from 1714 to 1830, London in particular witnessed a relaxation in hitherto rigid rules of propriety in social life. The establishment of 'pleasure gardens' at Vauxhall, Ranelagh and other sites around the capital introduced a new and very public frivolity from the 1730s onwards. Lavish masquerades – or fancy-dress balls – would take place, with wealthy folk and some of the growing, affluent middle classes enjoying dancing, flirting and intrigue. In theory, an entrance fee was designed to keep these pleasure gardens exclusive, but their reputation, among those who could only peer in from the outside, as louche, dubious and drunken playgrounds, hardly looked different from the 'gin craze' among the urban poor. The proliferation of shops selling cheap, unlicensed alcohol, often distilled in residential houses, caused a rise in drunkenness and associated problems. While the teetotal Wesley spoke out fiercely against such excess, too many of the leaders of Church of England turned a blind eye, lest they be accused of hypocrisy because of their participation in London society and intrigue.

The parish system was not in good repair. It has been estimated that, at this time, half of the incumbent clergy in English parishes were absentees. Priests would enjoy the proceeds of multiple livings, and give little back by way of service in return. Among those housed in large, often handsome Georgian rectories next to churches, there were plenty who would rather have been anywhere else than in the pulpit on a Sunday. They had little interest in the pastoral and spiritual care of their congregations or in setting them a good example. Instead, as in Wycliffe's day, they would pay poorly educated curates a pittance to hold the fort for much of the year as best they could.

What the appeal of Wesley and the Nonconformist preachers revealed was a taste for preaching of the first order that contained clear, Scripture-based, practical, moral guidance. The failure of too many parish churches to satisfy that, or to keep up with changes in the society in which they operated, is best summed up in 'The Sleeping Congregation', a series of engravings by the satirist William Hogarth, between 1728 and 1762. A bewigged, be-warted clergyman reads an interminable sermon from a high pulpit in a country church. His bored parish clerk passes the time leering into the cleavage of a woman in the congregation, while others in the pews catch up on their sleep. The very fabric of the building is quietly crumbling away, unnoticed by any of them as cracks appear across a fresco of an angel.

The lack of Communion services, especially in rural parishes, was a source of special dissatisfaction. It led to pressure on Wesley – who extolled the virtues of regularly receiving the Eucharist – to ordain ministers himself so as to make it more available. The lay preachers who would come to chapels, such as the one at Heptonstall, to deliver electrifying sermons could not celebrate Communion. Wesley consistently refused to change this, but finally in 1784 agreed to take several steps that carried him in that direction. There was a fast-growing Methodist circuit in the newly independent United States of America after 1776 that was critically short of clergy to lead Communion services. When the

Bishop of London refused to help, Wesley sent his own ministers and ordained them with the power to administer the sacraments. In the same year, he established an annual Conference, which would have the power to make decisions about Methodism (after his death, it elected leaders for one-year terms). And soon afterwards, Wesley also ordained more ministers to serve in England and Scotland.

They remained exceptions rather than the rule. As a Church of England clergyman, in theory Wesley had no powers of ordination – those belonged to bishops – so to go further would have provoked the confrontation with the Church authorities that he had always sought to avoid. In 1795, though, four years after his death, Conference broke free of the Church of England.

Shortcomings in the parish system became more noticeable with the surge in demand for labour that arose from the 1770s onwards with the Industrial Revolution and the coming of steam power, industry and mass production. Those who moved from rural areas like Heptonstall to the fast-growing towns, where they worked in collieries and factories, lived in overcrowded slums, with little sanitation, regular outbreaks of cholera and high infant mortality. The Sabbath was their one opportunity to attend church and hear that God was with them in the hardships of their new lives. Too few among the parish clergy saw fit to convey that message. Indeed, the French Revolution of 1789, and the sight of the national Church across the Channel being dismantled along with the monarchy as part of a despised *ancien régime*, caused many priests in the Church of England to recoil in horror and redouble their efforts to resist every aspect of modernity.

By contrast, Wesley and those who followed him, as well the broader Nonconformist movement, responded to the social ills that they saw afflicting their congregations. Wesley in many ways had come late to what is sometimes called the 'Evangelical Revival' of the eighteenth century. And while he stayed resolutely within the established Church, others chose religious freedom so as to be able to speak their mind and dirty their hands.

One of Wesley's earliest co-workers was George Whitefield. He had been part of that group at Oxford with the Wesley brothers and had gone forward to ordination. He had been in Georgia with Wesley, but formed a stronger bond with America, staying on to found an orphanage there and embark on preaching tours as far north as Massachusetts. Thereafter he travelled between America and Britain. It was the sight of him preaching to coal miners in the Kingswood area of Bristol that persuaded Wesley to embrace open-air meetings rather than the confines of a church pulpit.

Whitefield, too, laid the foundations for a 'Methodist' network, but he was not one who found it easy to tolerate others' opinions on theological matters or to trust them to do the right thing in his absence. In 1739, he and Wesley fell out over whether human-kind's eternal fate in heaven or hell was predestined – as Calvin taught and Whitefield believed – or whether it was something within each individual's grasp, influenced by how they lived their life, as Wesley upheld. And later, when Whitefield defended slav-ery in Georgia, Wesley denounced it as 'the sum of all villainies'.

It was Wesley, then, who was the one among that original Oxford group to take Methodism forward, though Whitefield's own, smaller strain, usually called Calvinist Methodism, grew to be quite a movement, especially after he was drawn into the orbit of another leading figure of the Evangelical Revival – Selina, Countess of Huntingdon. Widowed early, she was a significant figure in both aristocratic society and Nonconformity. Whitefield became her chaplain as the countess energetically evangelised the rich of her acquaintance and used her own wealth, and that of those she drew to her, to build an estimated sixty-four chapels in England and Wales, known as the Countess of Huntingdon's

Connexion, which was aligned with Whitefield and the Calvinist Methodist movement. Until the early 1780s, they were also part of the Church of England, using the Book of Common Prayer, but thereafter broke away.

After her death in 1791, most of her chapels passed into the hands of the Congregationalist Church, with some in the 1860s becoming part of a group known as the Free Church of England. It was Martin Luther, in breaking the stranglehold of Catholicism on Europe, who had encouraged his followers to base their beliefs on *Sola Scriptura* ('only Scripture') rather than on the teachings and traditions of the Church. But different passages of Scripture, sometimes in the same book of the Bible, can say different, even contradictory things, and quite what individual passages meant quickly became a matter of dispute within Protestantism, with fragmentation happening even in Luther's lifetime. The Evangelical Revival saw that pattern repeated again and again, as popular movements split over doctrinal matters into smaller and smaller clusters. Wesley's Methodists suffered just such a fate in the 1810s with the breakaway of the Primitive Methodists, who felt that mainstream Methodism, like the Church of England before it, had grown too comfortable, too fond of ornament in its chapels and of large manses for its ministers to live in, and therefore too far away from the lives of working people.

This constant fracturing may explain why some Evangelicals towards the end of the century preferred to remain firmly within the national structure of the Church of England and to rekindle Wesley's ambition of reform from within. Prominent among them were members of the 'Clapham Sect', which gathered in the 1790s around Holy Trinity Church in south London and its vicar, John Venn. A group of laity, some of them prominent in public life, including several Members of Parliament (William Wilberforce being one), they devoted themselves to religion and to philanthropic work with equal and seamless passion. Taking their lead

from the Quakers, among the causes they espoused was the abolition of the slave trade, as an offence to God as well as to those
exploited by it. Belatedly, the Church of England was waking up
to the challenges posed by commerce and industrialisation, just in
time for the age of Queen Victoria.

ALSO WITH A STORY TO TELL . . .

BUNHILL FIELDS, IN ISLINGTON, north London, across the road from Wesley's Chapel, was one of the first non-denominational cemeteries in the country. Established in the late seventeenth century on unconsecrated ground, and therefore outside Church of England control, it contains the graves of Susanna Wesley (died 1742), mother of John and Charles, of the Nonconformist hymn writer, Isaac Watts (died 1748), and also of William Blake (died 1827).

COUNTESS FREE CHURCH IN ELY was founded in 1785 by Selina, Countess of Huntingdon, after whom it is named. The plain brick building, close to the city's celebrated cathedral, has remained part of her 'Connexion' as one of twenty-two churches overseen by a trust established in her lifetime. It has been used down the years by Congregationalists, the Free Church of England and, more recently, Baptists.

DOLOBRAN FRIENDS MEETING HOUSE, NEAR PONTROBERT IN POWYS, was the first purpose-built Quaker Meeting House in Wales. It was constructed at the start of the eighteenth century by local landowners, the Lloyd family, who started the bank of the same name. Restored in the 1950s, the plain building houses a meeting room and a cottage. Its secluded location, accessed only via a footpath through woods, reflects the persecution Quakers faced at the time, a fate that made many emigrate to America.

CHAPTER 19

The Nineteenth Century

St Elisabeth's, Reddish: With God on Our Side

The Church as it now stands, no human power can save.
Thomas Arnold, head of Rugby School (1795–1842)

ST ELISABETH'S, IN the working-class district of Reddish in Manchester, captures Victorian Britain's brimming confidence. Not only was Britain the greatest power in the world, but it also had God on its side. Built in the 1880s, the church's design had been inspired by a visit to St Mark's Cathedral in Venice by devout industrialist Sir William Houldsworth and his wife Elisabeth (hence its name). Seeing the glories of an earlier empire prompted him to commission not just an elaborate landmark church with accompanying substantial rectory. With that sense of moral purpose that was so much a part of nineteenth-century Christianity in Britain, he wanted it to share the same site with a school, a working men's club with a bowling green, and homes for those who laboured in Houldsworth Mill, the largest cotton-spinning operation of its kind in the world when it had opened in 1865.

The combination of faith, learning and welfare in Houldsworth Model Village joined other similar ventures by philanthropic and religiously inspired fellow industrialists at Port Sunlight, Bournville, Saltaire and Bromborough Pool where, in return for their labour, workers' spiritual, educational and material needs were catered for by benign, God-fearing employers. The six giant polished Aberdeen granite pillars that line the nave of St Elisabeth's arrived with the sort of flourish expected of a man who named everything he created after himself or his wife: first by sea to Manchester docks, then on to Reddish by narrow boats on the city's thriving network of canals, and, on the final, brief leg of their journey, on a cart pulled by two elephants borrowed by Houldsworth for the task from nearby Belle Vue, the first privately financed zoo in the world, opened in 1836. It must have been, as he surely intended, an awesome sight for the workers who lined the route.

As, undeniably, was St Elisabeth's itself when it opened, designed in the dominant Gothic style of the age by one of its leading architects, Alfred Waterhouse, who was also responsible for Manchester Town Hall and the Natural History Museum in London. It cost Houldsworth £20,000 at the time, the equivalent now of getting on for £2.5 million. Seen today from across the green that stands in front of it, this red-brick colossus, its almost-freestanding tower topped by four pyramidal pinnacles, continues to dwarf the low-rise terraced housing that surrounds it.

The interior, completed in 1883 and large enough to accommodate 750 people effortlessly, used only the finest materials and craftsmen that money could buy. There is an alabaster font next to the main entrance, with a fine oak cover that lifts through a typically ingenious bit of Victorian engineering. The marble screen between nave and choir stalls was modelled on the one in St Mark's and features figures of the four Gospel writers. Decorated ironwork separates off a Lady Chapel big enough in itself to serve as a parish church, and exquisite stained glass throws a warm light onto the mellow, patterned red-brick interior walls even on the chilly December day when I visit.

The journey from the eighteenth-century Church to this monument to Victorian Christianity's liking for pomp, piety and presumptuousness is in some ways a straightforward one. Nineteenth-century Britain was booming, at home and abroad, as its colonial expansion turned a substantial part of the world map pink. The exodus from market towns and rural villages to industrial cities and ports trading with that empire was causing a demand for many new urban churches. While the Nonconformists and the now-separated Methodists had been quick to respond to this need, putting up chapels and meeting houses, the Church of England had been slower to realise that its existing parish network was woefully inadequate. When it finally cottoned on in 1818, a Church Building Society was set up to extend existing churches and build many new ones. The funds came in part from a £1 million grant – a fortune at the time – given by the government in celebration of the victory over the French at Waterloo three years earlier. The intention was that the visible presence of the Church in the city should be every bit as distinctive and unmissable as the Church in countryside villages.

At the start of the nineteenth century, there were around ten thousand parish churches in England and Wales. A survey carried out in 1872 recorded 3,204 new ones, plus 925 that had been completely rebuilt.[1] Such progress went far beyond what even the well-endowed Church Building Society could afford. Such rapid growth was therefore often paid for by the wealthy industrialists of the Victorian age, men like Sir William Houldsworth, keen to cut a dash. Like the landowners and nobility of old, these titans acted out of benevolence but also from enlightened self-interest, seeing in the Church a force for social stability and defence of the established order, under which they were prospering as never before.

Yet the nineteenth-century Church was not a building project. Whatever the impression churches such as St Elisabeth's sought to convey of shared moral purpose connecting all levels in society, this was also an age of questioning, adjustment, threat and turmoil. With the departure of the Methodists from the Church of England before the century had even started, there was a real risk that many more of the Evangelical clergy in the ranks of Anglicanism, as it increasingly came to be known, might follow them. Bishops were often reluctant to offer parish livings to those who shared the commitment of Wesley and the Nonconformists to a more vigorous personal engagement with those at the bottom of society.

One zealot in this regard, Herbert Marsh, Bishop of Peterborough from 1819 to 1836, had such antipathy to anyone who was so much as touched by Calvinism that he insisted every humble curate wanting to work in his diocese had to answer in writing a series of eighty-seven questions before being granted a licence to determine whether they belonged in the Church of England. It prompted a public dressing-down for the bishop from the writer, humorist and (to make ends meet) cleric, Sydney Smith, about episcopal prejudice against the diligent but hard-pressed priest: 'How any man of Purple, Palaces and Preferment can let himself loose against this poor working man of God, we are at a loss to conceive – a learned man in a hovel, with sermons and saucepans, lexicons and bacon, Hebrew books and ragged children.'[2]

Smith's plea for toleration and respect did not fall on deaf ears. Gradually, Evangelical clergy changed less-fixed minds than Bishop Marsh's by showing themselves to be exemplary in translating their own personal 'conversion experience' of God into a thoroughgoing calling to serve others in some of the toughest Church of England parishes up and down the land. They led wholly admirable lives in the newly industrial cities and towns. Their dedication to practical, pastoral care of downtrodden flocks who worked in brutal and often degrading conditions won them admirers among those who did not share their theological outlook. So did their efforts to educate in the faith those among their parishioners who could read, through the millions of cheaply produced texts of the Religious Tract Society that began to be widely distributed in the early decades of the century. Indeed, if the now-familiar stereotype of Victorian respectability existed anywhere, with its reading, praying, Sunday observance, family values and keen eye for moral standards, it was in the creation of the Evangelical wing of the Church of England.

In 1815, recognition of its importance as one of the component parts of a broad Anglicanism saw the bench of bishops welcome its first Evangelical member, Henry Ryder, as Bishop of Gloucester and then, from 1824, of Lichfield. He and those like him may have remained a minority in such upper levels of the Church well into the twentieth century, but they were over-represented not just in the cities but also in rapidly expanding overseas missionary work. The Charter Act of 1813, which extended the mandate of the East India Company, made provision for the first time for the Church of England to start operating there, something that had previously been resisted. The following year, T. F. Middleton, who had won plaudits as a socially active vicar of St Pancras in London, was sent as the first Bishop of Calcutta (Kolkata) to establish a seminary there, and was given oversight of Church activities in both the Indian subcontinent and Australia.

Yet the good example set by Evangelical churchmen did not easily shake the more mainstream parochial clergy of the Church of England in the countryside out of their eighteenth-century habits. Absenteeism remained a big problem, with an estimated six in every ten parishes in 1827 served only irregularly by the paid incumbent. In Jane Austen's 1814 novel *Mansfield Park* there is general surprise expressed in their social circle that Edmund Bertram is actually going to reside with his wife, Fanny, in the living he is given by his father.

And it wasn't only novelists who were keen to draw attention to this continuing abuse. It contributed to the popular anticlericalism that regularly bubbled up to the surface, as in 1831 when the palace of the Bishop of Bristol was burnt down by rioters.

That protest had a more immediate target – those members of the House of Lords, including bishops, who had opposed the Great Reform Bill that would extend the electoral franchise. In Bristol, just 6 per cent of the population was at that time allowed to vote for their Member of Parliament. With the end of the Napoleonic Wars in 1815, a movement for social reform had been growing in the country, drawing on the Enlightenment principles of liberty and reason that had been at the heart of the French Revolution. It had gathered sufficient momentum that (in spite of opposition from Lords and the Church leadership) a well-disposed Whig government was eventually able, in 1832, to pass the Great Reform Bill into law. As well as extending the franchise to many more householders, it abolished some of the more corrupt practices used to elect Members of Parliament.

The same drive for political and social change also targeted the privileges of the Church. Attendance at the universities of Oxford and Cambridge remained restricted to those who subscribed to the 39 Articles of the Church of England. To cater for those who were excluded by this regulation, progressive figures joined forces in 1828 to establish University College, London, as an alternative, with no faculty of theology and no religious tests for anyone wanting to study. (The appeal of its radical 'godlessness' prompted a backlash, with the founding in the following year of the rival King's College, London, just down the road, which had religion very much at its heart.)

For the first half of the nineteenth century, the Church of England as an institution – again most obviously through its bishops in the House of Lords – resisted all attempts to involve the State in the primary education it provided, often through the clergy, as part of the parish system. Nonconformist schools, run by voluntary societies, were demanding that the government provide funds for them to employ trained teachers, but the Church refused to join forces with them, wanting above all to retain its independence of the State and its dominance in educating the young. The first government grants to the voluntary educational societies came in 1833, but it wasn't until 1870 – with an estimated one-third of all children still receiving no basic education – that legislation was passed to set up 'provided' schools, funded by national and local taxes, in areas where there was no Church alternative. These were, by 1882, educating about one million children, half the number in Church establishments. Repeated efforts by the Nonconformists to join forces with the Church of England in a single school system, funded by taxes and run by educationalists, were resisted. The refusal of the Anglicans delayed progress and was eventually to give rise to the development of 'dual' State and Church systems that persist to this day.

In other areas, the Church's exclusive role in national life was more effectively removed. Religious tests, such as the ones Oxford and Cambridge applied to their undergraduate intake, had been central to the partnership of Church and State since the Reformation, but were increasingly seen as restrictive, outdated and unfair. Often, they were simply overlooked when recruiting to public office, but in 1828 any remaining uncertainty was removed when they were formally abolished by Parliament. You could now be a good citizen without having to attend the state Church.

In the mid 1830s, the registration of births, deaths and marriages also ceased to be exclusively a Church of England function. A civil registrar was appointed, and it was henceforth possible to have a civil ceremony for marriage rather than a Church of England wedding. By 1880, exclusive Church control of religious burials would go, too.

The repeal of the Test Acts saw the open admission of Nonconformists to Parliament. This development was regarded as a major challenge by many in the Church of England since Parliament exercised formal authority over it by passing the bills that regulated its inner workings. Even if the reality was that Nonconformists had long sat in the Commons by disguising their true religious convictions, now their presence was official, it raised questions about where authority truly lay in the national Church. Could Nonconformists vote on matters that pertained to a Church to which they did not belong?

The suggestion that followed next – that Catholics should also be admitted to Parliament and hence have a say through their votes in the governance of the Church of England – caused even more anguished soul-searching. Previous monarchs – George III in particular – had drawn the line at any suggestion of Catholic emancipation because he claimed it would violate his coronation oath. Efforts to remove a fraction of the restrictions placed on Recusant Catholics – many of them gentry or aristocracy – had prompted riots in the late 1770s, but the arrival of large numbers of Irish Catholics into the labour-hungry new industrialised areas of England, Wales and Scotland, and their demand for a place to worship freely on a Sunday other than the local Anglican parish church, were creating new pressures.

Of greater significance, though, was the growing unrest in Ireland since the Acts of Union of 1800 had abolished the separate Dublin parliament.

The principal agitator for change was the barrister and gifted orator Daniel O'Connell, who gathered his nation (or the Catholic majority within it) behind him in his argument that, if Ireland were now to be properly represented at Westminster, then laws that stopped Catholics standing and voting for candidates had to be repealed. Otherwise, he said, Parliament would lack legitimacy. Repeatedly rebuffed by the British authorities, in July 1828 O'Connell stood for election as an MP in County Clare. He won handsomely, even though as a Catholic he was barred from taking up his seat in Westminster. The very real threat that his exclusion could cause an Irish uprising prompted the Prime Minister, the Duke of Wellington, the victor over Napoleon at Waterloo and hitherto an implacable opponent of reform, to push through the

Catholic Emancipation Act of 1829 in the face of opposition from his own benches, the Cabinet and the King.

By 1850, the number of Catholic immigrants had risen to more than half a million, and this was swollen by a further wave of emigration that followed the disastrous famine caused by potato blight in Ireland from 1845. Meanwhile, as many as one in four of the population of England and Wales was reported to be attending some form of Nonconformist worship on a Sunday. Not just tolerance but religious pluralism was in everyday life becoming the hallmark of Christianity in Britain and Ireland.

Anglicanism's fight to retain its privileged position was beginning to resemble a losing battle and created an appetite from within for change. But what form should it take? In the 1830s, Ecclesiastical Commissioners were appointed to sort out its administrative failings, notably the tangled and unequal finances of the dioceses, including the incentives for those with no real vocation to collect parish appointments so as to line their pockets. The Pluralities Act of 1838 made it much harder for anyone to hold more than one living.

The most significant attempt at reform, however, came from 1833 onwards, not from the ranks of Evangelical clergy facing the everyday challenges of the age in industrial areas, but from an elite group at Oxford University who felt something had been lost in Anglicanism because of its separation from Rome. The Tractarian Movement was so named because its largely academic membership wanted to infuse new life into the Church by sharing reform-minded papers, called 'Tracts for the Times'. Popularly, though, it was known as the Oxford Movement.

Its leaders – Edward Bouverie Pusey, John Keble, Richard Hurrell Froude and John Henry Newman – shared a determination to redefine the *via media* or 'middle way' (between Roman Catholicism and Nonconformity) that had become the chosen course of the Church of England. They wanted to do so by a spiritual *and* practical renewal. For inspiration, they looked back to the early seventeenth century and figures such as Nicholas Ferrar at Little Gidding and his circle. Yet to return the Church of England to being, as they sought, holy, catholic and apostolic (though not Roman Catholic), they went back even further in time to claim as the source for the authority of its priests and bishops the 'apostolic succession'. In Roman Catholicism, this is the teaching that Jesus anointed Saint Peter as the first pope. So every ordination that Peter and those he had ordained made linked the person being anointed in a divine chain that led back to Jesus. In such a scheme, the Reformation had not therefore severed this connection with God's Son, the Oxford Movement sages argued, because the Church of England (unlike the Church of Scotland and other Protestant Churches) had kept its bishops. They stood in that line back via Peter to Jesus.

At a time when the Church of England's identity and authority was being challenged from all sides – 'the fashionable liberality of the generation', as John Keble bemoaned it – the Oxford Movement sought to reform it from within by making priesthood something more than a comfortable career option for younger sons of the gentry. Instead, it was about entering into a super-natural bond with Christ himself that imparted, among other things, a practical mission to serve the poor, exploited and marginalised, in imitation of Jesus. Not only did the Oxford Movement look back to find a new *raison d'être* for the Church beyond the whims of monarchs (it was noticeably cool about Henry VIII's Reformation, and declined to support an Evangelical-inspired scheme in 1837 to erect a 'Martyrs' Memorial' in Oxford to Thomas Cranmer and others), it was also about elevating an ideal of priesthood that would both purify it *and* make it answer the pressing social challenges of the industrial age.

Such ambiguity about the Reformation inevitably roused the suspicion of the Evangelical wing, while for many rank-and-file members of the mainstream of the Church, the Oxford Movement reeked too much of Rome. Its members – thought to be never more than 1,000 clerics at its peak (of a total of 18,000 clergy in England and Wales) – spent the 1830s vigorously rebutting any such suggestion, in person and in their tracts. In 1841, though, Newman, whose preaching and intellectual gifts had made him stand out as the leader of the group, published Tract 90, arguing that the 39 Articles of the Church of England were fundamentally in harmony with Roman Catholic teaching. Any difference was down to the 39 Articles condemning corrupt practices in the Church of Rome, not its essence. A furore followed. A line had been crossed, and at the request of the Bishop of Oxford no further tracts appeared.

Since his appointment in 1828 as vicar of the University Church of St Mary the Virgin in Oxford, Newman had lavished attention on its benefice – one of the smaller churches that came under its care – just south of the city in the village of Littlemore. To better serve its hard-pressed inhabitants, Newman had built a chapel and a school, in line with the Oxford Movement's combined spiritual and social commitment. After the outrage that Tract 90 caused, he retreated increasingly to Littlemore, where he established a quasi-monastic community (something absent from the Church of England since the Reformation) that lived under a rule of strict discipline. If he were hoping it would be sufficient to keep him within Anglicanism, it failed. In 1845, he announced publicly that he had become convinced that Rome represented the 'fullness of truth' in Christianity and was received into the Catholic Church.

It was a shattering blow to the Oxford Movement, and once again plunged the Church of England into crisis. In the years that followed, some 500 clergy followed Newman in 'crossing the Tiber', but the remaining Tractarians – though less well remembered now than Newman, who went on to become a Catholic cardinal in his lifetime, and in 2019 a saint – stayed put and ultimately did leave a lasting mark on the character of the Church of England. That was and continues to be seen in the elaborate liturgical rituals of High or Anglo-Catholic Anglicans, such as Sir William Houldsworth, carried out by preference in elaborate, beautifully decorated Gothic churches like St Elisabeth's, Reddish, whose architecture harked back to the medieval age.

It went much deeper, though, than ritual and a style sometimes dismissively referred to as 'smells and bells'. With the Church of England's confidence being eroded by growing religious pluralism and liberal, secular efforts to erode its footprint in national life, the Oxford Movement helped it find a new purpose and identity. The Evangelical wing, too, played its part, ensuring that it remained broad, inclusive and stable. Moreover, the large number of young men who came to Oxford with ordination in mind made the university the perfect place for influencing the following generations of Church leaders, and the Oxford Movement's greatest legacy was seen going forward in Anglicanism, with the emphasis placed not just on the Eucharist at the centre of worship, but also on other sacraments. Right up to the historic vote to ordain women as priests in the 1990s, nineteenth- and twentieth-century Anglicanism nurtured within itself, thanks to the Oxford Movement, a belief that its legitimacy lay in it staying close in doctrinal matters to the Church of Rome.[3]

Another part of this legacy was the rebirth of religious orders in Anglicanism; first for women in the 1840s, including the Community of St Mary the Virgin at Wantage and the Society of St Margaret at East Grinstead; and later for men, beginning in 1866 with the Society of St John the Evangelist, better known as the Cowley Fathers.

Emancipation for Catholics and Newman's 'going over' to Rome, along with a sizeable minority of the Oxford Movement, was followed in 1850 by Pope Pius IX restoring the Catholic hierarchy in England and Wales. A parallel system of bishops that over-lapped the Anglican dioceses was established (though efforts were made to avoid the two denominations' bishops in the same area holding the same title, with the Anglican diocese of Manchester, for example, covering much of the same territory as the new Catholic diocese of Salford). The arrival of Nicholas Wiseman from Rome as the first Catholic Archbishop of Westminster saw crowds once more take to the streets with cries of 'No Popery', and a leader in *The Times* condemning 'the grossest act of folly and impertinence which the court of Rome has ventured to commit since the crown and people of England threw off its yoke'.

Some of the vitriol was caused by Wiseman's triumphal tone in a message he sent ahead to his new flock, which reportedly caused Queen Victoria, on reading it, to remark, 'Am I Queen of England, or not?' There was open talk, too, in Catholic circles of 'reclaiming Mary's dowry' – a reference to a prayer long said more in hope than expectation by English Catholics in the post-Reformation years. Tensions and mutual suspicion were slow to abate between Church of England and Church of Rome in the decades that followed, as they operated and sometimes competed in inner-city areas. These were only further inflamed in 1895 when a papal bull, *Apostolicae curae* (still on the statute book), declared Anglican orders 'absolutely null and utterly void', rubbishing the Oxford Movement's claims to be part of the apostolic succession.

Nowhere, though, was the hostility between Anglicanism and Catholicism felt more strongly in the nineteenth century than in Ireland. The reach of the state Church had never been strong there, with the principle of *cuius regio, eius religio* – whose realm, their religion – invoked by Henry VIII at the Reformation largely rejected in practice by the Irish. The Church of Ireland had been established in law at the insistence of English monarchs. It was the religion of the ruling class as well as the prerequisite for hold-ing official posts. Yet, at best, it accounted for no more than 10 per cent of the population and did not constitute a majority in any single county (by its own estimates).[4] Meanwhile, the other 90 per cent resented the tax (or tithe) that they were obliged to pay to support this minority Established Church. Most of them were Catholics (driven during periods of persecution to attending Mass in the open air and sending their children to informal 'hedge schools' because Catholic education was banned), or Presbyterian and Nonconformist descendants of those who had arrived in the 'settlements' from the sixteenth century onwards, especially in parts of the northern province of Ulster.

The Catholic Emancipation Act of 1829 had made the privi-leges of the Church of Ireland ever harder to justify, and fuelled agitation for wider freedom from British rule. The Fenian Rising of 1867, organised by the Irish Republican Brotherhood with support from expatriate Irish in the United States, may have turned out to be something of a damp squib, but its reverbera-tions were felt strongly in mainland Britain among Irish commu-nities in Manchester, Liverpool and London. So concerned was the Liberal leader William Gladstone (in his youth closely associ-ated with the Oxford Movement) at this spread of discontent and potential unrest across the Irish Sea that he became convinced of the need for better ways to 'pacify' Ireland. One of the first meas-ures he brought forward when elected as Prime Minister in 1868 was a bill to disestablish the Church of Ireland. The passage of legislation the following year encountered substantial opposition, not least from Queen Victoria, who made her disapproval known, but Gladstone prevailed.

The British Crown no longer had any part in appointing Ireland's Anglican bishops, whose four allocated seats in the House of Lords were removed. The tithe system was scrapped, and the Church's substantial assets and property transferred to

Ecclesiastical Commissioners whose task it was to use it to enable the Church of Ireland to pay its own way. Governance was henceforth to be carried out by a General Synod of representatives, clerical and lay, of the Church.

The new arrangements in Ireland spurred on the Welsh. There were obvious parallels. Since its arrival in Wales in the eighteenth century, Nonconformity had been growing everywhere, most recently in the industrial areas of the south and north east. The Anglican Church was now in the minority. In 1910, a Royal Commission reported that the Nonconformist churches drew congregations of 550,000 each week, while the Established church had just 193,000 communicants. The belief was promoted from the pulpit of many a chapel house at the time that 'chapel people' were the only true Welsh, and that Welshness – and the Welsh language – was somehow synonymous with Nonconformity.

The Society for Liberating the Church from the State, which began in 1844, attracted strong support in Nonconformist areas from the 1850s, turning chapelgoers into activists. Cultural, political and religious issues were mixing with economic discontent. Tithes paid to the Anglican parish were just as disliked as in Ireland. In the late 1880s, Tithe Wars saw farms forcibly sold off after their owners refused to pay their dues to the local vicar. Rioting followed, notably in Denbighshire, the headquarters of the Welsh National Land League, modelled on the similar Irish Land League. Troops had to be deployed to keep the peace.

The first bill to disestablish the Church in Wales was introduced into the British Parliament in 1870 by Watkin Williams, himself the son of an Anglican clergyman, a Liberal MP in a party dominated, especially in Wales, by Nonconformist members. It failed. By 1887, disestablishment had become the official policy of the Liberal party, supported by Gladstone and the future Prime Minister, David Lloyd George. Again, in 1894 and 1895, it was voted down by the House of Lords. It took until

1914 to get through, once the power of the Upper Chamber had been reduced to blocking the will of the House of Commons for only two years. The Welsh Church Act came into force in 1920.

Despite seeing its position reduced throughout the century to that of one among many, Anglicanism's status as the Established Church still carried certain uncomfortable responsibilities. In 1859, the publication of Charles Darwin's *On the Origin of Species* proved a sensation, with its central argument, based on evidence he had collected from around the world, in favour of natural selection, a theory that took issue with the Christian narrative of the origins of the world as God's creation, found in the story of the Garden of Eden in Genesis. Twelve years later, in *The Descent of Man, and Selection in Relation to Sex*, Darwin sought to replace the Adam and Eve narrative with his scientifically based theory that humankind is descended from apes.

While other churches and their leaders largely remained silent in the face of such a challenge, or restricted themselves to sweeping condemnation of Darwin, the Church of England did try to muster a response. It would take it years, if not decades, to formulate a properly considered theological reply to Darwin (and 150 years to apologise publicly for the personal attacks they launched on him at the time), but the best-remembered Church attempt at the time to contribute to what was a national debate came from Bishop Samuel Wilberforce. The son of the anti-slavery campaigner William Wilberforce, he had been Bishop of Oxford since 1845. An admired public speaker, and credited with dealing effectively and calmly in his diocese with the fallout from Newman's conversion, he agreed in the summer of 1860 to take part in a discussion at the Oxford Museum with a group of philosophers, including Thomas Henry Huxley, who supported Darwin's ideas.

It didn't go well. Was it, the bishop provocatively asked Huxley, through his grandmother or grandfather that he was descended from a monkey? Huxley replied that there was no shame in having a monkey as an ancestor, and that would be preferable to a connection with a man [like Wilberforce] who used his great gifts to obscure the truth. The exact words spoken are disputed, as are their context, but the account that has survived in the public memory eloquently highlights how the Church was wrongfooted by Darwin's theories.

For all the bottomless Victorian confidence that St Elisabeth's still manages to convey, the nineteenth century was a time when Christianity in Britain and Ireland was struggling to adapt in a world that was changing faster than ever before. And the questions were only to get harder to answer in the coming century.

ALSO WITH A STORY TO TELL . . .

The Norman CHURCH OF ST MORWENNA AND ST JOHN THE BAPTIST, MORWENSTOW, on the north coast of Cornwall, was for forty years in the middle of the century under the care of the Rev. R. S. Hawker, poet, antiquary and eccentric. His devoted service to his parish, which included wreckers, poachers and smugglers, is recalled by the figurehead of a ship lost on the rocks beneath the Church that stands in its graveyard. Neither High nor Low in his ministry, Hawker was received into the Catholic Church on his deathbed.

ST MARY AND ST NICHOLAS, LITTLEMORE, near Oxford, was built between 1835 and 1836 for John Henry Newman, then vicar of the University Church in the centre of Oxford, under which Littlemore parish then came. It contains Newman's pulpit. Here, surrounded by a community of like-minded individuals, he made a life-changing decision to abandon the Church of England for Rome in 1845.

WESTMINSTER CATHEDRAL, LONDON, was built between 1885 and 1903, as the mother church for Catholics in England and Wales following the restoration of the hierarchy in 1850. Designed by John Francis Bentley in Neo-Byzantine style, using only brick, its tall campanile or bell tower is said to have provoked the wrath of Queen Victoria, who complained it spoilt the view from nearby Buckingham Palace.

CHAPTER 20

The Twentieth Century

Liverpool Metropolitan Cathedral:
The People's Church

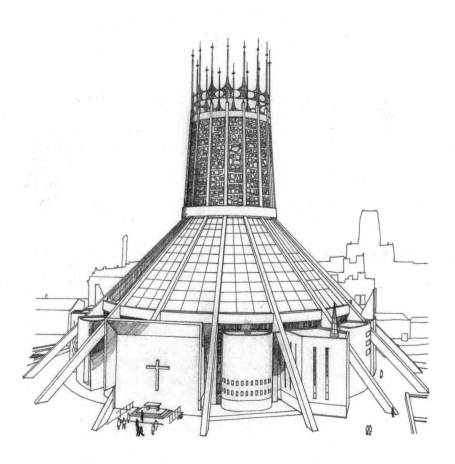

It is significant that the architect of the Metropolitan Cathedral was a non-Catholic. I don't regard [it] as Catholic property, but as belonging to you all.

John Heenan, Catholic Archbishop of Liverpool, 1967[1]

IN THE BASEMENT of Liverpool's still strikingly modern Catholic Cathedral lies a crypt. At first glance, with its monumental brick vaulted arches and marble trimmings, it appears to be a relic of the Victorian age, with little to do with the rest of the building. It was actually started on Whit Monday 1933, intended as the first stage in a grand design by Edwin Lutyens, the architect of Empire and creator of New Delhi, capital of the British Raj. His vision was of a Liverpool Catholic Cathedral, topped off with towers and a dome bigger than St Peter's in Rome, that would be so large and so magnificent that it would dominate the ridge that stands above and behind the Pier Head on the city's celebrated skyline.

Such eye-catching proportions were well suited to a Liverpool that was then booming as 'the port of Empire', and where to this day local pride morphs into a kind of fierce patriotism. Moreover, the arrival on its quaysides of generation after generation of Irish Catholic immigrants over the previous hundred years had made it the proud and pre-eminent centre of re-emerging Catholicism in England.

But there was another impetus, too, for the audacious scale of what was planned. Of the all the cities on the British mainland to be divided by vicious religious sectarianism in the twentieth century, Liverpool was the most blighted by suspicion, hostility and often violence that spilt onto the streets between Catholics and Protestants, with its working-class areas around Scotland Road close to the docks akin to rival ghettoes. In that un-Christian spirit, the new Catholic Cathedral was intended as a bigger, better, bolder rival to trump the equally gigantic but architecturally backward-looking red sandstone Gothic Anglican Cathedral that, since 1904, had been rising ever higher out of the ground a few hundred metres further along the same ridge. Lutyens' design, it was boasted, would be fifty metres taller than its neighbour.

It took the Second World War to spell the beginning of the end for such religious one-upmanship. At first there wasn't much evidence of a change of heart on the part of the protagonists. Schoolchildren at neighbouring Catholic and Protestant (the word Anglican was never used) schools would hurl abuse and sometimes stones at each other. 'Mixed' marriages between the two groups were frowned upon or forbidden.[2] Work resumed after 1945 on the Anglican Cathedral, but painfully slowly, as if the thrill had gone out of the chase. It wasn't completed until 1978.

For the Catholic leaders in the city, there was a more pressing problem. They could no longer afford the costs, which had spiralled since the construction of the crypt was started before the war. The final bill for the whole project was now edging towards £30 million, just as the city's economy was shrinking as postwar trading patterns altered to its disadvantage and the repair of wartime bomb damage swallowed any public money available. So, in 1957, John Carmel Heenan (himself of Irish immigrant parentage), newly installed as Archbishop of Liverpool, launched a competition for an alternative building that would be every bit as remarkable, but with a price tag of closer to £1 million. The result was Frederick Gibberd's radical drum-shaped, concrete, almost airborne Metropolitan Cathedral, which opened in 1967.

It sits on top of Brownlow Hill, once the site of a workhouse, and on top of the old crypt, rather like a rocket on its launch pad. This was, after all, not only the time when the city's music was putting it at the heart of Swinging Sixties culture, but also the new age of exportation of the final frontier of space. The central spire is a circular stained-glass lantern (with designs from John Piper and Patrick Reyntiens) that rises up as if about to blast off to heaven. The overall design spoke, as Lutyens' planned cathedral would also have done, of a new confidence in English Catholicism, reinforced by Irish immigration and now accounting for almost 10 per cent of the British population.

'Paddy's Wigwam', as it is affectionately known locally, also resonated with an unmistakable commitment to doing things in a new, more open way, in line with a reforming energy that was gripping the universal Catholic Church. In the first half of the 1960s, its cardinals and bishops gathered in Rome under Pope John XXIII for the Second Vatican Council with the aim of redefining in a more positive way its relationship with the modern world, other churches and other faiths.

The 2,500-strong congregation in the new cathedral was seated in a circle around a modest altar in the centre of the building. The traditional barrier that the nave-and-chancel arrangement of churches had placed between clergy and laity was thereby demolished. And the building's comparatively modest cost (albeit bringing with it decades of snagging problems because of the rushed finish to such a revolutionary design) had been met largely by small donations from those who would use it, rather than some grand philanthropist or factory owner wanting a memorial to himself. The names of all these donors, including my parents, are included in the Remembrance Book in one of the eight meticulously maintained side chapels that nestle round the circular core.

By virtue of its design and its location, Liverpool Metropolitan Cathedral embodies both a timeless spiritual power – the daylight that streams in through the coloured glass of the great lantern, moving round the pews as the day progresses like the hands of a clock, has a transcendent quality – and an urgency as Christianity struggled to claim its place in post Second World War Britain and Ireland. Church attendance figures had been going down since 1945, faster initially among Anglicans and Nonconformists than Catholics (where Sunday Mass attendance was compulsory), but by the 1960s were tumbling across the board. New solutions to reverse this trend were being sought.

An internal Anglican report in 1945, *Towards the Conversion of England*, inspired by two Church of England bishops on the Evangelical wing, was among the first to confront the stark fact that the country could no longer call itself Christian, as it had between the reigns of King Alfred in the ninth century and Queen Victoria in the nineteenth. Its recommendations were a mixed bag, some familiar – such as a more energetic proclamation of the Gospels – others more creative. The suggestion of an advertising campaign was, however, vetoed by both the Archbishop of Canterbury and the Church Assembly, which since 1920 had taken over Parliament's role in legislating for the Church and was later to become General Synod.

Religion, it was pointed out, had already been getting plenty of airtime and exposure on the BBC, which had been founded by a devout Presbyterian, John Reith, in the early 1920s, first on its radio stations and later on television, where it was a protected part of its public service remit. The same obligation was placed on new commercial broadcasters as they arrived on the scene from the 1950s onwards, and remained in place until the end of the century. Yet being beamed into living rooms was doing little to halt the ebb in numbers of worshippers in parish churches up and down the land.

More successful was a new emphasis on Christianity taking its message out of churches and into the community in practical, no-strings-attached ways to those in need of its help, whether or not they were believers or churchgoers. Between Liverpool's two great cathedrals runs Hope Street, lined by theatres, concert halls, hotels and Georgian houses. Its name resonated afresh from the late 1970s onwards when it became a thoroughfare for a remarkable and rapid rejection of the city's sectarian past by two prelates, one Catholic and one Anglican, and its replacement by a shared and practical commitment to addressing the economic and social problems facing Liverpool. Their statues, in the form of a pair of bronze doors (again paid for by the people of Liverpool), today stand halfway along it – Derek Worlock, the Catholic Archbishop from 1976 to 1996, and Derek Sheppard, who was Anglican Bishop from 1975 to 1997. Together they took God into the everyday lives of the people of Liverpool. Their efforts may not have refilled the pews of either of their cathedrals but, as this memorial in a city street (rather than a side aisle) demonstrates, they won an enduring place for themselves and for the type of Christianity they represented in the hearts of the people they served.

The two were very different characters – Worlock, a shy, awkward, back-room type, animated by the spirit of the Second Vatican Council, and Sheppard, a good-looking former England cricketer with an easy public manner and a passionate belief in social justice. The motto they adopted was 'Better Together', and they worked shoulder to shoulder over two decades, promoting community initiatives, stepping in when the local council imploded, making sure the voice of the city was heard in the corridors of power in London and ensuring that much-needed investment came its way.

Their double act on the national stage rallied a city that, especially in the late 1980s, was sinking under the weight of labour disputes and an exodus of major employers. And they rallied those within the churches who saw the future as championing social and societal justice. In the process, they reignited the debate about the role of the churches in politics (especially among the politicians they shamed into action).

More significantly, their ecumenical partnership thrived in apparently unpromising soil, setting an example of how to bring together the different and hitherto hostile branches of Christianity (they also included in their efforts the local Methodist leaders) in one shared and concerted effort for the common good. That was to become the hallmark of the endeavours of Christianity in Britain and Ireland in the second half of the twentieth century and beyond.

Anglican leaders were prominent at the outbreak of the First World War in encouraging young men to sign up for service in the trenches, building on the work in church halls in the preceding decades of the Boys' Brigade and Church Lads' Brigade in blending Christianity with patriotism in the minds of their young members. The popular Bishop of London, Arthur Winnington-Ingram – known for his outreach work as an assistant bishop in Stepney in the East End of London – led the charge from the pulpit with fervour. He was often to be found wearing a military uniform and preaching about a 'holy war' in the four years of a conflict that cost twenty million lives, split in roughly equal proportions between soldiers and civilians.[3] Other more measured voices, such as that of Randall Davidson, Archbishop of Canterbury from 1903 to 1928,[4] refused to allow clergy to sign up for combatant roles, but still the sheer scale of the slaughter on the Western Front caused a backlash against organised religion, which seemed incapable of offering any real explanation for such unfathomable suffering. Those who returned alive from active service often had little time for churchgoing, even if they had benefited in their hour of need from the pastoral care of outstanding army chaplains such Geoffrey Studdert Kennedy. Known as 'Woodbine Willie', his ministering to troops in the trenches included handing out cigarettes to soothe frayed nerves on the eve of battle.

It took until 1927 for numbers of Anglican communicants to recover from a nadir in 1917 to pre-war levels. It peaked in 1931, before declining slowly but steadily thereafter. Regardless of Sunday attendance, when peace returned, the Church successfully reclaimed its 'national' role in remembering the war dead, resisting government efforts to treat as a purely secular ceremony the unveiling on 11 November 1920 of the Cenotaph in Whitehall in central London (designed by Lutyens) as a memorial to the fallen. After some resistance from Whitehall and even from the King, George V, it was agreed that events at the Cenotaph should be followed by a procession to Westminster Abbey where a funeral service would take place before the interment of an unidentified solider from the Great War just inside the West Door. This grave – along with those laid out across the former battlefields in northern France by the Imperial War Graves' Commission (again using Lutyens' designs) – became a focus for grieving relatives throughout the years that followed, while Anglicanism's role in leading national acts of commemoration since has faced little real challenge.

The moral case for combat – set out in Christianity in the Just War principles as long ago as Saint Augustine in the fourth century – was arguably more clear-cut and less infused with nationalism in the Second World War, especially as the appalling reality of the Holocaust emerged during the conflict. There was a greater role, too, in this conflict for the churches, with days of public prayer drawing large congregations. Some prelates, notably Bishop George Bell of Chichester, went so far as to question in the House of Lords the saturation bombing of German cities and the civilian casualties they entailed. At the time it made him an unpopular figure, even among his fellow bishops, but subsequent generations have looked back on his humanitarian concerns, and his courage, with greater respect.

The same cannot be said of the Church's public intervention in the abdication crisis of 1936. The role of the monarch, as Supreme

Governor of the Church of England, had been enhanced in the public imagination from 1932 when George V began what have become regular Christmas broadcasts to the nation, first on radio and subsequently on television, where the affinity of Crown and altar was reinforced. When, however, his son and successor, Edward VIII, wanted to marry an American divorcee, Wallis Simpson, the new Archbishop of Canterbury, the Scot Cosmo Lang, sided with the Prime Minister, Stanley Baldwin, in insisting that the King must choose between what he regarded as the Christian institution of monarchy and the sinfulness of association with (in God's eyes) another man's wife.

Two days after Edward VIII had abdicated on 11 December 1936, Lang gave a radio broadcast that left a lingering impression of an overly judgemental, intolerant Christianity, at odds with popular sympathy for the King and with changing ideas around personal morality. 'Strange and sad it is,' Lang intoned, 'that [the King] should have sought his happiness in a manner inconsistent with the Christian principles of marriage, and within a social circle whose standards and ways of life are alien to all the best instincts and traditions of his people'.[5]

While first Edward VIII's younger brother, as George VI until 1952, and then his daughter, Elizabeth II, thereafter re-established both the good standing of the monarchy and its enduring link with the Established Church by their strong sense of duty and quiet, undemonstrative but deeply held Anglicanism, subsequent archbishops did not learn from Lang's misjudgements. Just short of twenty years later, his successor-but-one, Geoffrey Fisher, once again stepped in very publicly to oppose a royal marriage, this time of Elizabeth's only sibling, Princess Margaret, to Group Captain Peter Townsend, on the grounds that he was a divorcee. In a statement announcing that she was abandoning her plans, the Princess referred to being 'mindful of the Church's teachings that Christian marriage is indissoluble' and to her 'duty' as a senior member of the royal family. Once again, the spirit of the times was running fast against such a stance, leaving the Church to appear stranded in the past.

Defending what many saw as outdated rules did nothing to reverse a growing gap between the churches and those who no longer filled their pews. Embracing social justice and social mobility, by contrast, affirmed their continuing relevance. Successive education Acts from 1902 to 1944 extended a taxpayer-funded universal right to first primary and then secondary education for all children, and saw the Church of England, Methodists and the Catholic Church ever more firmly rooted in serving their local communities in some of the country's most deprived neighbourhoods. (Residual anti-Catholic prejudice saw local authority-funded Catholic schools attacked into the 1960s as 'Rome on the rates'.)

With its presence in the slum areas of big cities daily exposing priests, vicars and ministers of all denominations to the cost of rapid economic change, Christianity had already, in the mid nineteenth century, come into contact with the new creed of socialism. Church people had been there, too, at the dawn of the Labour party, with the Christian Social Union founded in 1889 and active branches established by the middle of the first decade of the twentieth century in the big industrial centres of Birmingham, Manchester, Leeds, Glasgow, Liverpool and London.

In the same year, and for many of the same reasons, the second Catholic Archbishop of Westminster since the restoration of the hierarchy, Cardinal Henry Manning, sided very publicly with striking dockers in the East End of London against their employers. His intervention proved decisive, persuading both parties to what was a bitter and protracted dispute to reach a compromise over pay and conditions. It was greeted by the workers as a victory. In the May Day procession of 1890, Manning was feted as a hero, his portrait carried alongside that of Karl Marx, co-author in

1848 of *The Communist Manifesto*, the most celebrated pamphlet in the history of the socialist movement (and a proponent of atheism).

Manning's courage and outspokenness was to find an echo almost a hundred years later when a 1985 commission headed by Robert Runcie, Archbishop of Canterbury, issued a report, *Faith in the City: A Call for Action by Church and Nation*. It chastised both the Church of England for its failure to do more to sustain blighted urban areas, and the hardline Conservative government of Margaret Thatcher for its free-market economic reforms and their social impact. Few column inches were spent reporting its criticisms of the Church. Instead, what made the headlines was the report's advocacy of higher child benefit and welfare payments and more investment in job creation for the inner cities. The Prime Minister declared herself 'absolutely shocked' by its findings, while an anonymous Cabinet minister labelled as 'Marxist' recommendations defended in public by an archbishop who had served as tank commander and won a Military Cross in the Second World War. At a time when the Conservative government was largely without a strong opposition in Parliament to challenge its record, the Church of England stepped into the role, just as in Liverpool, at the same time, Archbishop Worlock and Bishop Sheppard became the spokespeople for a city whose elected representatives were failing to make its case.

They would all insist, in the face of relentless criticism that they were 'meddling' in politics, that their concerns were not party political but pastoral, rooted first and foremost in the Gospels, as well as in theological developments in the second half of the twentieth century. These challenged the existing perception of God as a remote figure, available if at all only to believers via their monks, priests and bishops. In 1963, the Anglican Bishop of Woolwich, John Robinson, sold a million copies of his book

Honest to God, which translated theological conversations going on in ivory towers into more popular language to argue that the understanding of God had to change to embrace the real challenges of faith in a fast-changing world.

Taking an outspoken stance on social justice – at home, as well as abroad through its work with development agencies such as Christian Aid and CAFOD – may have revealed the Church as more in touch than some might have imagined, but it also came at a price. With the retirement of Robert Runcie, begetter of the controversial *Faith in the City* report, the Conservative government used the Prime Minister's remaining powers of appointment over senior Church positions (as the representative of the Supreme Governor, the monarch) to pass over better qualified candidates for the role of Archbishop of Canterbury and appoint a little-known bishop from the Evangelical wing in the person of George Carey.

The biggest change in the twentieth century in the role of Christianity, though, came with its embrace of ecumenism. Progressing at noticeably different speeds in different parts of Britain and Ireland, it ultimately achieved more in fostering mutual understanding of shared roots and respect between hitherto self-consciously separate traditions than it did in terms of formal mergers between denominations. Efforts to reunite Anglicanism and Methodism floundered in 1972, and discussions in the 1950s along the same lines between the Church of England and the Church of Scotland, national churches on either side of Hadrian's Wall, similarly started promisingly but failed to reach a final agreement. And if Liverpool's sectarian divide crumbled in the 1970s, in Glasgow the tribalism of supporters of Rangers (Protestant) and Celtic (Catholic) football clubs still retained a noticeable religious dimension at the end of the century despite all efforts to the contrary.

Above all, in Northern Ireland the different branches of Christianity too often sat on either side of a political, cultural, nationalistic *and* religious civil war over the fate of six northern counties, carved out from the rest of Ireland in 1921 with the support of the Presbyterian (Unionist) majority there who wanted to continue to be part of the United Kingdom. Meanwhile the other twenty-six counties threw off British rule and were governed under a system that for decades gave a 'special place' to the Catholic Church in the workings of what was initially known as the Free State. That position of trust was subsequently abused through the actions of some bishops, priests and nuns, as later revelations about clerical abuse and the treatment of unmarried pregnant women made plain.

Yet for all its failures to achieve the ambitious goals it had set, the ecumenical movement of the twentieth century redefined Christianity in the British Isles and challenged the popular stereotype in an increasingly secular, sceptical age that religion was the cause of conflict in the world. The term ecumenism was, at the start of the century, largely restricted to theological and academic circles, but it quickly took on more practical connotations. In 1909, the charismatic, free-thinking Hensley Henson, a future Bishop of Durham but at that time a Canon at Westminster Abbey, and with a reputation as a socially active priest in east London, caused major controversy by fraternising with Nonconformists. He accepted an invitation to preach at a Congregationalist chapel in Birmingham, ignoring the ban subsequently placed on his visit by the local Anglican bishop.

For four years from 1921 another boundary was crossed when informal inter-church discussions about the eventual reunion of Anglicanism and Catholicism took place at Malines in Belgium between a group of English clerics, attending with the blessing of the Archbishop of Canterbury, and a Catholic team, headed by the local Archbishop, Cardinal Mercier, with the approval of the Pope.

Though the talks were eventually brought to an end when some of the participants felt the exchange of ideas of a new shared future had gone too far, seeds were sown that were reaped later.

After the Second World War, the reluctance to return to pre-war certainties that saw the birth of the Welfare State, public ownership of key industries and the National Health Service also inspired fresh thinking about the fragmentation of Christianity. In the late 1950s, a proposal emerged formally to unite the ministries of the Methodists and Anglicans. It won approval from the Methodists in 1968 but failed in 1972 to receive the necessary three-quarters majority in the Church of England's General Synod to go ahead.

It was part of a pattern. Cooperation in the field led to broader theological discussions about putting such shared work and principles on a more formal footing, only to be defeated by entrenched minorities (in both Evangelical and Anglo-Catholic wings in the case of the Anglican–Methodist plan) wedded to their own particular identities, history, practices and prejudices.

The Anglican-Roman Catholic International Commission (ARCIC) was established in 1969, following a highly successful visit to Rome by Michael Ramsey, Archbishop of Canterbury. Pope Paul VI, recently emerged from the Second Vatican Council where the spirit of ecumenism featured large in the key document *Nostra Aetate*, gave him a warm welcome, and presented him with the bishop's ring he had worn as Archbishop of Milan. Hopes inevitably grew that the breach of the Reformation might just be healed. They were at their highest in 1982, when Pope John Paul II came to Britain and knelt to pray next to Archbishop Robert Runcie in Canterbury Cathedral.

Yet what many liked to think of as 'merger talks' subsequently stalled, unable to find a way or the will to navigate around what for some, including the essentially conservative John Paul II, were non-negotiable differences about authority, ministry and Eucharist between the two denominations. Whatever optimism remained further drained away after the Church of England voted in 1992 to ordain women to the priesthood, an option that the Catholic leadership continues fiercely to resist.

If institutional-level exploration of common ground failed to find a path forward, many individual Christians voted with their feet as the century neared its close. The decision around women priests saw some Anglican bishops, priests and laypeople joining what was presented at the time as a fresh wave of 'going over to Rome'. Though predictions of large numbers proved unfounded, some did it quietly, others with more fanfare, with Catholicism offering special arrangements to allow married Anglican vicars to serve as priests in a Church that insisted its own clergy remained celibate. Though it made fewer headlines, there was traffic in the opposite direction, too, from Catholicism to Anglicanism, seen as more flexible in interpreting the Gospels in the light of developments in society around, for example, the role of women and the sanctity of same-sex love. The democratic structures of the Church of England's elected General Synod appealed to many disgruntled Catholics who felt their voices were not being heard by the hierarchy of their Church.

At grass-roots level, by the end of the century, day-to-day relationships between the Church of England, the Catholic and the Reformed Churches had never been closer, whether at local or national level, with the sight of cardinals, archbishops and moderators working together as equals an unremarkable everyday sight. Often, they were joined by other faith leaders. The long history of Christian antisemitism, often violent, stretching back centuries, was acknowledged and repented of, and new understandings of shared origins were forged. Those attending Sunday services were much smaller in number going into the new millennium than a hundred years previously, made worse, some argued, by the abolition in 1994 of most of the restrictions on Sunday opening of shops (though the changes had little effect in some coastal areas of Scotland where Free Presbyterianism remains strong).

If congregations were made up of more elderly people, individual churches on the whole emptier, and many merged or declared redundant, the pastoral work carried out by people of faith continued and grew, especially in areas of national life where the need was most urgent.

ALSO WITH A STORY TO TELL . . .

The medieval church that housed COVENTRY CATHEDRAL was destroyed by the Luftwaffe in 1940. A breathtaking new building was consecrated in 1962, designed by Sir Basil Spence, and containing artworks by Graham Sutherland, John Piper and Jacob Epstein. It sits within the preserved ruins of the old one, creating a living cathedral dedicated to the cause of reconciliation and peace.

SANDHAM MEMORIAL CHAPEL IN BURGHCLERE, HAMPSHIRE, was built in the 1920s to contain a series of seventeen paintings by the artist Stanley Spencer, inspired by his experience of serving in the First World War. The resurrection scene, behind the simple altar at what is sometimes called 'Stanley's Holy Box', has soldiers laying the white crosses that mark their graves at the feet of Jesus.

The CHURCH OF CHRIST THE CORNERSTONE IN MILTON KEYNES, Buckinghamshire, was opened in 1992 by Queen Elizabeth II and is shared by five denominations – Anglicans, Baptists, Methodists, Catholics and the United Reformed Church. Conventional in design, it is a radical example of working together on the basis of shared covenant that speaks of 'one Faith, one Baptism' and 'common witness'.

Epilogue: A Twenty-First Century Church?

It is, of course, far too soon to know what shape the history of Christianity in Britain and Ireland will take in the twenty-first century. At a little more than one-fifth into its term, what may today seem distinctive and enduring features could well end up as footnotes in the story by the year 2100. Who, writing in 1521, would have been able to foresee on the basis of Henry VIII's policies and behaviour up to then all that was to happen in the turbulent seventy-nine years that followed? In 1521, he was working hand in hand with the Pope to see off the challenge of Martin Luther.

In general, though, history flows, rather than stops and starts, even if at times it can pick up speed at an alarming and head-spinning rate, all the more so given the technology we now have at our disposal. Looking back over the centuries that have witnessed so many radical, unsettling changes, it is possible with the benefit of hindsight to spot the signs that trouble was bubbling up. Yet looking forward is hazardous.

So a great revival in churchgoing may come about. All that can be said at the moment is that the tide is flowing in the other direction right now, though the effect of the COVID trauma on our hard-wired assumption that the world will generally and inevitably get better has yet to play out. And then, if COVID has been disruptive, it will potentially be nothing compared to some of the predictions of what climate change will bring to humankind, in these islands and elsewhere. Might such perils, if we don't do the sensible thing and change our ways, be the sort of catastrophe that brings people back to God or their gods?

How exactly such a return might happen, in Britain and Ireland at least, could be already playing out in the first two decades of the century. There are now many more people seeking out the spiritual rather than the material, but doing it not via the conventional route of gathering in churches for services. They go on pilgrimages in ever-greater numbers along rediscovered trails whose very soil is soaked in the prayers and hopes of earlier generations of believers. And they pick out the parts of the Christian heritage of these islands that they feel are still relevant to their lives. While one in three people say that they believe in angels – in Christianity, messengers of God – in the same surveys only a quarter describe themselves as very or fairly religious.[1]

So while the statistics unambiguously show a collective turning of backs in these islands on formal religious or denominational allegiance, they also report a rise in those openly and actively exploring whether there is something more than meets the eye to human existence than our secular orthodoxy allows. That hunger presents an opportunity as well as a challenge to Christianity in this century. Neither have as yet been grasped.

In many of the centuries covered in this book, the attitude of monarchs has been a key, if not the key, determining factor in the development of Christianity. What would have become of Saint Augustine in 597 when he landed in Kent if King Ethelbert had not welcomed him ashore? Today the throne no longer holds such raw power in Great Britain, but, by her longevity, her sense of duty and the clear faith that she reveals in her annual Christmas broadcasts, its current incumbent, Elizabeth II, has what we now call soft power aplenty. In the early part of the twentieth century, in the wake of ecclesiastical reforms to meet the national aspirations of Ireland and Wales, questions were being asked repeatedly about the disestablishment of the Church of England – including on occasion by leading Anglican clerics such as Hensley Henson, Bishop of Durham in the 1920s and 1930s. That debate is little heard at present, in part because of the pastoral role the Church plays to all, regardless of faith, in its still functioning parish network, but also on account of the coming together of national identity and belief in the person of Elizabeth II as Supreme Governor of the Church of England.

Whether disestablishment will remain on the back burner in the decades to come is debatable. Queen Elizabeth's son and heir, the current Prince of Wales, has spoken in the past about being 'Defender of Faiths' rather than, like his mother, 'Defender of the Faith' (as we have seen already, a title originally given to the English monarch by the Pope in the days of Henry VIII). In 2015, he clarified those earlier remarks to say he would want to remain 'Defender of the Faith' but also to be, in ecumenical, interfaith times, 'a Protector of Faiths'. It is a thoughtful approach from a thoughtful if not universally popular man to living in a much more diverse Britain, but where it leaves the Church of England is not obvious.

So far in these pages, the history of all but one century, the first, has been told through buildings. And churches continue to be built in Britain and Ireland in the twenty-first century, even as formal attachment to Christianity dwindles and footfall through their doors shrinks. The numbers of such new constructions are inevitably small, compared with what has gone before, and the majority largely functional in design. Most are commissioned by independent Evangelical churches, where numbers in the congregation buck the general trend and are growing.

There are, though, still some that catch the eye and the imagination, such as the oval-shaped Bishop Edward King Chapel, opened in 2013 at Cuddesdon, an Anglican training college in Oxfordshire. Niall McLaughlin's creation was runner-up in the prestigious Stirling Prize for architecture, hailed as 'a showcase for British craftsmanship' in its use of natural materials, with larch and ash in a light-filled interior that is dominated by great wooden arches. The overall approach is self-consciously new-century, mirroring that of Christianity as it seeks to define its place in changing times. The chapel blends in with its setting rather than stands out from or above it, as has been the tendency with churches, particularly in the English countryside or on the skyline of our cities.

If that modesty is to become a mark of twenty-first-century Christianity, then one step further down the same road is to dispense with church buildings altogether and to gather in the open air. At the end of this still young century, there is every chance that the building that tells the story (or part of it) of Christianity in Britain and Ireland is not a building at all in the conventional sense.

The first experiment in this direction came in the wake of the First World War, with Whipsnade Tree Cathedral in Bedfordshire, conceived by Edmund Blyth as a memorial to friends who had died in the conflict. Tracing the shape of Liverpool's Anglican Cathedral in trees, it uses poplars planted at intervals to create the pillared effect of a nave, with a graceful silver birch to mark the high altar, and other species for transepts and side chapels. 'Neither garden nor arboretum' was how Blyth described his creation. It remains in the custodianship of the National Trust, true to his founding goal – to create 'an enclosure for worship and meditation, offering heightened awareness of God's purpose and transcendence'.[2]

Blyth's experiment was replicated in the mid 1980s in the new town of Milton Keynes in Buckinghamshire, where landscape architect Neil Higson created another Tree Cathedral by similar means, this time based on Norwich Cathedral. Bark and leaves serve as its walls in place of bricks and mortar.

If church structures can harmonise with and learn from nature, so too can churchgoers. The notion of taking church outdoors is certainly contemporary, aligned with a flourishing theological debate around Christianity's Bible-signposted duty of 'steward-ship of creation' in the age of climate change.[3] Yet it is also as old as faith itself, in the worship of nature spirits in pre-Christian belief systems, borrowed by Irish, Welsh and Scottish Christian monks from the fourth to the seventh centuries. And when Jesus' followers gathered in the Gospels, it was more often outdoors than in. Likewise in the early Church, the threat of persecution by the Roman authorities, in Britannia as elsewhere in the second and third centuries, meant it could be safer for believers to assem-ble in the open air, far away from crowds, rather than in anything so easy to target as a church building. As late as the early decades of the fifth century, as we have seen, Bishop Germanus, on a visit from Gaul to Saint Alban's shrine, was surprised at quite how many believers in Britain still worshipped under trees.

If the ecumenical movement was one hallmark of twentieth-century Christianity in bringing closer together than ever the different Christian denominations, as well as other faith tradi-tions, then the question of humanity's relationship with nature, and the potentially irreversible damage being done to the planet, is a leading candidate as the biggest concern of twenty-first-century Christianity in these islands. And the two – ecumenism and climate change – have come together in the growing numbers of believers who reject formal institutional ties and the structures that are so much a part of those institutions, and instead join with other like-minded individuals to seek the sacred in the natu-ral world.

Tree cathedrals do have a sense about them, for me at least, whatever their high-minded creators' spiritual intentions, of primarily being art installations. Those mavericks who gather on the Sussex coast on the first Saturday of each month under the banner of Wild Spirit – 'Looking for something, out in the open' is their tag line – are altogether less lofty and prescriptive in their approach to a place in which to worship. It began in 2011 at

Birling Gap, a beach close to Beachy Head, with a handful of like-minded individuals from Christian backgrounds agreeing to assemble once a month at ten o'clock on a Saturday morning in an attempt to return to something elemental. As one of the founders, the writer Cole Moreton puts it, 'We instinctively felt that the need to step outside of buildings and institutions to explore a bigger, wider landscape and sky.'[4]

From the start, anyone of faith has been welcome, though a Christian element is still there in the make-up of Wild Spirit. The location changes month by month to encompass other spots on the coast, and sometimes inland places in woods or on downland. Those who are signed up receive an email or text to tell them where to gather. Deliberately informal, unstructured and unhierarchical, it refuses to be constrained by details such as owning and running premises. As Giles Fraser, the outspoken former Canon Chancellor of St Paul's Cathedral in the City of London, has written in his 2021 memoir, institutional Christianity can turn its custodianship of church buildings 'into an idol, a museum for the 1 per cent'.[5]

Numbers at Wild Spirit have grown steadily since those early days. Today, groups of thirty and more are not unusual, across all ages and backgrounds, faith traditions and none. With some it supplements other religious practice; for others, not. For an hour each month Wild Spirit comes together for something that avoids the predictability of ritual but still contains ingredients that have an appeal for all: drinking in the history of the selected place, its scale and its spirit; sharing in a reading of words of wisdom, whether from spiritual texts or resonant poems; reflecting in silence and prayer; exploring the immediate area in groups and then reassembling to share food and discussion; and an activity that touches on nature and the divine, whether it be kite-flying in the breeze or making paper boats to float in the stream. To close there is a final blessing, sometimes taken from Celtic traditions, seen as more in tune with nature's patterns than official Christianity. The only bit of formality comes when all recite a form of words that joins them in their endeavours. 'We are here because we want to be. We recognise where we are, and we are grateful for it.' No mention of any sort of God there.

The various COVID lockdowns that stretched from March 2020 into the spring of 2021 saw Wild Spirit gatherings put on hold, and hence my planned participation in them. I have therefore had to rely on accounts from those involved. The pandemic, though, is reported to have given fresh impetus to other similar outdoor experiments in new/old types of Christianity, such as 'Forest Church' in its various and substantial manifestations both in Britain and Ireland. The health benefits of meeting outdoors no doubt played a part when indoor locations became synonymous with transmitting infection.

When it comes to religion, small, simple and freelance appears to have an edge in this century over the large, complex and institutional endeavours of previous ones. The successful live-streaming by the major denominations of their services during the lockdown – 'attendance' is said to have gone up by between one-third and half compared to numbers in the pews beforehand – may further weaken the place of the church building.

But, to echo the health warning I have already posted, enthusiasm for bricks and mortar may return. Stranger things have, after all, happened over the past 2,000 years. To learn from them, and other aspects of Christian history in the past two millennia, is simultaneously to consider where that past has led us to now, as individuals, as congregations or as fairly agnostic but still spiritually curious nations bearing some of the hallmarks of Christianity. And there is no better resource to do that than the ancient and not-so-ancient churches that are on all our doorsteps.

Acknowledgements

This book was originally conceived in 2018 as a series of leisurely research trips around ancient and modern churches the length and breadth of Britain and Ireland. That, though, was in the golden age when I assumed that global pandemics didn't wash up on our shores. History, of course, could have told me otherwise if I had given it a thought, but now I know better.

Working round lockdown restrictions on church opening and travel ended up making it more of an obstacle course, and I am grateful to the following for assisting me in navigating the unforeseen roadblocks, often putting themselves out to make it possible in the topsy-turvy times through which we were living: Simon Banner, Rachel Billington, Vanessa Crooks, Margaret Coupe, Elena Curti, the late Evelyn Davies, Brian Daly, Mark Dowd, Margiad Eckstein, Richard Finn, Mark Griffin, Richard Holloway, Sara Maitland, Rachel Mann, Cole Moreton, Margaret Morgan, Julia Muir Watt, Angie Stainton, Caroline Willson and Duncan Withers.

Extracts from 'Little Gidding' by T. S. Eliot (*Little Gidding*, Faber & Faber, London, 1942) are reproduced by kind permission of the T. S. Eliot estate.

One wonderful artist, James Gillick, introduced me to another, Stephen Tsang, who has done a brilliant job with the illustrations that go with the text. I feel privileged to be working again with the team at Hodder – Katherine Venn, Jessica Lacey, Nicki Copeland and Rachael Duncan – and to have Piers Blofeld as my agent watching out for me.

Even though the various journeys to visit the churches featured were often on a wing and a prayer because of the ebb and flow of the pandemic, the constant steadying support and often presence of my children, Kit and Orla, and of my wife, Siobhan, with whom I am blessed to share my life, made it all not only doable but also the pleasure I had always intended it to be before circumstances intervened.

Notes

Prologue

1 Rose Tremain, *Sacred Country* (London: Sinclair-Stevenson, 1992)
2 'Exploring Churches with Diarmaid MacCulloch', *Financial Times*, 26 July 2019, which gave birth to a Radio 3 series in April 2021.

1. The First Century – Glastonbury Abbey

1 Regius Professor of Divinity at Oxford (1959–69), in an essay 'The Route from Galilee', in Henry Chadwick (ed.), *Not Angels, but Anglicans: A History of Christianity in the British Isles* (Norwich: Canterbury Press, 2000).
2 Matthew 27:57; Mark 15:43; Luke 23:50–6; John 19:38.
3 John Scott, ed., *An Early History of Glastonbury: An Edition, Translation and Study of William of Malmesbury's De Antiquitate Glastonie Ecclesie* (*On the History of the Church of Glastonbury*) (Suffolk: Boydell Press, 1982).
4 ibid.
5 See Professor Roberta Gilchrist, 'Glastonbury: archaeology is revealing new truths about the origins of British Christianity' (*The Conversation*, 23 March 2018).
6 'The Glastonbury Abbey Archaeological Archive Project', Glastonbury Abbey Archaeology, https://research.reading.ac.uk/glastonburyabbeyarchaeology/about.
7 The text in English is available on the Project Gutenberg website – http://www.gutenberg.org/

359

8   Romans 16:3–5.

9   Matthew 16:18.

10 Michael Grant, trans, *Tacitus, The Annals of Imperial Rome* (London: Penguin, 2003).

11 Mark 16:15.

12 Paula Fredriksen, 'Christians in the Roman Empire in the First Three Centuries CE', in David Potter, ed., *A Companion to the Roman Empire* (Oxford: Blackwell, 2006).

13 Luke 10:1–24.

14 John Williams, *The Ecclesiastical Antiquities of the Cymry; or, The Ancient British Church, its History, Doctrine, and Rites* (1848).

15 John I. Morgans and Peter C. Noble, *Our Holy Ground: The Welsh Christian Experience* (Ceredigion: Y Lolfa, 2016).

16 Serenus de Cressy, *1605–74, The church-history of Brittany from the beginning of Christianity to the Norman conquest under Roman governours, Brittish kings, the English-Saxon heptarchy, the English-Saxon (and Danish) monarchy . . .*, published in Rouen in 1668, now available in the University of Oxford text archive, https://ota.bodleian.ox.ac.uk/repository/xmlui/handle/20.500.12024/A34964

17 ibid.

18 From the preface of William Blake (c. 1808) *Milton: A Poem*.

2. The Second Century – Saint Alban's Shrine

1   Edward Gibbon, *The History of the Decline and Fall of the Roman Empire* (London: Penguin, 2000).

2   This is in line with a paper, 'The Date of Saint Alban', published in *Hertfordshire Archaeology* in 1968 by the English historian, John Morris, best known for his 1973 book, *The Age of Arthur*.

3   D. H. Farmer, ed., Bede's *Ecclesiastical History of the English People* (London: Penguin, 1990).

4 Geoffrey of Monmouth, *Historia Regum Britanniae* (*Histories of the Kings of Britain*) https://www.sacred-texts.com/neu/eng/gem/index.htm.

5 Farmer, Bede's *Ecclesiastical History*.

6 ibid.

7 ibid.

8 Robin Lane Fox, *Pagans and Christians in the Mediterranean World from the Second Century* AD *to the Conversion of Constantine* (London: Penguin, 1986).

9 Victor Turner and Edith Turner, *Image and Pilgrimage in Christian Culture* (New York: Columbia University Press, 1978).

10 F. R. Hoare, trans. and ed., *The Western Fathers* (New York: Harper Torchbooks, 1965).

11 The text in English is available on the Project Gutenberg website – http://www.gutenberg.org/

12 Farmer, Bede's *Ecclesiastical History*.

13 The figure quoted in Christopher de Hamel, *The Book in the Cathedral: The Last Relic of Thomas Becket* (London: Allen Lane, 2020).

14 ibid.

15 Michael Swanton, trans. and ed., *Matthew Paris' The Lives of the Two Offas* (Devon: Medieval Press, 2010).

16 D. J. Hall, *The English Medieval Pilgrimage* (London: Routledge, 1965).

17 However, during the disputes of the English Reformation, Lucius was quoted as evidence that papal writ ran in Britain as early as the second century.

3. The Third Century – Lullingstone Villa

1 J. R. H. Moorman, *A History of the Church in England* (London: A&C Black, 1963).

2 Mary Beard, 'Sculpture puzzles', *Times Literary Supplement*, 29 September 2020.

3 G. A. Williamson, trans., Andrew Louth, ed., *Eusebius: The History of the Church from Christ to Constantine* (London: Penguin, 1989).
4 Exodus 34:14.
5 Revelation 22:13.

4. The Fourth Century – Ninian's Whithorn

1 R. S. Thomas, *Collected Poems 1945–1990* (London: Orion Publishing Group, 2000). Used with permission.
2 Farmer, Bede's *Ecclesiastical History*.
3 Ian Bradley, *Celtic Christianity: Making Myths and Chasing Dreams* (Edinburgh: University of Edinburgh Press, 1999).
4 The text in English is available on the Project Gutenberg website – http://www.gutenberg.org/
5 As reported in the *Chronicles* of Prosper of Aquitaine, who in the 430s was secretary to the popes.
6 'The Life of Germanus', in Hoare, *The Western Fathers*.
7 Athanasius of Alexandria, *Ad Afros Epistola Synodica (Synodical Letter to the Bishops of Africa)*.
8 A. W. Haddan and W. Stubbs, *Councils and Ecclesiastical Documents* (Oxford: Clarendon Press, 1871).
9 Including Saint Jerome.
10 Bradley, *Celtic Christianity*.

5. The Fifth Century – St Martin's, Canterbury

1 *De Excidio et Conquestu Britanniae (On the Ruin and Conquest of Britain)*. The text in English is available on the Project Gutenberg website: http://www.gutenberg.org/
2 ibid.
3 Farmer, Bede's *Ecclesiastical History*.
4 ibid.
5 Michael Swanton, ed., *The Anglo-Saxon Chronicle* (London: Phoenix Press, 2000).

6 Many historians question whether Hengist ever existed, though they accept the story of mercenaries coming over and seizing power by force.

7 Matthew 16:18.

8 Eamon Duffy, *Saints and Sinners: A History of the Popes* (London: Yale University Press, 1997).

9 ibid.

10 Farmer, Bede's *Ecclesiastical History*.

11 ibid.

12 Jacqueline Simpson and Steve Roud, ed., *A Dictionary of English Folklore* (Oxford: OUP, 2003).

6. *The Sixth Century – Clonmacnoise*

1 Saint Patrick, *Confession*, https://www.confessio.ie/etexts/confessio_english#

2 J. Wyn Evans, 'The Legacy of the Watermen', in Chadwick, *Not Angels but Anglicans.*

3 Peter Brown, *The Cult of the Saints: Its Rise and Function in Latin Christianity* (Chicago: University of Chicago Press, 2014).

4 ibid.

5 Richard Sharpe, ed., Adomnán's *Life of Saint Columba* (London: Penguin, 1995).

6 However, the Anglican Archbishop of Armagh, James Ussher, in his seventeenth-century historical writings, suggests Palladius was, in fact, British.

7 Liam De Paor, *St Patrick's World* (Dublin: Four Courts Press, 1993).

8 Heinrich Zimmer, *The Celtic Church in Britain and Ireland* (London: David Nutt, 1902).

9 Saint Patrick, *Confession.*

10 ibid.

11 ibid.

12 Sharpe, Adomnán's *Life of Saint Columba.*

7. The Seventh Century – All Saints', Brixworth

1 Quoted in Bertram Colgrave, *Two Lives of St. Cuthbert* (Cambridge: CUP, 1940).

2 John Betjeman, *Guide to English Parish Churches* (London: Collins, 1958).

3 Christopher Winn, *I Never Knew That About England's Country Churches* (London: Ebury Press, 2014).

4 As set out in 'The Councils of Clofesho', a lecture delivered in 1993 in All Saints' by Simon Keynes, reader in Anglo-Saxon History at Cambridge University.

5 Notably by Professor R. H. C. Davis, Professor of Mediaeval History at the University of Birmingham.

6 Farmer, Bede's *Ecclesiastical History*.

7 ibid.

8 ibid.

9 As recorded in the twelfth-century W. T. Mellows, ed., *Chronicle of Hugh Candidus, a Monk of Peterborough* (London, 1949).

10 Farmer, Bede's *Ecclesiastical History*.

11 The text in English is available on the Project Gutenberg website – http://www.gutenberg.org/

12 Morgans and Noble, *Our Holy Ground*.

13 Farmer, Bede's *Ecclesiastical History*.

14 ibid.

15 R. A. B. Mynors, R. M. Thomson and M. Winterbottom, eds, *William of Malmesbury Gesta Regum Anglorum (The History of the English Kings)* (Oxford: OUP, 1998).

16 Farmer, Bede's *Ecclesiastical History*.

17 ibid.

18 David Rollason, 'To Whitby For Easter', in Chadwick, *Not Angels, but Anglicans*.

8. *The Eighth Century – Jarrow Abbey*

1   Diarmaid MacCulloch, *A History of Christianity: The First Three Thousand Years* (London: Allen Lane, 2009).

2   The Vulgate (from the Latin *editio vulgate* or 'common version') was the Bible compiled in Latin by St Jerome in the fourth century on papal orders as an authorised version.

3   Roger Rosewell, 'Stained Glass in Anglo-Saxon England', *Vidimus*, issue 42 (the online magazine on medieval stained glass: https://vidimus.org/issues/issue-42/features/).

4   John 9:5.

5   Peter Hunter Blair, *The World of Bede* (Cambridge: Cambridge University Press, 1990).

6   'The "Paenitentiale"', in A. W. Haddan and W. Stubbs, *Councils and Ecclesiastical Documents*.

7   ibid.

8   ibid.

9   ibid.

10 ibid.

11 Charles Plummer, ed., *Baedae Opera Histoica* (Oxford: Clarendon Press, 1896).

12 Dr Anna Ritchie, 'Alcuin of York: ambassador and scholar' published on the BBC History website in 2011.

13 Rolph Barlow Page, *The Letters of Alcuin* (New York: Forest Press, 1909).

9. *The Ninth Century – Sherborne Abbey*

1   Christopher Dawson, *Religion and the Rise of Western Culture* (London: Sheed and Ward, 1950).

2   Swanton, *The Anglo-Saxon Chronicle*.

3   ibid.

4   ibid.

5   ibid.

6   Catherine Cubitt, 'Rape, Pillage and Exaggeration', in Chadwick, *Not Angels but Anglicans*.

7   Simon Keynes and Michael Lapidge, trans., *Alfred the Great: Asser's Life of King Alfred and Other Contemporary Sources* (London: Penguin, 1983).

8   ibid.

9   ibid.

10. *The Tenth Century – St Andrew's, Greensted*

1   Simon Keyes, 'Apocalypse Then', in Chadwick, *Not Angels but Anglicans*.

2   Farmer, Bede's *Ecclesiastical History*.

3   Swanton, *The Anglo-Saxon Chronicle*.

4   Mynors, Thomson and Winterbottom, *William of Malmesbury's Gesta Regum Anglorum*.

5   Swanton, *The Anglo-Saxon Chronicle*.

6   J. A. Robinson, *The Times of St Dunstan* (Clarendon, 1923).

7   Peter Stanford, *The She Pope* (London: Heinemann, 1998).

8   Canterbury, Rochester, London, Winchester, Dorchester, Ramsbury, Sherborne, Selsey, Lichfield, Hereford, Worcester, Crediton, Cornwall, Elmham, Lindsey and Wells.

9   York and Durham.

10 Moorman, *A History of the Church in England*.

11 Swanton, *The Anglo-Saxon Chronicle*.

11. *The Eleventh Century – Canterbury Cathedral*

1   R. W. Southern, *The Making of the Middle Ages* (London: Yale University Press, 1953).

2   A seal of 1104 of Christ Church Priory, the first one used after the Norman Conquest.

3   The Church of St Alfege, rebuilt by Nicholas Hawksmoor in the eighteenth century, stands on what is reputed to be the place of his death.

4 Swanton, *The Anglo-Saxon Chronicle.*

5 Alphege's body was brought back in 1023.

6 The original story, found in twelfth-century sources, used the example of Cnut being unable to turn back the tide, to demonstrate his (alleged) piety. His earthly authority was as nothing next to God's over the world and nature. It has, however, become in the retelling a cautionary tale of a deluded king who believes in his own omnipotence.

7 Marjorie Chibnall, ed., *The Ecclesiastical History of Orderic Vitalis* (Oxford, Clarendon Press, 1969–80).

8 Dom David Knowles and Christopher N. L. Brooke, eds, *The Monastic Constitutions of Lanfranc* (Oxford: OUP, 2002).

9 Giles Gasper, 'The Norman Arrow Finds a Ready Target' in Chadwick, *Not Angels But Anglicans.*

10 Moorman, *A History of the Church in England.*

11 Other versions substitute the words 'turbulent', 'meddlesome', 'low-born' and 'insolent'.

12 Mark 12:17.

12. The Twelfth Century – St Melangell's, Pennant Melangell

1 Usually attributed to Ezekiel Hamer, vicar of Pennant Melangell in the late 1700s.

2 John Davies, *A History of Wales* (London: Penguin, 1993).

3 T. Edmund Harvey, *Saint Aelred of Rievaulx* (London: H. R. Allenson, 1932).

13. The Thirteenth Century – Blackfriars, Oxford

1 Richard Vaughan, ed., *Chronicles of Matthew Paris* (Stroud: Sutton Publishing, 1987).

2 According to Jordan of Saxony, the second Master-General of the Order, in *Libellus*, in part his biography of Dominic.

3 Vaughan, *Chronicles of Matthew Paris.*

4 James McEvoy, *Robert Grosseteste* (Oxford: OUP, 2000).

14. The Fourteenth Century – St Andrew's Fillingham

1 Walter Skeat, ed., William Langland, *Piers Plowman* (Oxford: OUP, 1906).
2 Kantik Ghosh, *The Wycliffite Heresy: Authority and the Interpretation of Texts* (Cambridge: Cambridge University Press, 2001).
3 Moorman, *A History of the Church in England.*
4 Skeat, William Langland, *Piers Plowman.*
5 ibid.
6 Kantik Ghosh, *The Wycliffite Heresy: Authority and the Interpretation of Texts* (Cambridge: Cambridge University Press, 2001).
7 This was an argument advanced later by Thomas More.
8 Thomas Fuller, *The Church History of Britain* (1655).

15. The Fifteenth Century – Henry VII's Chapel, Westminster Abbey

1 Barrie Dobson, '1400: The Laity Begin to Take Control' in, Chadwick, ed., *Not Angels, But Anglicans.*
2 No one is sure.
3 One wonderful example is the parish church of St Mary's in South Creake, north Norfolk.
4 Gerard B. Wegener and Stephen W. Smith, eds, *The Essential Works of Thomas More* (Yale: Yale University Press, 2020).
5 Despite suggestions to the contrary in modern-day films and fiction.

16. The Sixteenth Century – St Giles Cathedral, Edinburgh

1 David Laing, ed., *Works of John Knox* (Oregon: Wipf and Stock, 2004).
2 J. H. Pollen S. J., *Papal Negotiations with Mary Queen of Scots* (Edinburgh: Scottish History Society, 1st series, 1901).

3 Laing, *Works of John Knox*.

4 John 2:13–16.

5 Henry Gee, *The Elizabethan Prayer-Book & Ornaments* (London, 1902).

17. *The Seventeenth Century – St John's Little Gidding*

1 George Herbert (1593–1633) , 'The British Church', in *The Temple* (London: Penguin Classic, 2017).

2 T. S. Eliot, 'Little Gidding', *Four Quartets* (London: Faber & Faber, 2001).

3 Herbert entrusted to Ferrar on his deathbed in 1633 his most celebrated poetry collection, *The Temple*.

4 Eliot, 'Little Gidding'.

5 Melvyn Bragg, *The Book of Books: The Radical Impact of the King James Bible* (London: Hodder & Stoughton, 2011).

6 Trevor Cooper, ed., *The Journal of William Dowsing: Iconoclasm in East Anglia during the English Civil War* (Woodbridge: Boydell Press, 2001).

7 In his 1646 poem, 'On the New Forcers of Conscience under the Long Parliament'.

8 John Leonard, ed., 'Sonnet 16', in *John Milton: The Complete Poems* (London: Penguin 1998).

9 Guy de la Bedoyere, ed., *The Diary of John Evelyn* (Suffolk: Boydell Press, 2004).

10 Robert Latham, ed., *The Diaries of Samuel Pepys* (London: Penguin, 2003).

11 Bedoyere, ed., *The Diary of John Evelyn*.

18. *The Eighteenth Century – Heptonstall Methodist Chapel*

1 Alice Russie, ed., *The Essential Writings of John Wesley* (Ohio: Barbour Publishing, 2013).

2 Fletcher was born Jean Guillaume de la Fléchère of French Huguenot stock and had only come to England in 1750.

3 Russie, *The Essential Writings of John Wesley*.
4 Quoted in Amy Binns, *Valley of a Hundred Chapels: Lives and Legacies of the Nonconformists* (Heptonstall: Grace Judson Press, 2013).
5 ibid.
6 Russie, *The Essential Writings of John Wesley*.
7 Antonia Fraser, *The King and The Catholics: England, Ireland, and the Fight for Religious Freedom, 1780–1829* (London: Weidenfeld, 2018).

19. The Nineteenth Century – St Elisabeth's, Reddish

1 'Church Furnishing in 19th-century England: An interview with James Bettley', Victoria and Albert Museum, http://www.vam.ac.uk/content/articles/c/church-furnishing-in-19th-century-england/.
2 Sydney Smith, *The Works of the Rev. Sydney Smith*, Volume 4, 1836.
3 The viewpoint was summed up in an adage attributed to Michael Ramsey, Archbishop of Canterbury (1961–74), that 'the Church of England had no doctrine of its own but that of the universal Catholic Church'.
4 'Disestablishment', APCK, Church of Ireland, 2019, available at: https://www.ireland.anglican.org/our-faith/apck/disestablishment.

20. The Twentieth Century – Liverpool Metropolitan Cathedral

1 Addressing civic dignitaries at a banquet to celebrate its opening.
2 This was the case with the author's own parents.
3 According to figures from the Robert Schuman Centre for Advanced Studies.
4 The first Archbishop of Canterbury to retire peacefully from the post.
5 Robert Beaken, *Cosmo Lang: Archbishop in War and Crisis* (London: IB Tauris, 2012).

Epilogue: A Twenty-First Century Church?

1 See ICM's survey for the Bible Society in 2016 and YouGov's poll on religious belief in the same year, both reported in Peter Stanford, *Angels: A Visible and Invisible History* (London: Hodder, 2019).

2 See 'Whipsnade Tree Cathedral', Historic England, https://historicengland.org.uk/listing/the-list/list-entry/1439326

3 The phrase is not used in the Bible but developed as a theological concept using a variety of passages, including Psalm 24:1.

4 In conversation with the author.

5 Giles Fraser, *Chosen: Lost and Found between Christianity and Judaism* (London: Allen Lane, 2021).

Index

abdication crisis 339–40
Acts of Union (1707) 302
Adelphius 45
Adomnán 56, 92, 93, 116
Adrian IV, Pope 188
advowson 211
Aelred 187
Aidan, St 53, 106, 108
Ailbe of Emly, St 25
Alaric 65
Alban, St 23–32
Alcuin of York 122–4, 125
Aldhelm 126, 132
Alexander, Archbishop of St Andrews 249
Alexander I of Scotland, King 248
Alexander II, Pope 164, 167
Alfred the Great, King 131–6, 138–40, 146, 148, 149
Alfriston Clergy House (E. Sussex) 224
All Saints', Brixworth (Northants.) 97–100, 101
alms-houses 271
Alphege, Archbishop of Canterbury 160, 161
Amphibalus 24
Anabaptists 257, 286
ancient Greece 25–6, 47
Andrew, St 62
Andrewes, Lancelot, Bishop of Winchester 269
Anglican-Roman Catholic International Commission (ARCIC) 345
Anglicanism 16, 206, 302, 315–17, 321, 324
    and decline 336, 338–9
    and ecumenism 344–6
    and Ireland 325–7
    and *Towards the Conversion of England* 336
    and Wales 327–8
Anglo-Saxons 65–7, 68–9, 72, 97–100, 180–1
    and Vikings 130, 131–2
Angus, King 62
Annals of Inisfallen 81
Annals of St Neots 135
Anne Boleyn, Queen 254

Anne of Cleves, Queen 236
Anne of Great Britain, Queen 290, 302–3
Anselm 168–70, 204
anticlericalism 317–18
antisemitism 33, 188–9, 201, 303, 346
Antonine Wall 43
Antoninus Pius, Emperor 43
Aquila 12
archaeology 78, 86, 118, 137, 178
    and Glastonbury 10–11
    and Lullingstone Villa 39, 40, 41, 46
    and St Martin's, Canterbury 67, 68
    and Whithorn 55, 60
Archbishops of Canterbury 102–3, 124–5, 183; *see also* individual archbishops
architecture 117, 292, 330
    Gothic 206, 224, 314
    Norman 167, 174, 177, 179
    Perpendicular Gothic 227, 232–3, 241
    Romanesque 164, 167–8, 177
Aristobulus of Britannia 15–17, 23
Arles, Council of (314) 45–6, 56
Arranmore (Ireland) 81, 82
Arthur, King 17
Arundel, Thomas, Archbishop of Canterbury 227–8
Ashdown, Battle of (871) 134
Asser, Bishop of Sherborne 133, 135
Athanasius of Alexandria 56
Athelney (Somerset) 140
Auchenblae (Scotland) 89
Augustine, St 68, 70–1, 73–7, 93, 99, 101
    and Archbishops of Canterbury 102–3
    and Ethelbert 159, 350
Augustine of Hippo, St 57–8, 186
Augustinians 186
Aurelian, Emperor 44
Austen, Jane: *Mansfield Park* 317
Australia 317
Avignon (France) 215

Babington Plot 261
Baldwin, Stanley 340
Ball, John 210, 214

373

Index

Index

Johnston, Andrew 249
Jones, Inigo 292
Jörmungandr 141
Joseph of Arimathea 9–10, 17–18, 19, 20
Judaism 43–4, 286; *see also* antisemitism
Julian of Norwich: *The Revelations of Divine Love* 217
Julius II, Pope 238
Justus, Archbishop of Canterbury 76
Jutes 65–6, 68

Keble, John 321, 322
Kennedy, Geoffrey Studdert ('Woodbine Willie') 338
Kenneth II of Scotland, King 174
Kent 104–5, 129, 131; *see also* Canterbury Cathedral; Holy Rood of Boxley Abbey; Isle of Thanet; Lullingstone Villa; Rochester; St Martin's, Canterbury
Kilwardby, Robert, Archbishop of Canterbury 198, 203
Kings College Chapel (Cambs.) 241
Kings Langley (Herts.) 203
Kirkmadrine (Scotland) 53–4, 55
Knox, John 245–7, 249, 250, 252–3, 255, 264
  The First Blast of the Trumpet Against the Monstrous Regiment of Women 259
  The First Book of Discipline 254

Lambay (Ireland) 129
Lancashire: Old St Leonard's Church, Langho 264
land 121, 189
Lane Fox, Robin 26
Lanfranc, Archbishop of Canterbury 160, 165, 166–8, 204, 248
Lang, Cosmo, Archbishop of Canterbury 340
Langland, William: *Piers Plowman* 212, 217–18
Langton, Stephen, Archbishop of Canterbury 199, 200
Langton, Walter 203
Last Judgement 146–7
Latin 122, 139, 167, 220
Latinus Stone 51, 53, 54–5
Laud, William, Archbishop of Canterbury 269, 277
Laurence, Archbishop of Canterbury 74
Lavagna, Frederick de 202
learning *see* education
Leicester (Leics.) 125, 137
Leland, John 232
Lent 153
Leo III, Pope 124
Leo X, Pope 234

Levellers 287
Lewes, Battle of (1264) 202
Lewes Priory (E. Sussex) 174
Lichfield Cathedral (Staffs.) 101, 125, 126
Lincoln Cathedral (Lincs.) 137, 191
Lincolnshire 101, 148; *see also* Lincoln Cathedral; St Andrew's Church, Fillingham; St Andrew's Church, Sempringham; St Mary, Stow-in-Lindsey; St Paul in the Bail 78
Lindisfarne (Northumbria) 58, 106–7, 108, 125, 129, 147
Liudhard, Bishop 69, 72
Liverpool Metropolitan Cathedral (Merseyside) 333–6
Llantwit Major (Wales) 16, 58
Lloyd George, David 327
Llywelyn ap Gruffudd, Prince of Wales 182, 185
Lóegaire Mac Néill 90
Loki 141
Lollards 210–11, 214, 221, 238
London 14, 40, 76, 304, 318
  and Vikings 134, 136, 160
  see also Bunhill Fields, Islington; Henry VII Lady Chapel, Westminster Abbey; Queen's Chapel; St Etheldreda's Church, Ely Place; St Paul's Cathedral; Westminster Abbey; Westminster Cathedral
Lords of the Congregation 253
Lucius 34
Lullingstone Villa (Kent) 39–42, 45, 46, 47–8, 67
Lupus of Troyes 58
Luther, Martin 221–2, 234, 238, 250, 297, 308, 349
Lutheranism 237–8
Lutyens, Edwin 333, 334, 335, 339

MacCulloch, Diarmaid 3
McLaughlin, Niall 351
Magna Carta 200, 206
Magnus, Maximus 55
Magyars 131
Malachy, St 187, 192
Malcolm II of Scotland, King 161
Malines (Belgium) 344–5
Manchester: St Elisabeth's, Reddish 313–14, 315, 324, 329
Manning, Henry, Cardinal 341–2
Marcellinus, Pope 45
Marcher Barons 179, 181
Margaret, HRH Princess 340–1
Margaret Beaufort 229, 232
Marsh, Herbert, Bishop of Peterborough 316

Index

On the Truth of Sacred Scripture (Wycliffe) 214
open-air worship 352–5
Order of Preachers 195–6
Orderic Vitalis 163–4
ordination 306, 324, 346
Ormond, Earl of 280
Orthodox Christianity 15
Oslac 154
Oswald, St 105, 106, 148, 151, 156
Oswiu of Northumbria, King 101, 107–8, 116
Oxford, John de Vere, Earl of 241
Oxford Movement 321–4
Oxfordshire see Bishop Edward King Chapel, Cuddesdon; Blackfriars; Community of St Mary the Virgin, Wantage; Society of St John the Evangelist (Cowley Fathers); St Mary and St Nicholas, Littlemore

Padarn 103
paganism 2–3, 25, 26, 66, 120, 353
    and Picts 51
    and water deities 40–1
    see also Norse gods
Palladius 87–8, 89–90
papacy 71–3, 151, 163, 169, 183, 228–9
    and Avignon 215, 249
    and Wycliffe 216, 218–19
    see also individual popes
Paris (France) 195
Paris, Matthew:
    Chronica Majora 201–2
    The Lives of Two Offas 30
parish churches 152–3, 189–90, 230–1, 315
    and absentee priests 214, 304–5, 317–18
Parker, Matthew 260
Parliament 197, 202, 317–18, 319–21, 327–8
    and Charles I 276, 277, 283–4
    and religion 303, 304
Parry, Blanche 264
Parry, Sir Hubert 18
pastoral care 152, 316–17, 347, 351
Patrick, St 53, 54, 89–91
patriotism 338
Paul, St 12, 15, 16
Paul IV, Pope 249, 259
Paul VI, Pope 345
Paulinus, Bishop of York 76, 104–5, 111
Peada 101
Peasants' Revolt (1381) 210, 217, 219
Peckham, John, Archbishop of Canterbury 203
Pelagius, Pope 57–8, 71, 88
Pembrokeshire 181
Penda of Mercia, King 30, 101

Pennant Melangell (Wales) 177–9, 189
persecution 13–14, 23–4, 26–7, 32–3, 42–5, 353
Pertinax, Emperor 41, 42
Peter, St 13, 71, 108, 322
Philip II of France, King 200
Philip II of Spain, King 258, 259
Philip IV of France, King 215
Picts 51, 54
Pilgrim Fathers 275–6, 286
pilgrimage 146, 147, 190–1, 221, 350
    and All Saints', Brixworth 97
    and Clonmacnoise 83, 84
    and Glastonbury 10, 17, 19
    and Pennant Melangell 178
    and St Alban 29, 30, 56
    and St Ninian 52
    and Whithorn 59, 60
Pilgrimage of Grace (1536) 237
Pilton (Devon) 138
Piper, John 119, 335, 348
Pius V, Pope 261
Pius IX, Pope 325
plague 44, 71, 83, 109, 155; see also Black Death
Plautius, Aulus 12
pleasure gardens 304
Plunkett, Oliver, Archbishop of Armagh 301
Pluralities Act (1838) 321
Pole, Reginald, Cardinal 258–9
politics see Parliament; socialism
polytheism 11, 66–7, 81–2
Popish Plot (1678) 301
poverty 195, 218, 271
Powys 180, 181
Presbyterianism 60, 254, 289, 276–7, 326
priests 105, 107, 121, 152–3, 186; see also ordination
Primitive Methodism 308
Prisca 12
Prosper of Aquitaine 87
Protestantism 59, 222, 280, 333–4, 336–8; see also Nonconformists; Puritans; Reformation
Ptolemy of Alexandria: Almagest 87
Puritans 274, 275–6, 282–3, 289
Purvey, John 220
Pusey, Edward Bouverie 321

Quakers 286–7, 288, 303, 308–9, 310
Queen's Chapel (London) 292

Raedwald of the East Angles, King 100–1
Ramsey Abbey (Cambs.) 156
Ramsey, Michael, Archbishop of Canterbury 345